SIR NINIAN COMP

Sir Ninian Comper (1864–1960). Photograph: Allan Chappelow.

SIR NINIAN COMPER

An introduction to his life and work
with complete gazetteer

Anthony Symondson SJ
and Stephen Arthur Bucknall

with *Of the Atmosphere of a Church*
by Sir Ninian Comper

Spire Books & the Ecclesiological Society • 2006

ISBN 1-904965-11-3
ISBN 978-1-904965-11-4

First published 2006 by Spire Books Ltd in association with the Ecclesiological Society

Spire Books Ltd
PO Box 2336
Reading
RG4 5WJ
www.spirebooks.com

The Ecclesiological Society
c/o The Society of Antiquaries of London
Burlington House
Piccadilly
London
W1V 0HS
www.ecclsoc.org

The views expressed in this publication are those of the authors, and do not necessarily represent those of the Ecclesiological Society or of Spire Books Ltd.

Printed in Great Britain by the Alden Group Ltd., Osney Mead, Oxford

Front cover illustration: St Mary, Wellingborough, the church widely regarded as Comper's masterpiece (discussed on page 190). *Photograph: Martin Charles.*

Rear cover illustration: Morse for the cope of the Bishop of Norwich, worn at the Coronation of King Edward VII in 1902 (discussed on page 102).

Contents

List of illustrations

References in *italic* type are to the page(s) on which illustrations will be found. References in normal type in the right hand column are to the page on which begins the main discussion of the work being illustrated.

Publisher's acknowledgements

We are grateful to the late Richard Surtees, Sir Ninian Comper's literary executor, for permission to republish *Of the Atmosphere of a Church*.

The following kindly gave permission to reproduce images: the *Architectural Review* (St Cyprian, Clarence Gate, looking east, and looking west; St Alban, Holborn, tomb canopy of the Stanton chantry; Westminster Abbey, Warriors' chapel, exterior, and interior looking east); the National Gallery (the *Mass of St Giles*); the National Monuments Record (St Wilfrid, Cantley, chancel screen, and Virgin and Child; St Mary Magdalene, Paddington, crypt chapel looking west, and crypt chapel organ case; St Mary, Egmanton, interior from west; St Barnabas, Pimlico, crypt chapel; Wymondham, general view of the screen, and details of the reredos; St Alban, Holborn, looking east at Stanton chantry, and effigy of Fr Stanton; Southwark Cathedral, interior looking east, and Lady Chapel; St Mary, Wellingborough, external view from south-east, and looking north-east from south aisle); RIBA Library Drawings Collection (design for St Cyprian, Clarence Gate); *The Times* (St Cyprian, Clarence Gate, the arrangement of the east end, and the rood and screen); the *Western Mail* (the Welsh National War Memorial, Cardiff, two images). We apologise for any breach of copyright, and will correct the matter in any future edition.

Ecclesiological Society preface

The Ecclesiological Society is delighted to publish this book, the second we have issued in association with Spire Books. It presents an introduction to Comper, many fine historic photographs, a reprint of an important article written by Comper, and a complete Gazetteer of all his work.

The introduction to Comper is based on a selection of contemporary illustrations, chosen to allow a chronological narrative of his life and work, and displaying the development of his approach to church design and furnishing. This is not intended to be a full biography, nor a systematic discussion of all his achievement, but to provide the reader with the framework needed to appreciate his work and put it in its wider context. The decision was taken not to provide detailed references to this section of the book, as to some extent it foreshadows the much fuller biography of Comper by Anthony Symondson which it is anticipated will appear in the future.

We have reprinted Comper's well-known but scarce pamphlet, *Of the Atmosphere of a Church*, which describes his views on church design and furnishing. Published in 1947 in response to a particular set of circumstances, it is to some extent a period piece, and Anthony Symondson has therefore written an introduction putting it into context. In the process he has thrown light on the complex interrelationships between Betjeman, Piper and Comper, and the effects of Betjeman's advocacy on Pevsner's attitude to Comper's work.

The Gazetteer speaks for itself. It is the result of many years' dedicated and painstaking work by Stephen Bucknall, and with some six hundred entries is intended to be comprehensive. Anthony Symondson kindly undertook the significant task of reviewing the entire gazetteer in its final form, to make any necessary corrections, and we hope that it is now as complete and correct as such a thing ever can be on its first outing.

We are proud to be associated with this book, which we believe will be invaluable as an introduction and guide to Comper, both to those who have already discovered his work, and to those for whom it will be a journey of exploration.

TREVOR COOPER
Chairman of Council of the Ecclesiological Society

Additions and corrections to the Gazetteer may be notified directly to the Society, preferably by email (the Society's details are on the reverse of the title page), and will be passed on to Stephen Bucknall, and posted on the Society's website.

Part 1: The life and work of Sir Ninian Comper

Anthony Symondson SJ

To J. B. Sebastian and Zoë Comper, and Richard and Elizabeth Surtees

Foreword to Part I

Anthony Symondson SJ

IN 1933 THE CENTENARY OF THE OXFORD MOVEMENT was celebrated with great fervour. Anglo-Catholicism was then the most powerful religious force in the Church of England and promised to change not only the face of the national Church but the Anglican Communion. At no time, before or since, had the triumph of the Anglo-Catholic cause seemed so certain. It commanded spiritual and pastoral success, reinforced by a formidable battery of academic and scholarly plausibility. Some of the leading Oxford and Cambridge academics, biblical scholars and theologians gave their support to the Movement. This was reinforced by intellectuals, artists, writers and architects who embraced Anglo-Catholic ideals and devoted their work to the promotion of a Catholic understanding of the Church of England.

An indication of the achievement of Anglo-Catholicism is given in a collection of studies published in 1933, entitled *Northern Catholicism: Centenary Studies of the Oxford and Parallel Movements*, edited by N. P. Williams, Lady Margaret Professor of Divinity in the University of Oxford, and Charles Harris, Prebendary of Hereford Cathedral. One of these essays, 'The aesthetic side of the Oxford Movement', by Sir Stephen Gaselee, a Fellow of Magdalen College, Cambridge, contains these words:

> I have ordinarily been unwilling in the course of this essay to mention the names of persons still living; but even this brief mention of Church architects would be incomplete without a mention of Mr J. N. Comper, whose work, which may be seen all over the country, in church fittings as well as in their fabric, is perhaps the high-watermark of all that is artistically best as a result of the Movement.

Comper was sixty-nine when this tribute was made and past the zenith of his creative powers and influence, yet he still had the capacity to surprise. But within Anglicanism as a whole he was seen as the best and most influential church architect of his generation whose work achieved an unequalled standard of accomplishment shared by few of his contemporaries and immediate successors. Gaselee was exact in associating Comper's work with the Oxford Movement. Comper was a child of the Movement, many of the leading protagonists of the second phase of development known as ritualism were among his personal friends, and friends of his family, and some of the most influential of them were his patrons. Comper and his contemporaries believed that the ornaments rubric of the Book of Common Prayer authenticated sacramentals. In one of his early papers Comper wrote that the ornaments rubric was 'the outward token of our union with the rest of Catholic Christendom, both past and present'. Catholicism was his inspiration and well-spring. Comper saw his work as an expression of Catholic unity. It was admired as much by the young as his own peers.

Employing the highest artistry and workmanship on a broad craft basis Comper was able to give credibility and conviction to a Catholic understanding of the architectural setting of Anglican worship. His work had a numinous quality that fulfilled the spiritual and aesthetic ideals of many who held Anglo-Catholic tenets. Comper believed he was building for the future and helped to forge a distinct Catholic identity in the national Church. He effected a transformation of Anglican taste and had a strong influence, through his work, on liturgical worship.

Among those who came to know Comper in old age was John Betjeman. In August 1935 he and Frederick Etchells went on a three-day church crawl in Huntingdonshire and Northamptonshire and took in Wellingborough, a 'good heartily ugly Midland town'. They visited the 'exquisite' St Mary's church: 'Enriched Perp ... Comper will spoil it if he puts on any more colour ... C is a first-class architect.' St Mary's is the most beautiful Anglican church of the twentieth century and embodies Gaselee's claim that Comper's work brings together all that is artistically best as a result of the Oxford Movement. The strength of a religious movement is symbolically expressed by architecture. No other church so completely fulfils developed Anglo-Catholic spiritual and liturgical aspirations with such finished artistry. History may well come to see it as the most poignant monument to the Movement.

Betjeman was an Anglo-Catholic, but he was frivolous. He met Comper in 1937, formed an immediate friendship, and quickly became one of the most ardent admirers of the younger generation. Another was the writer, Peter Anson (he had first met Comper in 1903), who wrote perceptively of Comper's originality as a liturgical planner in the Benedictine periodical, *Pax*, published by Prinknash Abbey. The ambivalence of Betjeman's reaction to St Mary's, Wellingborough (his first response thought the interior 'pleasingly effeminate' and the painted glass 'execrable') ran through his subsequent friendship but, as he came to discover more of Comper's work and understand it better, Betjeman modified his early reservations and became his principal supporter.

Soon after the end of the Second World War Betjeman wanted to write a book about Comper, composed of a short monograph with illustrations, the republication of his liturgical papers and a list of works in the form of a *catalogue raisonné*. He hoped its format would be designed by Stanley Morison, the leading typographer of the time. It would have been a handsome volume but it was never written, though its scope remained in Betjeman's mind for the rest of his life. The research and discoveries that have gone into Stephen Bucknall's list were not then available and it would have been difficult to compile such a gazetteer in Comper's lifetime as he discouraged investigation into his early work. A balanced record of his achievement would have been hard to write and by now such a book would have become a period piece.

Betjeman and his friend John Piper did more to further Comper's cause in his old age than any other influence. Betjeman began by seeking him out as a joke but became persuaded by the beauty, integrity and mental rigour of his architecture. He established a cult and many came to see it through his eyes. Betjeman wrote and broadcast at a time when cultural Anglicanism was at its height. That fruitful episode is long over and will only be remembered by an older generation. There were complications in Betjeman's championship and they had repercussions that would have dismayed him if he had foreseen their consequences. They unintentionally ended in the blighting of Comper's reputation. The essay on this event tries to examine them, set them in context and rescue Comper from their malign effects.

The Church and the world have dramatically changed since Comper's death and the presuppositions that lay behind his work are either lost or have become academic. Comper ruled a kingdom that no longer exists and he needs to be interpreted for a new audience. Anglo-Catholicism has become a residual part of contemporary Anglicanism. With its decline the spiritual values embodied in Comper's work are now rarely understood or applied. He is regarded, if he is remembered at all, as part of an historical episode fast retreating into the past. While not attempting to achieve what Betjeman proposed in the way he would have approached it, the survey of Comper's work that accompanies the illustrations in this book tries to present an abridged account of his life, architectural development and ideas, and to describe it as Comper himself and his contemporaries would have understood it. I hope that it will dispel some of the ignorance and misunderstanding that surrounds it.

It would be inappropriate in a book of this size to republish Comper's liturgical papers in their entirety, for (despite their value in setting out his theories) they are now mostly of historic, rather than practical, interest. Nevertheless, it is essential to read them if his work is to be properly understood. *Of the Atmosphere of a Church* has been chosen for republication because it is a distillation of Comper's thought that has perennial application and accessibly sums up his mature conclusions.

There is no better introduction to Stephen Bucknall's careful and pains-taking list of Comper's work, to the completion of which he has dedicated many years, much enthusiasm, work and patience. The list will accomplish a great deal by making Comper's achievement familiar on a scale of compre-hensiveness hitherto unattempted. If it is used after reading *Of the Atmosphere of a Church*, the churches to which it will take the visitor should begin to make sense in a new way. He or she will come to understand them better for knowing what was in Comper's mind when he designed them.

Many of Comper's churches and restorations have been spoilt in the last forty years, others have suffered from the ravages of vandalism, theft and neglect; some of his work has been destroyed by war, demolition and change of use. Yet more is misread, but a few churches remain much as Comper left them, dignified if anything by time. He often said that the full beauty of his work would not be seen for hundreds of years hence. That was based on the assumption that the Church would remain immutable. Comper would have been astonished by the changes in the Western Church since his death, and, I suspect, dismayed by the loss of common assumptions which he would have taken for granted in those who sought his work. But among those works that do survive some could, with little difficulty, be returned to their original form without ossifying their function.

The principle behind the choice of photographs is twofold. It is intended to show a chronological development of Comper's work, using characteristic examples. It attempts to present it in its original integrity, rather than as it is now, compromised by change. Contemporary photographs have been used, many taken under Comper's direction, and some are published for the first time. Comper had strong views on photography. He disliked wide-angle lenses because he thought they distorted scale and he preferred photographs taken in early morning or late afternoon light, especially if they had happily chosen effects of sunlight. Many of the illustrations were taken soon after the work was completed, some when it was partly finished, and the best convey a little of the atmosphere of the time as well as making an accurate record. While the number of plates is limited, and no attempt has been made to represent Comper's work in its entirety, it is hoped that the choice of subjects will provide a useful overview.

Comper was an artist. He is presented in these pictures as a church architect, not simply as a church craftsman and glazier. Comper's artistry was subordinate to architecture. His work was governed by a severe and learned liturgical, architectural and aesthetic discipline. Representative examples of painted glass, textile design, metalwork and embroidery have not been included, due to a limited compass. Those samples that do appear take their place in an existing architectural context because that was how they were designed to be seen.

Unfortunately it has not been possible to include colour photographs in this book. On the other hand, many of the illustrations are not only of great historical interest, taken under Comper's direction, and showing his work in its original state, but are also of high quality. For Comper's work was recorded by some of the leading architectural photographers of the time. First came Cyril Ellis, about whom little can now be established beyond his early association with the *Architectural Review*, and that he lived at Alexandra Park, North London. He photographed much of Comper's early work, and that of his contemporaries, and continued to do so until *c*.1908. Sebastian Comper, Comper's eldest son, made record photographs and so did John Samuel Bucknall, his great-nephew. But it was not until the Thirties that major twentieth-century English photographers were used. Foremost among them were Dell & Wainwright, photographers who recorded the Modern Movement, and who were commissioned in 1939 by the *Architectural Review* to illustrate John Betjeman's pioneer article on Comper's work. Their work is among the finest ever taken of Comper's buildings and church furniture. John Piper photographed Comper's work in the Forties and after the war came Eric de Maré, Edwin Smith, A. F. Kersting, and Sydney W. Newbery. In recent years Paul Barker, Gordon Barnes, Peter Burton, Martin Charles, Christopher Dalton, Martin Harrison, and Harland Walshaw have added their studies.

Among the illustrations are several that may be said to be definitive. St Wilfrid's, Cantley, (page 33) by Cyril Ellis; the chapel of the convent of the Holy Name, Malvern Link, (page 42) by Christopher Dalton; St Cyprian's, Clarence Gate, (page 94) by Dell and Wainwright; St Philip's, Cosham, (pages 167, 169) by J. S. Bucknall; and St Mary's, Wellingborough, (page 193) by Edwin Smith.

A choice of William Bucknall's fine pen and ink presentation drawings has been included. So has the perspective of St John of Jerusalem, Clerkenwell, (page 185) drawn in 1944 by Comper, Arthur and J. S. Bucknall and E. J. Lucas; Comper himself added the tinted washes. William Bucknall drew with accomplishment and delicacy: his heavy line and subtle perspective owed a great deal to Dürer and Schongauer. His work is pictorial and precise, marked by modest reticence, and represents a remarkable artistic achievement in its own right. Bucknall's drawings translated Comper's sketches into perspectives and thus did much to recommend his work to clients and further his ideals.

Comper's ultimate objective was to bring man to worship God through beauty. He believed that 'the church of intrinsic beauty speaks today to many a cultured mind of youth and age; to win such minds by beauty of architecture and music may not be everything, yet it is by way of beauty that all are won. And it is by mediocrity in beauty and goodness and by half-truths that men are turned away.'

'What is so sad,' wrote Gavin Stamp in a review of the exhibition of Comper's work at the Heinz Gallery in 1988, 'is that all Comper sought to achieve through design combined with painstaking historical research is utterly irrelevant to the modern Church of England. It is not only that Anglo-Catholics are oblivious to the English liturgical tradition that so obsessed Comper's generation, but also that the refinement, scholarship and careful splendour of Comper's work is totally out of fashion in the modern Church. Many clergymen, indeed, now seem to regard Beauty as a wicked snare and delusion.' And the same may be said, with rare exceptions, of the Roman Catholic Church in these islands.

Effectively the artistic legacy of church art of the first half of the twentieth century has been discarded, and is now rarely taken seriously beyond a dwindling band of enthusiasts. Comper was a high priest of beauty but, in modern times, the beautiful has become the merely beautiful. It has lost its converting power because few are able to recognise it. Where once beauty bestrode an artistic continent, its fiefdom has now dwindled down to the size of a small island. Despite this unfavourable climate I hope that the illustrations and their commentary will encourage people to rediscover, if elegiacally, Comper's work and appreciate its lasting value.

ANTHONY SYMONDSON SJ

Acknowledgements: I would like to acknowledge the following for their help with my introduction to the life and work of Comper, and my essay, 'John Betjeman, John Piper and Sir Ninian Comper: *Of the Atmosphere of a Church* in Context': the Revd Michael Beattie SJ, the Revd Kevin Donovan SJ, Michael Hall, Peter Howell, Dr Alan Powers, the Revd Dr John Sharp and Dr Gavin Stamp. I am deeply indebted to Candida Lycett Green and the Betjeman estate, for generously permitting the printing here of John Betjeman's letters; to Richard Brain for finding and copying Betjeman's book reviews in *The Times Literary Supplement*; and to Pamela Griffin, archivist to the Arts Council, for finding and copying the catalogue of *The Artist and the Church*. I am grateful to John Francis Bucknall for his help with the choice of photographs and valuable observations, some of which I have incorporated in my text, and to David Bucknall for providing further illustrations. I would like to thank the Revd Gerard Mitchell SJ, parish priest of the church of the Sacred Heart, Wimbledon, for giving me time to write this short study. Finally, I must also thank the Very Revd Michael Holman SJ, Provincial of the British Province of the Society of Jesus, for authorising its publication.

Sir Ninian Comper:
an introduction to his life and work

Anthony Symondson SJ

UNITY BY EXCLUSION

COMPER'S WORK WAS GOVERNED BY PLATONIST PHILOSOPHY drawn from *The Symposium*. The speech of Socrates provided a basis for his thought: 'A man should, from his youth, seek for forms which are beautiful. At first he should love but one of them; then recognise the beauty which resides in one as the sister of that which dwells in another.' 'Philosophy helps, from Plato onwards,' Comper wrote, 'because it puts beauty in the right place as one of the three eternal values equal with truth and goodness so that what applies to one of them is true of the others.'

Comper sought beauty in a lifelong quest. His youthful appreciation of beauty was confined to Northern European Gothic of the fifteenth century but he also recognised this period as the Northern Renaissance. Inspired as it was by the work of a single historic era, the work of the first part of his career he afterwards characterised as 'unity by exclusion'. He later came to recognise the Greek Classical inheritance of architecture from antiquity, and found a way to fuse elements from various traditions into a coherent whole – 'unity by inclusion'.

His early interest was not antiquarian, because he believed that late-medieval architecture should be equated with a national expression and applied to the liturgical needs of modern times. Due to the gains of the Oxford Movement, modern worship was seen by Anglo-Catholics to be Eucharistic in distinction to the prevalence of the offices of Morning and Evening Prayer that had become the staple form of English worship.

Comper's emphasis on Englishness should not be mistaken for provincial insularity. Throughout Europe at the turn of the century, each nation sought

*St Lawrence, Nuremberg, 1445–72. The 'Northern Renaissance' – an inspiration for
Comper's early work.*

the roots of its own culture. The contemporary rebirth of English identity
spearheaded the move towards modernity by investigating England's medieval past. 'By medieval architecture I mean the best developments of our
national English architecture which is no less medieval than is Shakespeare.
Both were developments of the middle ages, but both usher in the modern
world.' In his churches, restorations, furniture design, and painted glass
Comper conceived his achievement as a unified work of art subservient to one
controlling thought. Working from a perfectionist sensibility, nothing was left
to chance.

Comper's early work was inspired both by East Anglia and Germany. He
had been fired with enthusiasm for German church furniture by C. E. Kempe

and G. F. Bodley who both regarded the heavily carved richness, colour and iconography of late-medieval Germany as the fullest expression of a Gothic ideal. They applied the results of their own travels and observation in the Rhineland to their sumptuous, if at times ponderous, work.

In 1896 Comper, at the age of thirty-two, went on an extended tour of the Rhineland, primarily to look at late-Gothic church furniture. At St Lawrence's, Nuremberg, he discovered a densely furnished church with diffused light pouring from two tiers of traceried windows onto the images displayed inside. During the English Reformation and continental Counter-Reformation, many parish churches had lost their Gothic sculpture, and the East Anglian Perpendicular churches of the fifteenth century were little more than stripped barns after the devastation of seventeenth-century Puritan iconoclasm. But St Lawrence's retained its medieval appearance, despite becoming Lutheran in 1525, partly because so much patrician wealth had been invested in it.

As will become apparent, Rhineland carving and imagery provided precedents for much of Comper's early church furniture. Of equal significance was the disciplined arrangement of the interior with closely set blocks of pews divided by wide aisles, and the clean definition and function of each element of the building. This is a theme running through all Comper's work, as strong as the differentiation between dark wood and gilded surfaces contrasted with white walls.

ST MARGARET OF SCOTLAND, ABERDEEN
Proposed additions and rebuilding, 1887

John Ninian Comper was born in Aberdeen on 10 June 1864, the eldest son and fourth child of the seven children of the Revd John Comper (1823–1903) and Ellen Taylor (1828–1908) his wife. The Comper family are of Norman origin, but settled at the Conquest in Pulborough, Sussex, and remained there as yeoman farmers until the first half of the twentieth century. John Comper's romantic belief that the family was Huguenot, of noble Breton ancestry, has no substance in fact, although the tradition was strongly held.

John Comper had left Sussex as a young man to seek work in Scotland as a schoolmaster with a view to ordination. His lack of an Oxford or Cambridge education disqualified him from taking holy orders in the Church of England. and he was ordained a priest of the Scottish Episcopal Church. He became a northern leader of the Anglo-Catholic phase of the Oxford Movement, known as ritualism, and was closely associated with the English ritualists, many of whom stayed at his home at St Margaret's Brae, on the Spital. Mrs Comper's visitors' book is a roll call of notable ritualists, northern and southern. Comper's work can only be fully understood within the context of the Oxford Movement and its later developments.

Comper's first school was Kingston College, Aberdeen. In 1874 he went as a boarder to Trinity College, Glenalmond, but left in 1880 at the age of sixteen and drew at the Aberdeen School of Art. He went on to study for a term at the Ruskin School, Oxford, but in 1882 he was introduced by Fr George Congreve, of the Society of St John the Evangelist, Cowley to Charles Eamer Kempe (1839–1907), a glass-painter and church craftsman, who arranged for him to work voluntarily in his drawing office in Beaumont Street, St Marylebone, while continuing his studies at the South Kensington School of Art. In later life Comper said that he owed little to his year with Kempe, but his brief training in drawing, wall- and glass-painting, gave him the eye and the technical ability to develop his vocabulary of workmanship and skill. It gave him the confidence to train workmen in many disciplines, and imbue them with his standards and aesthetic ideals.

Comper did not extol craftsmanship in the spirit of Ruskin, Morris and the Arts and Crafts Movement. Design was created, he believed, by the controlling thought of the architect, and control was continued in execution. The achievement was secured through the accomplishment of workmen trained by apprenticeship. 'I say deliberately workman and not craftsman,' he explained to Dom Michael Hanbury of Prinknash Abbey in later life.

> The craftsman abounds, as the schools of art and of architecture abound, but they do not, and I think cannot, produce workmen and architects. Apprenticeship alone has ever, and I think will ever, produce these. … There is no more fond illusion than that put forward so charmingly by Ruskin and, if I remember rightly, by Lethaby and their followers, viz, that you have only to give the carver and painter a really free hand and he will produce carving and painting like the old. The results of trying it are the proof of its fallacy. On the other hand I can shew proof of obtaining today the same skill of workmanship as in the past. That, however, is the result of following not merely a general design but most careful and often-corrected drawings, and of a continuous supervision; and, though I think the need of supervision of what is required grows, I have never seen an indication in support of the Ruskin theory. …The workman's happiness and pride, be he mason, carver or painter, is in doing good work and I do not think he naturally troubles himself about design, or is often good in his results if he does. Sometimes my experience is that he has no "taste" at all, but remains a good workman so long as he lets all notions of design alone.

These principles lay behind the practice of the Gothic Revival from Pugin onwards and were learnt from Kempe, and later from Bodley, and applied for the rest of Comper's life. It is tenuous to see him as an Arts and Crafts architect.

In 1880 Congreve had taken Comper to see the unfinished nave of Bodley & Garner's church of St Michael, Camden Town, (1880–94). The 'beauty of proportion and whiteness' of the nave effected a conversion to architecture and in 1883, on leaving Kempe, Comper entered the drawing office of George Frederick Bodley (1828–1907) as an articled pupil with a four-year indenture of £80 per annum. Bodley and his partner, Thomas Garner (1839–1906), were the leading church architects of the day whose work represented for

St Margaret of Scotland, Aberdeen. Design for proposed additions, 1887. Comper's first commission (not built). Drawing by William Bucknall.

Comper a standard of perfection unequalled by any other architect other than George Gilbert Scott Junior (1839–97). Their achievement is embodied in Bodley & Garner's church of the Holy Angels, Hoar Cross, Staffordshire (1872–1900), and Scott's St Agnes', Kennington Park, London (1874–91; destroyed 1941). Scott's architectural theories and St Agnes had a profound influence on Comper's own thought and work. Religiously and architecturally, he had a good pedigree.

In 1887 Comper was lodging with the Revd George Hollings SSJE at 6 Lloyd Street, Clerkenwell. Hollings was chaplain to the Sisters of Bethany and a noted spiritual writer and retreat giver. Comper began designing for the order's School of Embroidery, an association that would last until the end of his life, and soon the work of the school came exclusively under his direction. The school came to produce the finest church embroidery procurable – vestments, banners, altar frontals and linen – superior to the existing standards in other convent embroidery rooms, better than contemporary work on the Continent and commercial ventures. It was unequalled and came to exercise strong influence on church embroidery and ecclesiastical taste.

In that same year Comper's pupillage came to an end and he began to work independently from Lloyd Street. During his pupillage Comper had met in Bodley's drawing office William Bucknall (1851–1944), an improver who was a pupil of E. R. Robson (1836–1917), the architect to the London School Board. Bucknall had architects, builders and engineers in his background: he was a nephew of Benjamin Bucknall (1833–95), the translator of Viollet-le-Duc. They formed a partnership in 1888, and took a drawing office at 7 Queen Anne's Gate, Westminster: Comper was twenty-four, Bucknall thirty-seven; and in 1890 Comper married Bucknall's sister, Grace.

Comper's first commission was from his father, who had founded St Margaret's in the slums of the Gallowgate in 1867. It had a school-chapel built in 1870 by James Matthews, a pupil of Archibald Simpson. Comper was invited by his father to recast and extend Matthews's modest church.

The first proposal was to add a narthex, clad the internal walls in stone and plaster, add a cloister to the north, leading to a chapel of St Clement and a sacristy, and throw out a vaulted Lady Chapel behind the high altar. The altar is raised on many steps and has a gradine and six candlesticks standing before a screen of wrought iron that looks through to the chapel. The arch surrounding it is carved with angels in relief and above is a flat panelled ceiling, heavily decorated over the altar. There is a rood beam flanked by figures of St Mary and St John, and an organ in an ingenious case, enclosing a console within the base, stands on the south side of the sanctuary. The walls were intended to be painted in registers of colour with a counter-change and texts in black letter, and there is a floor of stone and red quarry tiles.

This was soon superseded by an ambitious proposal for an entirely new church. Modelled upon Bodley & Garner's St Augustine's, Pendlebury, Manchester (1870–74), it is influenced by Albi Cathedral translated into

St Margaret of Scotland, Aberdeen. Comper's second proposal, for an entirely new church (1887, not built), produced in association with William Bucknall. The design is influenced by Albi Cathedral. Drawing by William Bucknall.

St Margaret of Scotland, Aberdeen, the St Nicholas chapel, 1889. Mostly in Bodley's manner, with few signs of Comper's later development. Photograph, c.1890.

English Decorated Gothic, using internal buttresses to form a high arcade which includes recessed windows piercing a tall wall surface; the buttresses are pierced to form narrow passage aisles; above is an unbroken groined vault. A rood-beam was placed at a high level within the chancel arch, based on Butterfield's western arch at St Alban's, Holborn (1861–2). Beyond, the narrow chancel leads to the elevated sanctuary with the high altar forming a base for a high reredos of carved wood with a figure of the Virgin and Child occupying the main panel. To the north, projecting from the chancel, is the organ chamber standing before a vaulted chapel of the Blessed Sacrament.

The design anticipates the internal disposition of the chapels of the Community of St Margaret, Aberdeen, and the Community of the Holy Name, Malvern Link, four years later, and shows the influence of Bucknall in the powerful structural mass. Indeed, it demonstrates the complementary character of their early partnership. The drawing influenced A. H. Skipworth, a fellow pupil of Bodley whom Comper regarded as the most brilliant of his pupils, in his design for St Etheldreda's, Fulham (1894–7; destroyed 1944), which followed the lofty nave, with passage aisles, and narrow chancel raised above a crypt.

All that was built of these schemes was the vaulted chapel of St Nicholas at the west end, the first stone-vaulted building erected in Aberdeen since the Reformation, and the rood. Stylistically it favours Fountains Abbey rather than anything consciously Scottish. The designs are made in the manner of Bodley and show little anticipation of Comper's future development beyond a hint in the intensification of angels round the altar in the first design, and the scale of the proposal in the second. However, he was soon to investigate the authentic form of the Gothic altar.

In 1908 Comper added on the south a more definitely Scottish Founder's Aisle, in memory of his parents. The arcade contains suggestions of what he had proposed in 1887. There is a low open reredos of stone and a parclose screen with two figures of gilded oak representing St Helena and St Clement. The east window has in the centre a representation of Christ in Glory seated on a rainbow, flanked by St Margaret of Scotland and St John, and there is a kneeling portrait of John Comper. This is the first instance where Comper depicted Christ beardless 'as if in that moment of youth in his life on earth, which would seem to be the least inadequate figure of him who makes all things new, and is the same yesterday, today and forever'.

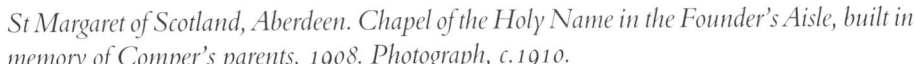

St Margaret of Scotland, Aberdeen. Chapel of the Holy Name in the Founder's Aisle, built in memory of Comper's parents, 1908. Photograph, c.1910.

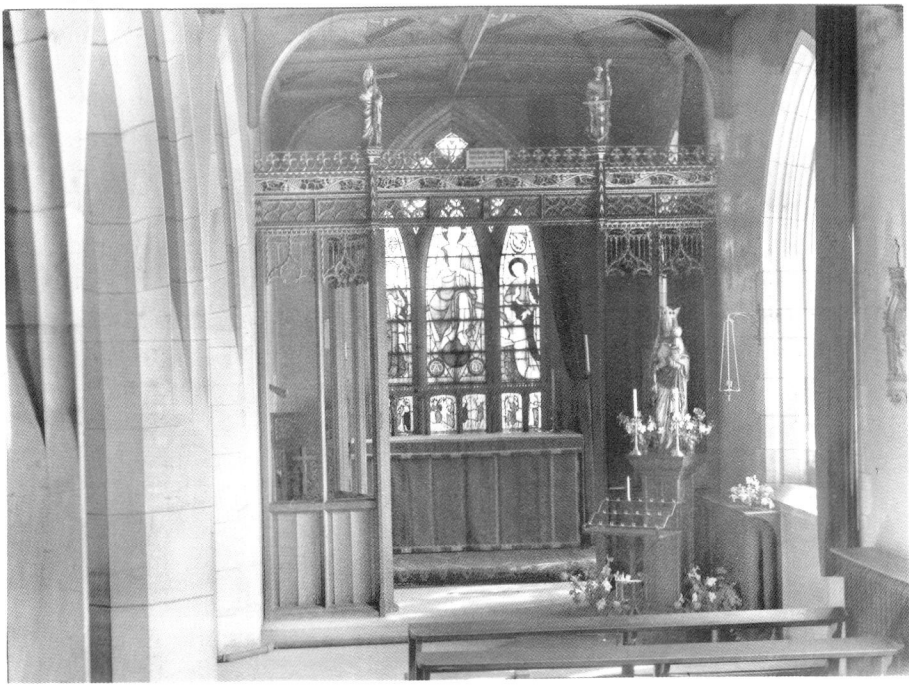

St Peter, Ely, Cambridgeshire. Painted rood screen, 1889. Note the structural loft, and winged seraphim, features developed in Comper's later work. Photograph: Cyril Ellis.

ST PETER, ELY, CAMBRIDGESHIRE

Screen, 1889

The rood screen was the visual centrepiece of every medieval parish church, the high altar was its heart. The screen divided the ritual enclosure of the chancel from the nave, and took its name from the crucifix, or rood, flanked by figures of St Mary and St John, which stood upon, or above, the loft. It is a common misconception that the rood screen removed the Mass beyond the reach and sight of the laity. Like the medieval originals, Comper's rood screens were easy to look through and sometimes designed lightly to enable the worshippers to see the high altar. They were conceived as a window frame through which the congregation watched the principal Masses and the most important elements in the liturgy, and were decorated with complex iconography that emphasised Catholic doctrine and the heavenly hierarchy. The screen also served as a piece of liturgical furniture by virtue of the gallery, called the rood loft, that ran along the top of it.

The screen at St Peter's was the first painted screen designed by Comper after he had formed his partnership with William Bucknall in 1888. The loft is inscribed in black letter with the antiphons for Matins and Lauds for the feast of the Exaltation of the Holy Cross, with plainchant notation from the Sarum Gradual. On the left (from the office of Matins): *Salva nos Christe salvator per virtutem sancte crucis qua salvasti Petrum in mari, miserere nobis* – Save us, Christ our Saviour, by the virtue of the holy cross, through which you saved Peter in the sea, have mercy on us. On the right (antiphon for Lauds): *Crux benedicta nitet dominus qua pependit, atque cruore suo vulnera nostra lavit* – The Holy Cross shines forth, on which the Lord hung in the flesh, and with his own blood washed our wounds. There are instances in Comper's work of lofts incorporating musicians' galleries, organs and even chapels. His screens all had a liturgical function and were never simply ornamental. 'An English parish church without a screen,' Comper believed, 'may be said to have ceased to be English almost as absolutely as an Eastern church without an iconostasis.'

Commissioned by Dr Salisbury James Murray Price (1858–1926), the Ely screen contains the elements of his later design, including a structural loft and figures of winged seraphim. Price was a well-connected man of means and has been described as an 'ultra-sacerdotalist medievalist'. His patronage and introductions were decisive for the future. Price later used Comper to restore the church at Kingston, Cambridgeshire, in 1893 and, in the following year, at St Ives, Huntingdonshire, he paid for the decoration of the magnificent organ screen and statuary. He later used Comper in the restoration of Stratton Strawless, Norfolk, and for the war memorial at Tintinhull, Somerset. It was Price who introduced Comper to some of his notable early patrons, including the squires Athelstan Riley and W. J. Birkbeck, and they introduced him to others. In company with the Revd A. H. Stanton, of St Alban's, Holborn, he

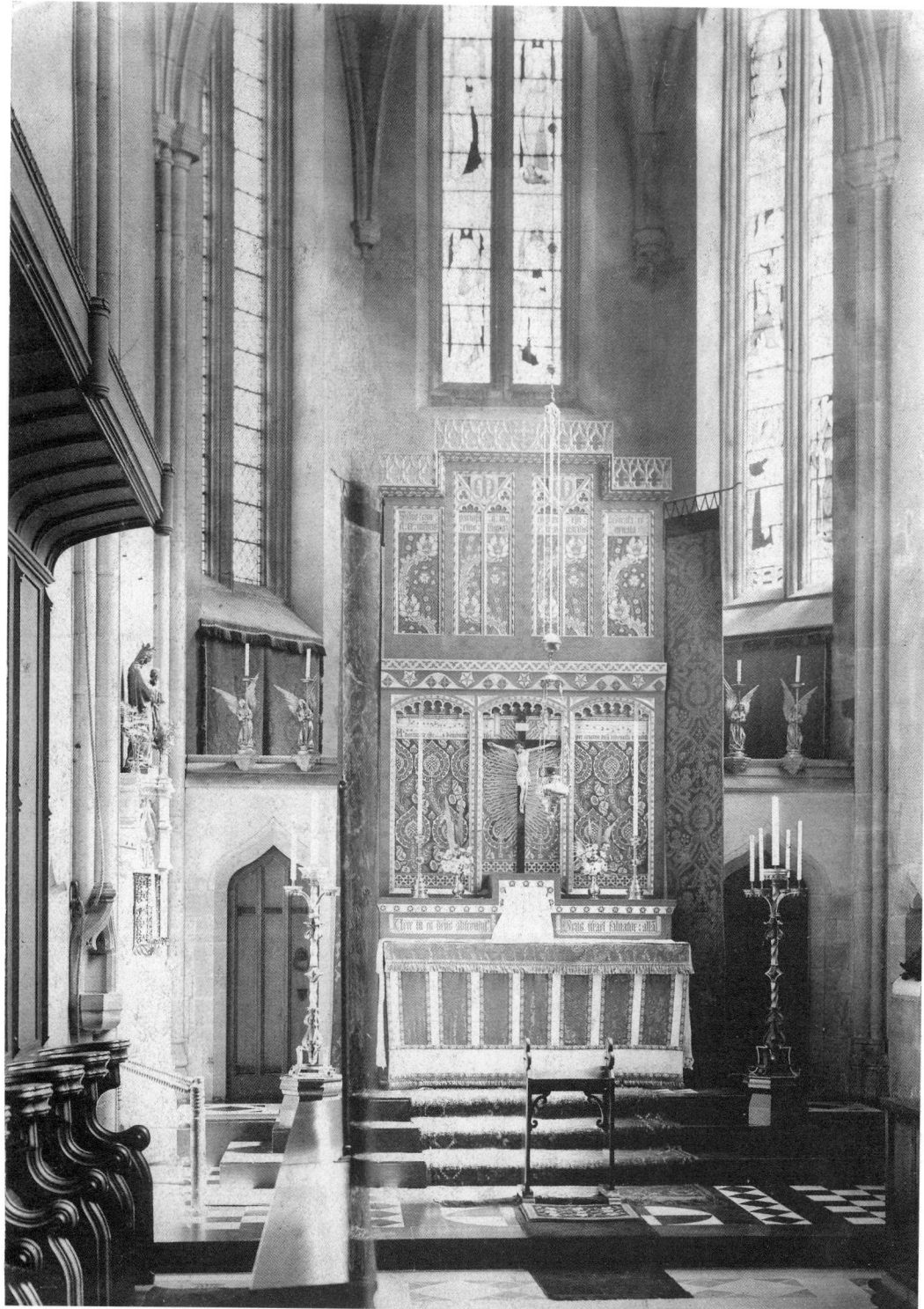

Community of St Margaret, Aberdeen. Chapel, 1892. The building is modelled on the fifteenth-century choir of the kirk of the Holy Rood, Stirling. Here Comper 'built his father's convictions in stone'. Photograph: Cyril Ellis.

persuaded Henrietta Sharman and her sisters to commission St Mary's, Wellingborough in 1904. The Revd T. J. Watts, of Fenstanton Manor, St Ives, the first Vicar of that church, was his choice and Price was a significant benefactor.

COMMUNITY OF ST MARGARET, ABERDEEN

Conventual chapel, 1891–2

Comper's second work in Aberdeen was the convent chapel for the Community of St Margaret. The order had been founded by John Mason Neale (1818–66), one of Comper's god-fathers, in 1855 at East Grinstead, Sussex. John Comper was the first to introduce Anglican sisters into Scotland in 1864 when he was rector of St John's, Aberdeen. He never ceased to foster the growth of the religious life and Dr Neale, because of his liturgical interest in the revival of local rites, was influenced in his decision to send sisters from East Grinstead by the elder Comper's love of the Scottish Liturgy. Comper's elder sister, Ellen, joined them and John Comper was their chaplain. It was originally proposed that Comper should design a new convent but only the chapel and a wing were realised.

Built of granite, the tower-like east end, raised high on the Spital for the sisters' new home at Bayview, is rooted in the Scottish vernacular tradition. It was modelled on the fifteenth-century choir of the kirk of the Holy Rood, Stirling, and has massive walls, rough-hewn, battering buttresses rising from foundations to parapet, and is roofed in red pantiles. The Aberdeen Ecclesiological Society considered that Comper had built his father's convictions in stone.

The interior is a sensitive essay in the manner of Bodley. The altar has a gradine, or shelf, containing a tabernacle, for the ornaments and has a tall reredos divided into compartments, decorated with diaper patterns. Riddel curtains of tapestry designed by Bodley and woven by Watts & Co. flank the altar at an angle of forty-five degrees. Gilded figures of kneeling angels, wearing apparelled albs and holding tapers, line the wall dividing the sanctuary from the retro-sacristy. The floor is paved in black and white marble and on the north wall is a Scottish sacrament house surmounted by a figure of the Virgin and Child.

Sister Mary Ellen SSM described the consecration in 1892: 'Looking down from the organ gallery at Vespers that evening, on the black and white veils of the sisters, the lofty vaults of the tower among which the flickering shadows were playing – the dim outline of the tall vast windows – and the gorgeous colouring of the reredos, which was lighted by the rays of the setting sun; it was difficult to realise that only a wall separated us from the busy, hurrying life of the nineteenth century.'

ST WILFRID, CANTLEY, SOUTH YORKSHIRE

Restoration and furnishing, 1893–4

The restoration of St Wilfrid's, Cantley, was the second of a sequence of restorations of medieval churches. (The first was of St Mary Magdalene, Geddington, Northamptonshire, in 1889–92.) The Revd William Tatham, supported by the parish patrons, the Childers family of Cantley Lodge (cousins of Charles Lindley Wood, second Viscount Halifax, the President of the English Church Union, and another of Comper's patrons who used him at Hickleton, Yorkshire), wanted to undo a mid-Victorian restoration by Sir George Gilbert Scott and return the church to its late-medieval cohesion.

Comper sought the evidence of medieval inventories, re-established the spacial logic of chapels contained within parclose screens and designed a loft to the rood screen. The surpliced choir was removed from the chancel and moved to the west end in benches close to the organ, thus freeing the sanctuary for Eucharistic worship and the offices. Comper allowed church architecture to breathe by restoring space to the chancel and sanctuary. His solution was architectural rather than decorative because it involved the manipulation and articulation of space and human activity. In recent years St Wilfrid's has been drastically enlarged and adapted and few of the surviving parclose screens any longer define liturgical space. Its logic and intensity of conception has been lost.

Opposite: St Wilfrid, Cantley, South Yorkshire. The screens and chancel, 1894, part of a restoration designed to re-establish medieval spacial logic. Photograph: Cyril Ellis.

Above: The high altar, 1894, Comper's first Gothic altar in a parish church, with a hanging pyx for reserving the Blessed Sacrament. Carnations are strewn on the floor. 'The old English 14th and 15th century miniatures seemed to have revived,' said Comper. Photograph: Cyril Ellis.

St Wilfrid, Cantley, South Yorkshire. Virgin and Child. The influence of German Gothic figure sculpture is typical of Comper's early work. Photograph: Gordon Barnes.

In its rearranged form it is difficult to imagine the delicate scale and unity of what Comper and Tatham accomplished. So convincing was the restoration, so captivating was its beauty, that when the interior of Cantley was damaged by fire in 1906 and the contents lay scattered in the churchyard, a visitor staying with Lord Halifax, on seeing the devastation, observed that this is what it must have been like when churches were sacked by the Puritans. He was Cardinal Gasquet, of Downside Abbey, whose books described the destructive effects of the English Reformation and were influential in Comper's circle.

Comper desired the revival of medieval rubrics and in preparation for his marriage ceremony in 1890 he had studied medieval manuscripts in the British Museum in order to seek directions for the rite. Coincidentally, the illuminations demonstrated to him that the Gothic altars designed by Bodley & Garner, with their overpowering reredoses, were foreign to the essential simplicity of the medieval originals. He repudiated the altar designed in this style at Aberdeen. In 1893 he had delivered a paper, *Practical Considerations on the Gothic or English Altar and Certain Dependent Ornaments*, to the Society of St Osmund and, at Dr J. Wickham Legg's invitation, read it again in that same year to the St Paul's Ecclesiological Society. In it he set out the evidence for the reconstruction of a genuine Gothic altar, the first example of which he had provided for the chapel of the clergy house of St Matthew's, Westminster, in 1892. Stacked though it is with the result of individual study, Comper's work never smells of research: it is learned and spontaneous.

In 1894 he was able at St Wilfrid's to erect a pure Gothic altar for the first time in a parish church. The altar was of stone and stood free from the east wall. Modelled on the evidence of medieval illuminations, it had four riddel posts, hung with curtains suspended by silk cords looped in split rings running on black iron rods. The posts supported gilded figures of kneeling angels holding tapers, taken from precedents discovered by Bodley in Nuremberg. There were no gradines, or shelves, for a crucifix and six candlesticks, only a low reredos, carved coloured and gilded. Two candlesticks lay on the *mensa* and the altar was covered by an embroidered, panelled frontal and narrow frontlet. There was an overhanging canopy, or tester.

Above the altar is a pyx designed to reserve the Blessed Sacrament, suspended 'with its gold and snow-white linen glittering in front of the expanse of silver glass … bearing its jewelled imagery of saints that ever surround the Presence'. The adoption of this method of reservation was then unknown in England. Experimentally it had been proposed by Pugin at St Mary's, Uttoxeter, Staffordshire, in 1839–40, which he described as 'the first Catholic structure erected in this country, in strict accordance with the rules of ancient ecclesiastical architecture, since the pretended Reformation'.

'At the sung mass this morning,' Comper wrote to his father immediately after the altar's completion in 1894, 'the spirit of the old English 14th and 15th century miniatures seemed to have revived – never so much before did it seem to me, simple as it was – or perhaps *because* it was so simple.'

Its legitimacy was made by an appeal to the Ornaments Rubric of *The Book of Common Prayer* which gave lawful authority to sacramentals and opened a way to their revival. The rubric states that 'chancels shall remain as they have been in times past', and continues: 'Such ornaments of the church and of the ministers thereof, at all times of their ministrations, shall be retained and be in use in this Church of England by authority of parliament, in the second year of the reign of King Edward VI': 1548–9.

At a later date the splays of the windows were painted with flowing diapers, images of St Peter and St Paul flank the altar, and there is a small image of St Wilfrid on the north wall of the chancel.

Gothic, or English, altars later became ubiquitous in the Church of England and were popularised by Dr Percy Dearmer, author of *The Parson's Handbook* (1899). So familiar did they become that the revolutionary character of their origin was lost. In 1940 Dearmer's widow, Nan, acknowledged Comper as their originator and conceded their beauty in *The Life of Percy Dearmer*. She also noticed the influence in their promotion of Dr Wickham Legg, 'one of the greatest of all liturgical scholars'. None equalled those designed by Comper. Writing to his friend, Lord Elmley, Dearmer recognised that 'The one man who does know is Comper but he is a mere copyist of Medieval work. So I always try and get a real artist, and then pour into him Comper's archaeological knowledge.' Dearmer was a late follower of the Arts & Crafts Movement and was prejudiced against stylistic authenticity. He did not share Comper's advanced Anglo-Catholic convictions, nor those of his patrons, and he led medievalism down a new and superficial path. Dearmer clung to aesthetic socialism, a cause that was regarded by Comper and his circle with distaste. Comper had moved from the influences of the Aesthetic Movement which he had imbibed from Bodley. He declined to follow the free expression of the Arts and Crafts and established an independent line of his own, basing his work on perfected late-medieval precedent. His work was consciously and deliberately anti-Victorian and his patrons shared the same reaction.

Comper was constantly accused by his critics of being archaeological, a mere imitator. His artistry is so original as an expression of the continuing tradition that it is wholly successful and rarely individualistic in the Aesthetic and Arts and Crafts sense. His work is in a way as self-effacing as the other movements were not. 'I think *The Parson's Handbook* may be taken as the most characteristic change in the Ecclesiological Movement after its first fifty years,' wrote Comper in 1933 in *Further Thoughts on the English Altar, or Practical Considerations on the Planning of a Modern Church*, 'when a new phase began, at once more technical and less spiritual. It was no longer out to suffer for the truth but gain by it. It had a most fatal effect upon architecture, leading to commercial degradation to the level of the church furnisher.'

Master of Saint Giles, The Mass of Saint Giles, *about 1500, oil and egg on oak, 62 x 46 cm. © The National Gallery, London. In the early part of his career, this and similar images strongly influenced Comper's thinking about the most appropriate form of the altar and its furnishings.*

All Saints, St Ives, Huntingdonshire. The organ case and screen of about 1894, one of the most elaborate of Comper's early designs, modelled upon that at King's College, Cambridge. Photograph: Cyril Ellis.

Comper's father and the persecuted first generation of ritualists had fought for externals because they believed in the meaning and value of sacraments. Dearmer and his followers encouraged doctrinal dilution and reduced the religious conviction which underlay Comper's work to hollow aesthetics, with meretricious results. 'It is the change from persecution, from hard fighting for purely spiritual values, to the material beauty which so quickly follows victory,' Comper wrote bitterly.

> Those extreme things for which the fight was hard, and often against honest opponents who really believed that the doctrines of which they were the expression were false, are now accepted by the bishops, and adopted by an ever increasing number of churches which attach to them no more than their 'aesthetic' value. Mere ritualism has become either popular, or a matter of indifference. The chasuble for which S. F. Green was imprisoned for two years without prospect of release is now worn even by the Archbishops on occasions in which it will give no offence. ... There is little doctrinal significance and little liturgical appreciation behind it, and little regard for the authority of the Church or for more than personal preference.

ALL SAINTS, ST IVES, HUNTINGDONSHIRE
Restoration, with organ case, screen and rood, 1894–9

All Saints, St Ives, Huntingdonshire is a noble Perpendicular church built in 1470. In the middle ages it had been splendidly furnished, as shown by the carved corbels on the pillars of the nave arcade.

Arthur Stapylton Barnes was appointed Vicar in 1891. He was an Etonian and had been a curate of St Agnes', Kennington, from 1884 to 1886 and it was there that he met Comper. St Agnes was the centre of revived medievalism and three of the curates went on to become Comper's patrons, including Reginald Camm who preceded Barnes into the Roman Catholic Church in 1890 and went on to become a Benedictine monk, and William Tatham who became Vicar of Cantley, Yorkshire.

Barnes was a serious liturgical scholar, persuaded by the Anglican appeal to the middle ages. He was also a convinced Anglo-Catholic and his research represented a more solid approach than Percy Dearmer's because he regarded a medievalist interpretation of the Book of Common Prayer as a vindication of its Catholic credentials. His ideal was the Dominican Rite which he believed represented the purest instance of medieval continuity.

He gave Comper a free hand to restore All Saints. A Gothic altar with iron riddels, now in the south aisle, was provided, with new pews, a fine brass lectern and much structural work. But the main centre of interest is the organ screen, the second designed by Comper after St Peter's, Ely, incorporating a rood, which was erected by Barnes and some friends in memory of his father, George Carnac Barnes CB. It is modelled upon the disposition of the organ screen of King's College, Cambridge, stripped of Classical references, and is the most elaborate of Comper's early designs for organ screens.

Barnes resigned in 1894 to go on to St Mary's, Ilford, and was succeeded by Dr Salisbury Price who readily continued the restoration. First came the colouring of the screen. As we have seen, Price was, like Barnes, a friend but Comper recalled that he was 'of the somewhat arbitrary type of priest who afforded, perhaps, a kind of excuse for the creation of parish church councils'. An instance was, after settling some detail of colouring with the foreman, Comper found on his return that Price had made him alter it. Needless to say it was put back again. The illustration shows All Saints immediately after the completion of the decoration, before the figures were added to the corbels in the nave.

One of Comper's best early windows, representing St Gregory, St William and St Richard, was erected in the south aisle by Dr W. R. Grove in 1895. Figures for the corbels came next. These represent St Nicholas and St Margaret; St Mary Magdalen and St Lawrence; St Stephen and St Andrew; St George and St Agnes; St Thomas of Canterbury and St John Baptist. The work was done at the height of Comper's enthusiasm for German wood-carving and was designed soon after a tour of the Rhineland in 1896. It ranks with his work at St Mary Magdalene's, Paddington, and in the reredos for St Anne's, Eastbourne. In later life Comper reacted against this influence which he saw as a decline from the Classical ideal of Greece and Rome that he was to discover in Rome in 1900, and did as much as possible to conceal it. He had not entirely shaken off the decorative influence of Bodley and the organ screen was sometimes mistaken for his work.

Salisbury Price resigned in 1899 and went to Kingston, in Cambridgeshire, where he wore the chasuble at the altar and the black gown in the pulpit. Comper did considerable restoration there, but little furniture. Price was succeeded at St Ives by Oscar Wilde, a curate of St Barnabas, Pimlico, who retained Comper for structural work but removed the Gothic altar and replaced it with a more conventional reredos, dependent on Bodley's altars, with a gradine, tabernacle, and six candlesticks that had no connection with Comper and spoils the chancel.

In 1918 the steeple was knocked down by a young airman who flew into it and was killed in the church beneath. It was rebuilt and new bells were hung. The tragedy provided an opportunity to replace the flat plaster ceiling of the nave with an open timber roof. A window in the north aisle in Comper's later style, representing the Risen Saviour flanked by figures of St Thomas More and St Alban, was designed as a memorial to the Watts family in 1929. Many years later Sebastian Comper improved the altar in the south aisle by adding rose-red hangings and gilded baroque ornaments.

All Saints, St Ives, is one of the most ambitious of Comper's early restorations. In the last decade of the nineteenth century medievalism began to move from the main centres of influence in urban churches like St Agnes', Kennington, St Augustine's, Haggerston, St Barnabas, Pimlico, St John the Divine, Kennington, and St Matthew's, Westminster, into lesser London and country parishes. Invariably Comper was responsible for their furniture and restoration and nobody more than he laid the foundations for a medieval liturgical revival applied in purist terms. Accomplished with faultless artistry, Comper made spacial sense of stripped church interiors and opened them up to a new understanding of worship.

COMMUNITY OF THE HOLY NAME, MALVERN LINK, WORCESTERSHIRE
Conventual church, dedicated 1893

The conventual church of the Holy Name, Malvern Link, is a rare example of the successful partnership of Bucknall & Comper in the early days. The commission for the Holy Name arose through William Bucknall's membership of the congregation of St Peter's, Vauxhall, for which parish the community had been founded.

Bucknall was not only a good draughtsman, he was, as a result of his pupillage to Robson, a sound constructor. But he was a pedestrian architect, as his independent work demonstrates, and it was the collaboration with Comper's artistry that produced buildings where the structure complemented the detail. The scale and form of the Holy Name is influenced by Bodley's chapel at Marlborough College, Wiltshire, (1883–6), St Augustine's, Pendlebury, Lancashire, (1870–74) and George Gilbert Scott Junior's St Agnes', Kennington, (1874–91). It is a single vessel with a nave of wide span, no structural division between choir and sanctuary, and tall bays without a clerestory, with arches dying into the piers in the manner of the arcades of St Agnes. It works on the plan and structural principles of Albi Cathedral adapted to conventual use.

The solid form, monumental scale and white walls complement the delicate sanctuary furniture, with a gilded Gothic altar-screen and imagery standing before a wall leading to a sacristy, a painted and decorated ceiling, stalls of dark oak and painted glass in which shining colour and faultless draughtsmanship were set in a white ground relieved by yellow stain. Above the altar hung a gilded pyx protected by a circular tent of rose-red silk.

Comper's copper-gilt pyx was not added until 1924. It was made by Frank Knight in the form of a gabled sexagonal vessel with a crocketted lantern and spire, standing on a broad foot. Three of the sides have angels standing on brackets holding shields bearing the Holy Name. There is not the slightest trace of Classical influence; it complements the Gothic altar and screen below.

Comper was convinced that reservation of the Blessed Sacrament in a pyx, uplifted and on high, was not only one of the most ancient, but the most desirable, method of reservation. The first unambiguous reference to the use of a suspended vessel for reservation occurs in the *Life of St Basil*, written by the pseudo-Amphilochius, probably in the ninth century. Here it is related that he 'caused a golden dove to be fashioned, and having placed in it a portion of the sacred Bread, hung it above the altar'.

Conventual Church of the Holy Name, Malvern Link, Worcestershire, dedicated 1893. A building which works on the plan and structural principles of Albi Cathedral adapted to conventual use. Photograph: Christopher Dalton.

Conventual Church of the Holy Name, Malvern Link, Worcestershire, dedicated 1893. The altar, with suspended pyx above. Photograph: Christopher Dalton.

Its use had never entirely died out in the Western Church and is still to be found in France. There is abundant medieval precedent and Comper believed that the east windows of East Anglian churches and their low cills are explained by the hanging pyx. He revived the practice first at St Matthew's, Westminster, in 1892, and in the following year at Cantley. Bishop Frere suspended the pyx that Comper had designed for Caldey Abbey, presented by Athelstan Riley, in Truro Cathedral. Bishop Gore had approved the introduction of one at the Grosvenor Chapel, Mayfair, where it still remains. Most exquisitely, Prebendary H. F. B. Mackay raised a *turris* of silver, like the steeple of a Wren church, above the high altar of All Saints, Margaret Street. It was presented in 1928 by the Duke of Newcastle as a memorial to the boys of the choir who had died in the Great War.

Reservation in a suspended pyx lasted for a brief time but, although it survives in rare instances, never took hold as it was considered to be unsafe, except in secure places like the convent chapels at Malvern Link and London Colney.

Drawing of altar and suspended pyx for the chapel of the clergy house at St Matthew's, Westminster, 1892. This was the first revival of a Gothic altar and hanging pyx in an Anglican setting since the Reformation (see page 43). Drawing by J. N. Comper.

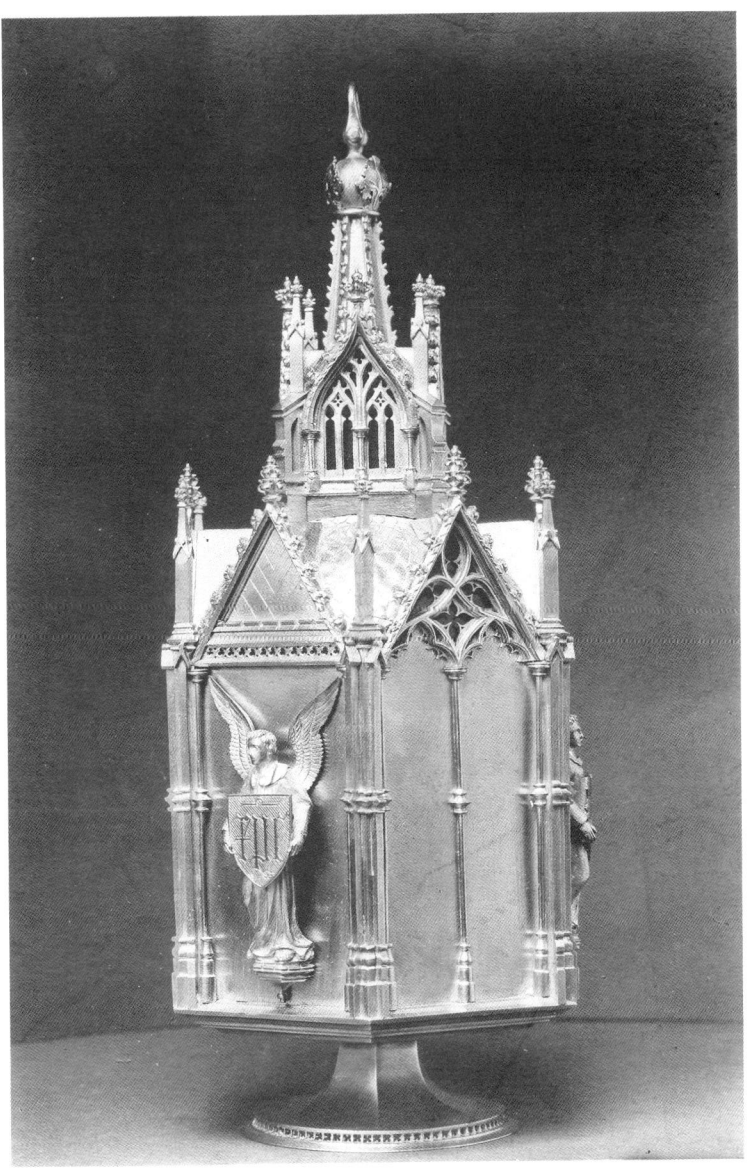

Conventual Church of the Holy Name, Malvern Link, Worcestershire. Hanging pyx, copper-gilt, 1924, one of a number introduced by Comper, who was convinced of the desirability of this method of reservation. Photograph: Frank Knight.

After the dissolution of Comper's partnership with Bucknall in 1904, the Holy Name remained in Bucknall's hands, but for the addition of isolated items of furniture. It did not return to Comper until after Bucknall's death. The Holy Name survived until recently as one of the most perfect and least spoilt survivals of Comper's early work The community decided to make a new foundation in 1988 and the furnishings and glass were later dismantled and vandalised. The chapel has now been converted for domestic use.

DOWNSIDE ABBEY, SOMERSET

Various works, 1896 onwards

Comper rarely worked for the Roman Catholic Church. A notable exception was Downside Abbey, in Somerset, where he established a long connection in 1896 that lasted until 1951. The abbey church contains some of his best work and charts the evolution of his style from the early late-Gothic work which he described as 'unity by exclusion' to the mature developments that synthesised the evolution of Western architecture in his theory of 'unity by inclusion'. But it is not only the evolution of Comper's style which is represented at Downside. He worked there in all media, and the abbey has outstanding examples of stone and alabaster carving, painted glass, metalwork and woodwork, embroidery and textiles. In a Catholic setting Comper's creative powers breathed with unbounded freshness.

Comper owed his introduction to Downside to Arthur Stapylton Barnes. In 1894 Barnes had moved on from St Ives to become warden of St Mary's Hospital, Ilford, in Essex. Two years later he was received into the Roman Catholic Church by Cardinal Merry del Val and spent the early months of his new life at Downside. At that time the abbey church was only fragmentarily built and consisted of the transepts and crossing and the start of a chevet of chapels surrounding the site of the unbuilt choir, including the completed Lady Chapel. This was the work of Dunn & Hansom and had been built in 1873–82.

The church is a fusion of the work of four Gothic Revival architects, and others contributed to the furniture. In 1905 Dunn & Hansom's plans for the church were superseded, after the death of Edward Hansom in 1900, by Thomas Garner's design for the choir; F. A. Walters added the sacristies in 1913; and the nave was built by Sir Giles Gilbert Scott in 1925–38. Downside Abbey is one of the most outstanding churches of the Gothic Revival. In the diversity of hands that have contributed to the design, in its lack of uniformity, it equals the building development of medieval Gothic. Pevsner declared that: 'The whole of the abbey church has become the most splendid demonstration of the renaissance of Roman Catholicism in England. But most of what makes Downside unforgettable belongs to the C20. With its commanding West tower it is Pugin's dream of English Catholicism at last come true.'

Comper had an integral influence on the liturgical and artistic purism of Downside and if he had not had such a long association with the abbey it is unlikely that it would have developed as it did. Barnes commissioned a Gothic altar for the Lady Chapel as an *ex voto* offering in thanksgiving for his conversion. It had four riddel posts of wrought iron, gilded angels bearing tapers, and hangings of figured tapestry that foreshadowed the work that was to come. The altar, raised on broad, shallow steps, was monumentally executed in stone, of great depth, and the posts and curtains were deep enough to form a ritual enclosure. Inspired by the sanctuary of Westminster Abbey,

Downside Abbey, Somerset. The altar of the Lady Chapel, 1896–1913, described as 'a striking novelty'. It is the finest of Comper's Gothic altars, modelled on Nottingham alabasters.

the east end of the chapel was made square by a stone wall, pierced by two oak doors, forming a small sacristy in the apse.

Delicate negotiations were needed before Comper was formally commissioned. First, Comper was asked if he would, as an Anglican, have any objections, on religious grounds, to making a design. He consulted his father, John Comper, and Lord Halifax and they both telegraphed 'Go'. The Prior needed assurance of Comper's sympathy with Catholic doctrine and, when it was given, asked if his proposals were in conformity with Roman rubrics. Surprisingly there were found to be no difficulties but it is only when early photographs are consulted that it is shown how these problems were overcome.

The community was accustomed to the altars designed by Dunn and Hansom where the altar was reduced to little more than a base for the gradines, tabernacle and exposition throne. For Comper's altar, the new wall was used as a gradine for a crucifix and six candlesticks; four candlesticks and altar cards stood on the *mensa*; and a painting of Our Lady was suspended from the back rod, in front of the *halpas*. Barnes presented a frontal of cloth of gold, executed by the School of Embroidery of the Sisters of Bethany. The altar immediately followed Cantley and was the third Comper designed in an authentic medievalist form. He intended a hanging relief of the Coronation of the Virgin (after the fifteenth-century Annunciation surrounded by the mysteries of the rosary, by Veit Stoss in St Lawrence's, Nuremburg) to hang before the altar but it was not executed. Later Comper planned a large square tester hung from the roof above the altar, a rood with attendant figures for the stone screen, four gilded Gothic relic-chests, and a retable of fifteenth-century design. It took some years for these to come to fruition. The altar was completed in 1898 and the first Mass celebrated on the feast of St Augustine of Canterbury, 28 May. The result was described in *The Downside Review* as 'all to us of striking novelty'.

Next came painted glass. Comper's first window at Downside was a small panel of heraldic glass, set in quarries of yellow stain, executed in 1896 in the new lower east cloister. In 1899 he was commissioned to design the east window of the Lady Chapel. The Annunciation was chosen as the subject. Although it is not possible to discuss Comper's glass in detail in this study the Downside windows present an opportunity to explain his principles for painted glass. It has proved the most controversial and misunderstood part of his work, admired as much as it is dismissed.

In his churches and furnishing schemes Comper wanted light for showing the beauty of colour on carved woodwork, painted and gilded screens and altars, textiles and embroidery. He turned for inspiration to English glass of the fifteenth century in York, Fairford, in Gloucestershire, the chapels of All Souls College and New College, Oxford, Great Malvern in Worcestershire, and in fragmentary survivals in East Anglia. For figure subjects he turned to English illuminated miniatures, Norfolk rood screens and stone sculpture,

Dürer, and the Netherlandish panel painters, of whom Memling was the foremost inspiration.

Comper was always keen to defend himself from the charge of antiquarianism and copyism. Defending the window in *The Downside Review* he wrote that it was

> undertaken without claim on the part of the maker of the window to have reproduced exactly any of the ancient examples which have suggested its various details. On the contrary, he would guard himself from any such misconception, by acknowledging that the aim of such a work is not to make a museum of antiquities, or to copy for the sake of copying, but simply to tell afresh, in glass, the old story of the Faith in its most beautiful manner, and by the most direct means attainable. It is with this end in view that, like the merchantman of the parable, its maker takes from his treasures things old as well as new: old, if what is old will best serve his end: new, if he cannot find what he requires in the store-house of the past.

What Comper liked about English late-medieval glass was the large scale, often full-size, 'as large as the lights will contain,' of the standing figures and the architectural effect they achieved in relation to furniture. 'Certainly the value of the large images in the Lady Chapel will better appear when all the windows have their painted glass, and when in front of them is seen the hanging image of the coronation in carved wood, painted and gilt, which is here designed to take the place of the open screen of a parish church.'

He admired late-medieval glass for its 'lightness and pearly whiteness, and that rarity of colour, as of jewels, which mark it off so absolutely from the glass first brought to England from abroad (such as may be seen in the Cathedral Church of Christ at Canterbury), and which was no sooner introduced than departed from'. Technically, he discovered that the glass-oven was favourable to these figures, 'allowing each to come out perfectly in almost one piece of glass. And here it may be remarked how large the pieces of glass were in the most developed old work, and how carefully the leading of even the plainer surfaces of the tabernacle work was ruled by their form; as witness Fairford and All Souls at Oxford.'

Above all it was the tonal effect the glass achieved that Comper admired, accomplished by controlled light. 'It is the glass of the whiter type that we associate with the Lady altars of English quires and the high altars of our parish churches, as their principal and most fitting ornament; and surely it is to this typical English glass with its mysterious effect of liquid silvery coolness, as of light seen through water, that Milton referred when he applied to it the expression "dim religious light", which is as frequently misunderstood for darkness as it is frequently quoted.'

And writing of the window of the Annunciation, Comper set the work in the context of past and future. 'It is the effect of this glass when it was new, and not as it is now after three centuries of exposure, that is aimed at in the present window. And if it must be acknowledged that age gives everything in architecture a charm which nothing new can have, still more must it be remembered that it is not within the province of architecture to imitate the effect of age. But under some conditions of light, as when the sun has gone down on a summer evening, the new glass will anticipate that mellowness which only the long course of the work of nature can permanently impress upon it.'

The window proved controversial. 'The new window in the Lady Chapel has formed a fertile field for divergent criticism,' forthrightly declared *The Downside Review*. The plumed robing of the angels, taken from a precedent in Kilmersdon church, not far from Downside, and the 'woman-shaped serpent' tempting Adam and Eve, taken from Fairford, caused greatest alarm. The figures of Our Lady and the Archangel Gabriel gave the exact impression of old examples and few were used to them.

'We can well understand why St Gabriel caused a great deal of consternation,' wrote Dom Augustine James many years later in *The Story of Downside Abbey Church*, 'face, hands and feet are bare, but his limbs, so far as they are not covered by a gracefully flowing dalmatic, appear in all the glory of an azure crop of feathers. His half smile reminds us of the charming beckoning angel of Rheims Cathedral. He is quite unlike the golden-haired, white-gowned angels of our nursery days … There are great splashes of glowing colour in the window: the reds seem to be on fire, and the blues match an Italian sky in purity. As for the leading, it is wrought so skilfully that it only adds to the decorative effect.' And he concludes that, 'Except for their perfect condition and the silvery whiteness of much of the background, not yet overlaid and darkened by the dirt of centuries, one feels that both lights might have been transferred to Downside from a fifteenth-century church.'

It was the unfamiliarity and novelty of the general treatment, as well as its archaic references, that attracted most comment. The monks were used to the heavy, opaque stained glass by Nathaniel Westlake in St Benedict's and St Isidore's chapels, and Hardman's rose window in the north transept. It was seen in the context of high art and had been chosen by Dunn & Hansom. These windows were as acceptable to the community as their altars.

Comper's window was praised by Francis Bligh Bond, an acknowledged authority on late medieval art whom Comper knew slightly, better known for his archaeological investigations of Glastonbury Abbey and expertise in rood screens. 'Easily the best modern glass in England,' he pronounced, 'comparing very favourably with the best of the old English glass.' This quietened the community's misgivings a little. In July 1904 it was announced that

Mr Comper has another window in hand for the Lady chapel. It is to represent the Visitation of our Lady … Mr Comper's glass is peculiar and excites keen criticism. Many, perhaps most, think it too light and cold. But the conditions of the chapel must be taken into consideration. The number and height of the windows and the narrow breadth of the chapel would make it light under any condition of glass, and would keep the details of the groining always in evidence; and it is desirable that this should be so. There is room to think that a more heavily coloured treatment of the glass and especially a more populously grouped representation of figures, would not harmonise with the architectural effect. The single-figured lights and the canopy work of Comper's window, all help in that soaring sentiment which is conveyed by the chapel.

In December of the same year a more positive tone was adopted: 'We must confess that the general opinion is in favour of the new glass.'

The glazing of the Lady Chapel continued until 1927 when the final window on the north side of the west end was inserted. The subjects of the scheme were the life of the Virgin and a typological interpretation of the Christian dispensation. Typology, with an increasing allegorical emphasis, was much employed by the early Church, especially by the Alexandrian Fathers, for whom almost everything in the Old Testament was capable of interpretation by this method. A Christian type differs from an allegory in that the historical reference is not lost sight of. Typology was revived in the nineteenth century and had profound meaning for Comper and his clients.

Architecturally the scheme achieved the controlled diffusion of light that Comper desired. The glass forges the link between the arcaded wall surface and vault and draws the chapel into unity. It also demonstrates the gradual evolution of Comper's glass techniques expressed in clarity of colour and refined, but tense, draughtsmanship. He came to use medieval recipes, in which sand and seaweed were used as a flux made in clay pots, instead of the modern chemical methods made in metal pots. To this is attributed the brilliance of the tones of white and the carrying power of the colour.

'Almost alone among modern workers in stained glass,' commented *The Downside Review*,

> Mr Comper has the courage to use pure whites, as the medieval workers did, instead of a pale greenish glass, and to trust in time to mellow down the tone, instead of faking an appearance of age with extra paint 'to dirty it down', as they say in the workshop. The superficial critic, who does not realize this, will often complain of his work as too thin, but we feel convinced that time will allow him to be right. Already, for example, his glass in the Lady Chapel has mellowed wonderfully, the dust of a few years and the Mendip mists combine to give it just the softened effect which the artist allows for; and this without losing the brilliancy which his pure whites secure so brilliantly.

Greatest effect, notably in the tones of blue and red, was achieved in the windows in the chapel of the Sacred Heart, erected in 1914. The design has a figure of Christ in the centre of the composition with the twelve seated Apostles enthroned, grouped below. This chapel opens from the south-west end of the Lady Chapel, the three windows provide a foil, in the form of a triptych, to the neighbouring glass, and are visible, glowing with ultramarine intensity, from almost every part of the building.

Downside Abbey, Somerset. A detail of the reredos of the altar of the Lady Chapel, 1913. It is made of alabaster and richly coloured and gilded, following medieval precedent.

'The result is something that must surely take its place in the history of stained glass,' recorded *The Downside Review* at the conclusion of the scheme, 'it is also a remarkable record of Mr J. N. Comper's work of a period not far short of thirty years, and one which should, we think, bring to him something like the satisfaction and pride which it causes us. Whatever is done in the future towards the adornment of our Church, the Lady Chapel windows will always remain one of the outstanding features and most precious ornaments.'

In 1913 Comper's plans for the elaboration of the altar of the Lady Chapel came to fruition. Barnes was a man of independent means but he was unable to decorate the chapel as fully as Comper wanted. In 1912 Sir William Butler presented a new retable, or reredos, riddel posts (the original angels were retained), the relic chests and crucifix to the chapel, and the east wall was decorated in blue and gold with Islamic patterns. They were given to commemorate the ordination to the priesthood of his son, Dom Urban Butler. Comper had an acquaintance with Alice Meynell, the writer and poet, whose sister, Lady Butler, the equine painter, was Dom Urban's mother. His work was already known to the Meynell circle independently of Downside. Lady Butler presented a set of embroidered red vestments to Comper's design for her son's first Mass. At the Meynell's house in Palace Court, Bayswater, Comper encountered Francis Thompson. 'Francis Thompson is a well remembered but silent figure, drooping over their hearth, an object of misery. To stumble in later years upon his *Hound of Heaven* was one of the greatest surprises this life can hold.'

The form of the reredos was five panels contained within an encircling Jesse tree. They were executed in English alabaster, and the canopies above each panel in oak. Reading from left to right the subjects are: the Nativity, with St Joseph and an adoring angel; the Adoration of the Magi; the child Jesus standing on a rose between Our Lady and St Anne; the Presentation in the Temple with Simeon and Anna; the traditional appearance of Christ to his Blessed Mother after the Resurrection. The figure of Jesse is in the centre of the frame, immediately below the Child Jesus, and to his left and right are David and Solomon, with other kings of the House of Judah on either side. In the right-hand bottom corner are the arms of the donor.

The work was based on surviving examples of the Nottingham school of sculptors, whose alabaster carvings were sent all over England, and to Germany, France, Italy and Spain in the fourteenth and fifteenth centuries. Following this precedent Comper decorated the whole in rich colour with large quantities of gold. The natural alabaster was left exposed for the faces and hands of the figures, only the eyes and hair were tinted. The draperies were decorated in gold leaf, with their turnovers, or linings, powdered with ermine spots on the alabaster. The background throughout is a pure cobalt blue, diapered with flower sprigs in gold, and very small touches of red, green and black are used here and there as a foil to the main colours. The gold leaf, of pale lemon colour and special quality, was beaten especially for the work. The carving was executed by Messrs J. McCullogh & Co. Ltd of Kennington, the precursor of W. D. Gough, and the decoration in gold and colour by the *atelier* of H. A. Bernard Smith.

With the later exception of the Stanton chantry, executed immediately after in 1913–17 at St Alban's, Holborn, no other work by Comper was of equal scale and splendour. Indeed, it contributed to the later design through finesse of workmanship. It is one of the finest works of religious art of the early twentieth century. 'What makes Mr Comper's work unique,' said *The Downside Review*, 'is not its material or even its exquisite detail, for many other architects have produced alabaster sculptures of great beauty; but rather his treatment of the whole work with the richest possible decoration in gold and colour.' It opened a vision of the medieval past obscured by later Puritan severity and crude Victorian restoration. 'We are now so accustomed to cathedrals, abbeys and churches which have first been whitewashed, then scraped and finally restored into chilly respectability, that few realize at all how very different was their appearance and how glorious their decoration in the heyday of their life as shrines of the Blessed Sacrament.'

The new work sealed Comper's acceptance by the Downside community and opened up a liturgical vision for the future. 'Still towards such an effect the decoration of the Abbey Church is tending and the Lady Chapel altar is a graceful foretaste of the beauties we may hope to realize when every altar, screen and statue shall be clad in gold and colour, so that the material Church, like the Bride of Christ herself, is literally "all glorious within".'

Comper wanted to complete the Lady Chapel by decorating the stonework with diaper patterns and the groined vault with gold and a firmament of stars on a cobalt ground. The effect would have been like the Sainte Chapelle in Paris, a building whose overall tonality of blue and gold and elegance of scale Comper greatly admired. He designed carved panelling and stalls for the entire length. These were arrested by the Great War. But in 1913 he laid down a pavement of grey Pennant stone in the ambulatory, given by Richard Howden, with a permanent flight of steps leading up to the chapel. In 1915 he designed for the same donor the tall gilded statue of the Virgin and Child of lime wood, wearing an ermine-lined cloak, and richly patterned underdress, which stands on a pedestal against the column which divides the western arch of the chapel; a tall, slender gilded and crocketted canopy rises above it. In 1929 he added the beautiful black iron gates with sinuous arabesque cresting in the form of Spanish *rejas*. They act as a screen to the chapel and frame the statue of Our Lady.

In 1902 Barnes went on to become Catholic chaplain to Cambridge University and helped Wilfrid Ward in editing *The Dublin Review*. He was made a Privy Chamberlain to the Pope in 1904, became a distinguished Catholic historical writer, and in 1916 he migrated to Oxford and became chaplain to the University until his retirement in 1926. Comper did not forfeit his friendship; he retained great affection for him and liked his books. 'Barnes was always an ecclesiologist of considerable power and a good opposition to J. Wickham Legg,' Comper noted, 'but his outstanding book is *St Peter in Rome and his Tomb on the Vatican Hill* of 1900. His thoroughness and, I believe, new conclusions were recognised alike by non-Catholic archaeologists and the Vatican which conferred upon him the title of Monsignor, but was shy of pushing his excavations to their extreme limit. It was characteristic of him to prove his case with such absolute certainty – and perhaps never more so than in his work on the Holy Shroud of Turin – that it leaves a doubt in the reader's mind.'

Barnes soon abandoned his medievalist enthusiasm and rarely referred to it in later life. But in 1926 he published *The Catholic Schools of England* and mentioned the altar of the Downside Lady Chapel. 'One piece of interior decoration stands out especially and calls for notice. It is the treatment of the

*Downside Abbey, Somerset.
The Virgin and Child in
the Lady Chapel,
lime-wood, gilded and
painted, 1915.*

Lady Chapel by Mr J. N. Comper. He has used gold and colour freely, but with great skill. The alabaster reredos, relieved only by gold, is one of the most beautiful things in all Europe.'

In the early days of Comper's connection with Downside he had provided a shape for a full Gothic chasuble. He designed several sets of vestments for the Abbey and they provided a precedent for the chasubles made in the abbey work room thereafter. In 1925 when Comper designed a set of High Mass vestments for Southwark Cathedral he referred back to Downside and found that the only alteration which the experience of thirty years had made was a slight widening of the chasuble 'bringing it, with the arms stretched out, to about the joint of the thumb'.

Comper's full Gothic chasubles were sometimes criticised for being too cumbersome in their medieval authenticity but his response was to encourage priests to know how to wear them. He made an appeal to the Sacred Congregation of Rites in Rome and was gratified to be told that 'a chasuble

Downside Abbey, Somerset. A posed photograh in the Lady Chapel of about 1913, showing a set of Gothic vestments designed for High Mass.

may reach a little beyond the wrists, or a little below the shoulders, but not in between'. 'To my eye,' he recalled, 'the "not in between" is very important; it is the blindness to this which has been I think responsible for the desertion of the full shape.'

The vestments shown in the illustration were made about 1913 for the Abbot of Mount St Bernard's Abbey, Coalville, Leicestershire, and show the continuity of Comper's influence on Downside. They are made of textiles designed by Comper, follow the cut of his vestments, and the group is posed in the Lady Chapel, creating an impression of what it was like when in use.

After the Lady Chapel, Comper went on to design much furniture for Downside Abbey, notably the statue of St Benedict in 1919, St Sebastian's Chapel in 1929, and the east window of the choir when Scott's nave was completed in 1936. 'To the community, which had been entirely converted to a full appreciation of Comper as a decorator, it seemed obviously right that he should be entrusted with this, the most prominent work of decoration in the church.' He had immense influence on the refined taste and liturgical life of the abbey. 'One of the first unchallenged acceptances of "the English altar" was in the Lady Chapel of Downside Abbey,' Comper wrote in his paper, *Further Thoughts on the English Altar: or Practical Considerations on the Planning of a Modern Church*, in 1933, 'where now, in the finished church, every new altar is in conformity with it. This is an important witness to a fact which is far too much forgotten, viz that between what is English and what is Roman there is no difference.'

When Scott's nave was opened in 1925 Abbot Ramsey sought Comper's view on the design of the high altar of Garner's choir. Garner's desire to erect a version of the pre-Reformation altar screen of Westminster Abbey as depicted in the funerary roll of Abbot Islip was deemed impractical. Comper came up with an entirely unexpected and revolutionary proposal. By then his early medievalism was long past. He suggested that 'we must look behind the middle ages for a clue to the solution'. He proposed an altar at the west end of the choir, with the choir stalls behind it, standing beneath a high, gilded ciborium of Classical design. 'Your church is now too long to admit of the ceremonies of the high altar where it now stands at the extreme east end of the choir taking their right relation to the worshippers in the nave. It is too isolated and far removed.' This proved too radical for the community, by now entirely medievalist in their preferences, and nothing was done about it. Comper prepared a ground-plan and in 1968 it was used by Francis Pollen when Scott's long stone high altar, shortened to ten feet, was moved to the place Comper had proposed and the choir stalls behind it. If Comper's designs had been executed forty years previously Downside Abbey would have had one of the most liturgically advanced plans of any church in the country, crowned by a stately ciborium of burnished gold and colour.

Comper was in complete sympathy with Downside and it encouraged his ecumenical hopes of the union of the Church of England with the Roman Catholic Church. One who understood him with sympathy and penetration, spiritually and artistically, was Dom Augustine James. He spoke for many of his generation who held Comper's work in high regard.

> To enter one of these churches, in which his planning and design has been fully carried out, is to find oneself in another world … As to the persuading of Mr Comper, he may be said to have belonged to that section of the established church to which differences from Rome are more apparent than real. Any step towards reconciliation and ultimate union between Rome and Canterbury would be acceptable to him; and the undertaking of decorative work in a great Benedictine church would have presented itself to him as a step in the right direction … Our church is, as far as I know, unique among Catholic churches in possessing much of his lovely work.

ERDINGTON ABBEY, BIRMINGHAM

Feretory, 1896

In 1896 Comper was invited to design a feretory to contain one of the skulls of St Ursula's eleven thousand virgins for Erdington Abbey, on the outskirts of Birmingham. The origin of the commission was circuitous. The donor was Dom Bede Camm OSB. Reginald Camm was an exact contemporary of Comper and, as previously discussed, had started his professional life as a curate of St Agnes', Kennington. There he was influenced by the architecture of George Gilbert Scott Junior and an admiration for the work of the late Gothic Revival defined his taste for the rest of his life. Dom Aidan Bellenger attests that 'grandeur seems to be what he was continually looking for', and this is confirmed by his patronage.

Erdington Abbey, Birmingham. Feretory of 1896, made of gilded wood, and showing the influence of Pugin. Photograph, 1896.

Camm was received into the Roman Catholic Church in 1890 at the Benedictine Abbey of Maredsous, in Belgium, which had been founded in 1872 as a daughter house of Beuron, in Germany. Maredsous was in the vanguard of monastic revival and liturgical reform and had an imposing Gothic Revival church. Camm entered the Maredsous community in 1891, was ordained priest in 1895, and went to Erdington after his ordination and remained there until 1912.

As an Anglican, he was drawn to the Society of St John the Evangelist, Cowley, and a Cowley Father with whom he maintained contact after his submission was Fr Congreve. Congreve recommended Comper's work to Camm when he expressed a desire to present a feretory for the skull to commemorate the elevation of Erdington to abbatial status in 1896.

Comper felt less at home at Erdington than he did at Downside, found the German monks cold, and Camm a humourless client, driven by convert zeal. 'There was a very deep kindliness and indeed simplicity, in the best sense, about Dom Bede,' declared his obituary in *The Downside Review*, 'though this was sometimes obscured by a certain brusqueness, even perhaps tactlessness, of manner which those who know him slightly did not always understand.' Comper and he disagreed over the claims of the Church of England and modern Roman devotions. When Comper expressed a dislike of Benediction 'the fact that he could say he had known it in the Anglican Communion from his childhood caused an expression of annoyance which betrayed a different spirit from Downside'.

Nor did Comper like relics. 'While nothing is more impressive and inspiring than to stand at the tomb of some great man, no matter whether it covers the whole of his mortal body or whether only a bone or ashes remain, the same bone or ashes enclosed in how magnificent a portable reliquary leaves me unmoved by anything but a sense of distress and discomfort.' He thought the relic cupboard at Downside, full of human fragments in glass cylinders, 'suggestive of a surgeon's collection'.

Nevertheless, the feretory went ahead. It took the form of a chapel-like structure of gilded wood with a steeple and shows the direct influence of Pugin. The only other relic chests that Comper designed were for the Lady Chapel of Downside Abbey in 1913 and the Erdington feretory is more elaborate. 'Its translation seemed of little moment to the German monks, but of great importance to the English convert who had invited me there. The most outstanding interest connected with the ceremony was the use of Pugin's tunicles from Oscott by the four bearers of the reliquary, the feature of which was a steeple, and the whole made a picture not unlike a medieval miniature.'

Camm was a generous benefactor to Erdington and his most sumptuous gift was a red silk altar frontal embroidered with half-length portraits of English martyrs enclosed in winding rose briars, with a jewelled figure of St Thomas Becket in the centre, and a set of pontifical High Mass vestments, including seven copes. They were designed by Thomas Garner, who had become a Catholic in 1896 following the condemnation of Anglican orders as invalid through defect of form and intention, and executed by the Sisters of the Poor Child Jesus, at Southam, Warwickshire. Camm continued to commission work from the Southam Convent after becoming affiliated to the Downside Community in 1913.

He became a noted martyrologist, promoted the cause of the English martyrs, and was responsible for the Oratory of the Martyrs at Tyburn Convent. But perhaps his most notable achievement was the preparation of the Anglican monks of Caldey Island and the nuns of St Bride's, Milford Haven, for their reception into the Roman Communion in 1913.

The Erdington feretory was destroyed after the Second Vatican Council by the Redemptorists, who succeeded the Benedictines after their return to Maredsous and Beuron after the First World War.

ST MARY MAGDALENE, PADDINGTON, LONDON
Chapel of St Sepulchre, 1895

The Revd Richard Temple West founded St Mary Magdalene's, Paddington, in 1865. He had been a curate of All Saints, Margaret Street, from 1860 to 1864, and it was there that he met George Edmund Street, a member of the congregation, with whom he formed a friendship. Street was commissioned to design the new church on a difficult site next to the Regent Canal. Completed in 1878, it is one of the best mid-Victorian churches in London, outstanding for the plan, polychromatic brickwork, sculpture and stained glass by Henry Holiday.

On his death in 1893, West was succeeded by William Henry Bleaden, one of his curates from 1889. Bleaden had been Vicar of St John's, Aberdeen, and knew Comper's father. He took an interest in Comper's work and invited him to design West's memorial brass. Comper designed many memorial brasses and they are distinguished by one feature: exact portraiture. The West brass represents him standing in Gothic eucharistic vestments, including an apparelled amice and alb, on a flowered sward, holding a chalice and paten, beneath an elaborate canopy, flanked by shields. Above is a text *In lumine tuo videvimus lumen* (In your light we shall see the light) inscribed in black letter on a scroll. The brass was executed by Barkentin and Krall. In 1915 Comper designed a monumental brass to Bleaden, executed by Harold Soper.

Bleaden went on to commission from Comper the undercroft chapel of St Sepulchre as a memorial to West. It represents the most extensive and challenging opportunity of Comper's first period. He transformed the south aisle of Street's severe and monumental crypt into a late-medieval votive shrine and chantry, using controlled delicacy and sweetness of effect to counteract the crushing context. The precedent is the fifteenth-century chapel of St Mary Undercroft in the crypt of Canterbury Cathedral, defined by stone screens. But he also brought to bear the influence of Flemish Primitive panel paintings in the tonality of colour and the detailing of the pavement, composed of red, green and white quarry tiles. The sanctuary lamp, candelabra and altar candlesticks are taken from Pugin's published working drawings for ecclesiastical metalwork.

The density of statuary in the altar screen is heavily dependent upon Germany. The Virgin and Child are in the centre standing upon the moon, surrounded by a mandorla and a wreath of roses, flanked by angels playing musical instruments. An open screen of geometrical design veils the altar, while the length of the north side of the chapel is lined by screens filled with

Chapel of St Sepulchre, St Mary Magdalene, Paddington, London. Brass to Richard Temple West (d. 1893), who founded the church. Brass rubbing.

attenuated mullions with ogival heads, painted and gilded, supported by a stone wall, shielding the eye from the oppression beyond. Germany also influenced the silver glass which has painted detail taken from Dürer and the Danzig 'Last Judgement', combined with the English influence of Fairford. Figures of saints stand on flowered swards. In the west window Dr West kneels before St Richard, his patron saint. The wings of the organ case depict the three Maries at the Sepulchre and the resurrection appearance to St Mary Magdalene. Above is a scroll held by angels containing the first verse of the Easter office hymn, *Chorus novae Jerusalem*, and at the corners are St Cecilia and St Gregory the Great, after whom the Gregorian chant is named. Introits, antiphons and the Easter Sequence from the Sarum Missal and Antiphoner, painted in black letter with plainsong notation, run round the walls. The screens and organ case are ornamented with West's armorial bearings.

The vault was originally given an impression of infinity by being painted dark blue (the present Mediterranean tone is a misrepresentation of his father's intentions by Sebastian Comper) relieved by gilded angels from whose praying hands were suspended candle branches of wrought iron. Between them are powdered stars of gilded lead, containing convex reflective

Opposite: Chapel of St Sepulchre, St Mary Magdalene, Paddington, London, 1895. The vault was given an impression of infinity by being painted dark blue, with stars of gilded lead. Photograph: Cyril Ellis, 1895.

Above: The altar, 1895, with a density of statuary influenced by Germany. Some of the altar furniture is taken from designs by Pugin. Photograph: Cyril Ellis.

Chapel of St Sepulchre, St Mary Magdalene, Paddington, London, 1895. Design for the altar and reredos, 1895, a fine example of William Bucknall's draughtsmanship. Drawing by William Bucknall.

glass. When candles were lighted at night the vault was transformed into a sparkling firmament representing the vault of heaven.

The function of the chapel was not solely that of a chantry but a place of reservation of the Blessed Sacrament. The sanctuary beyond the screen has a stone sedilia and piscina, and the stalls have misericords. A concealed tabernacle is hidden behind the centre panel of the reredos and from the tester hung a pyx for which the screen provided the imagery of saints. A frontal of yellow velvet embroidered with seraphim hung before the stone altar. St Sepulchre's glows with luminous Northern Gothic colour. Yet it had a fragile beauty that quickly deteriorated. When William Butchart repainted the chapel in 1937 he said that the damp from the adjacent canal was so bad that, when finished, the black letter inscriptions were beginning to deteriorate where he had started.

Chapel of St Sepulchre, St Mary Magdalene, Paddington, London, 1895, looking west. Although a consummate example of Comper's early church design, in later years he reacted strongly against this work. Photograph: Gordon Barnes, 1966.

Chapel of St Sepulchre, St Mary Magdalene, Paddington, London, 1895. The organ at the west end. Photograph: Gordon Barnes, 1966.

St Mary Undercroft may have provided a precedent but it is Flanders that furnishes the key. In 1894 Comper had toured the Low Countries. Of Flemish primitive paintings he wrote in 1893: 'We have no pictures nearer home than these that can be so entirely relied upon as accurate in what they show. … To go no further than the National Gallery, a careful comparison of these Flemish pictures with other work will show convincingly that they stand alone, amongst all schools of painting, in the way this carefulness of detail is maintained throughout the whole of each work.'

In later life Comper strongly reacted against the chapel of St Sepulchre. Referring to the figures he had executed in the nave of St Ives, Huntingdonshire in 1894 he wrote: 'The figures restored to the old corbels on the nave arcade, are, with those in the undercroft of St Mary Magdalene's, Paddington, perhaps the worst examples of bad copies of bad German figures, after the tradition learnt from Kempe and Bodley, but worse executed.'

And writing in *Further Thoughts* he gave his considered conclusions on German influence. 'There is no denying the Teutonic influence in the fifteenth century which, though itself modified by Italy, not only marked with its ugly mannerisms the fairer art of Flanders and Spain, but spoiled the painting and sculpture of Burgundy and the rest of France and, in its softened French and Netherlandish form, ousted in England also the keen sense of the beauty of the human form which has come straight from the Mediterranean and is part of the glory of our earlier Gothic.' Nevertheless, St Sepulchre's chapel remains a consummate example of Comper's early church design. There is no chapel of such elaborate and concentrated richness in the history of the Gothic Revival in England, fulfilling the ultimate expression of the Puginian ideal.

ST ANNE, UPPERTON, EASTBOURNE, SUSSEX

High altar and reredos, 1896–7

In 1896 the Revd W. P. Jay commissioned a new high altar and reredos for St Anne's, Eastbourne. St Anne's was an undistinguished church, designed by George Cowley Haddon of Hereford, and consecrated in 1882. It had an aisleless nave and an elevated chancel. Jay had been instituted in the previous year and wanted to dignify the church.

Here Comper designed perhaps the most elaborate high altar of the period of his enthusiasm for German fifteenth-century Gothic art, one that remains the least known example of his early work. Drawings for it no longer exist, nor does correspondence, it was never illustrated, and he never alluded to it in his professional recollections. Yet it ranks with his contemporary work in the Chapel of St Sepulchre in the undercroft of St Mary Magdalene's, Paddington, as one of the best, most considered examples of his early style. It is a significant casualty of Comper's later reaction against his early work.

St Anne, Upperton, Eastbourne, Sussex. High altar and reredos, 1896–7, an example of Comper's enthusiam for medieval German art. Photograph: Cyril Ellis.

The altar is composed of a retable divided into five panels, carved in shallow relief. In the centre is a group of the Annunciation flanked by figures of St Joachim and St Anne. To the left is the Nativity; to the right the Visitation; angels divide the panels. They stand against diapered tapestry hangings beneath crocketted tabernacles, enclosed in a moulded frame.

The reredos, in the form of an altar screen, is composed of a central figure of Christ in the act of blessing, holding an orb signifying his kingship, surrounded by six adoring angels. It is flanked by figures of St Richard and St George, while St Peter and St Paul occupy the outer niches, standing on corbels against a frame of blind tracery decorated with armorial bearings. The figures are contained within crocketted tabernacles standing beneath open-work brattishing, from which rise six poppy heads. Beneath, a cornice of four angels holding shields divides the retable from the upper structure.

The altar, without gradines, is enclosed within iron riddel posts decorated with fleurs de lys, crowned by four kneeling angels holding tapers. Comper designed the brass altar candlesticks. There is a panelled frontal made of cloth of gold, copied from the surcoat of a figure in Van der Weydon's diptych panel of the Exhumation of St Hubert in the National Gallery, woven by Perkins, embroidered by the Sisters of Bethany with a seraphim, flanked by sacred monograms.

St Anne's was destroyed in 1940 and the parish came to an end in 1955. The reredos was badly damaged but the retable survives and is now in St Mary Magdalene's, Coldean, Brighton.

ST MARY, EGMANTON, NOTTINGHAMSHIRE

Restoration, 1897

Of Comper's many restorations, the most beautiful and complete is Egmanton in Nottinghamshire, carried out in 1897 for the seventh Duke of Newcastle to whom he was introduced by Sir William St John Hope. It is a subtle fusion of English and German precedents. The Gothic altar had a hanging pyx. The solid panels of the screen, painted with tall figures of saints, are taken from Attleborough, Norfolk, a screen that exercised a permanent influence on Comper which was fulfilled at St Cyprian's, Clarence Gate. But the winged organ case is dependent upon Germany as interpreted by the Revd Frederick Sutton, Vicar of Brant Broughton, Lincolnshire. Sutton designed Bodley & Garner's organ cases and Comper met him during his pupillage to Bodley. This case lacks the faults which mar some of Comper's later organ cases. The front pipes and the scale are properly related to the small one-manual instrument it contains. Germany also influenced the design of the imagery. In 1897, the same year, Comper published the second of his liturgical papers, *The Reasonableness of the Ornaments Rubric Illustrated by a Comparison of the German and English Altars.*

Egmanton was one of two restorations commissioned by the Duke of Newcastle. The other was at East Markham and was only partly completed (see illustration page 74). The Duke had wanted Comper to work at his estate church at Clumber, a remarkable work of aristocratic patronage and Anglo-Catholic piety, completed by Bodley in 1889. Comper designed some imagery, vestments and altar frontals but their association was short-lived. Comper recalled that 'in 1897 the Duke (who had already quarrelled with the Vicar of Markham and stopped the rood loft and organ which he had put in hand) wanted to pull down the two ends of Clumber, rebuilding the east wall at the west end, substituting for it a blank wall to receive an elaborate reredos, and when his architect [Comper] had to tell him that he could not pull down his old master's work all the schemes fell through.'

Opposite: St Mary, Egmanton, Nottinghamshire, 1897. This is perhaps the most beautiful and complete of Comper's restorations. Photograph, 1950.

Above: The hanging pyx and tent at St Mary, Egmanton, 1897. The pyx is now in the Victoria and Albert museum.

St Mary, Egmanton, Nottinghamshire. Above: Design for the restoration, carried out in 1897. Beautifully proportioned, the screen is based on Norfolk precedents, the organ on German examples. Drawing by William Bucknall, 1896. Opposite: Photograph of the interior: Cyril Ellis, 1897.

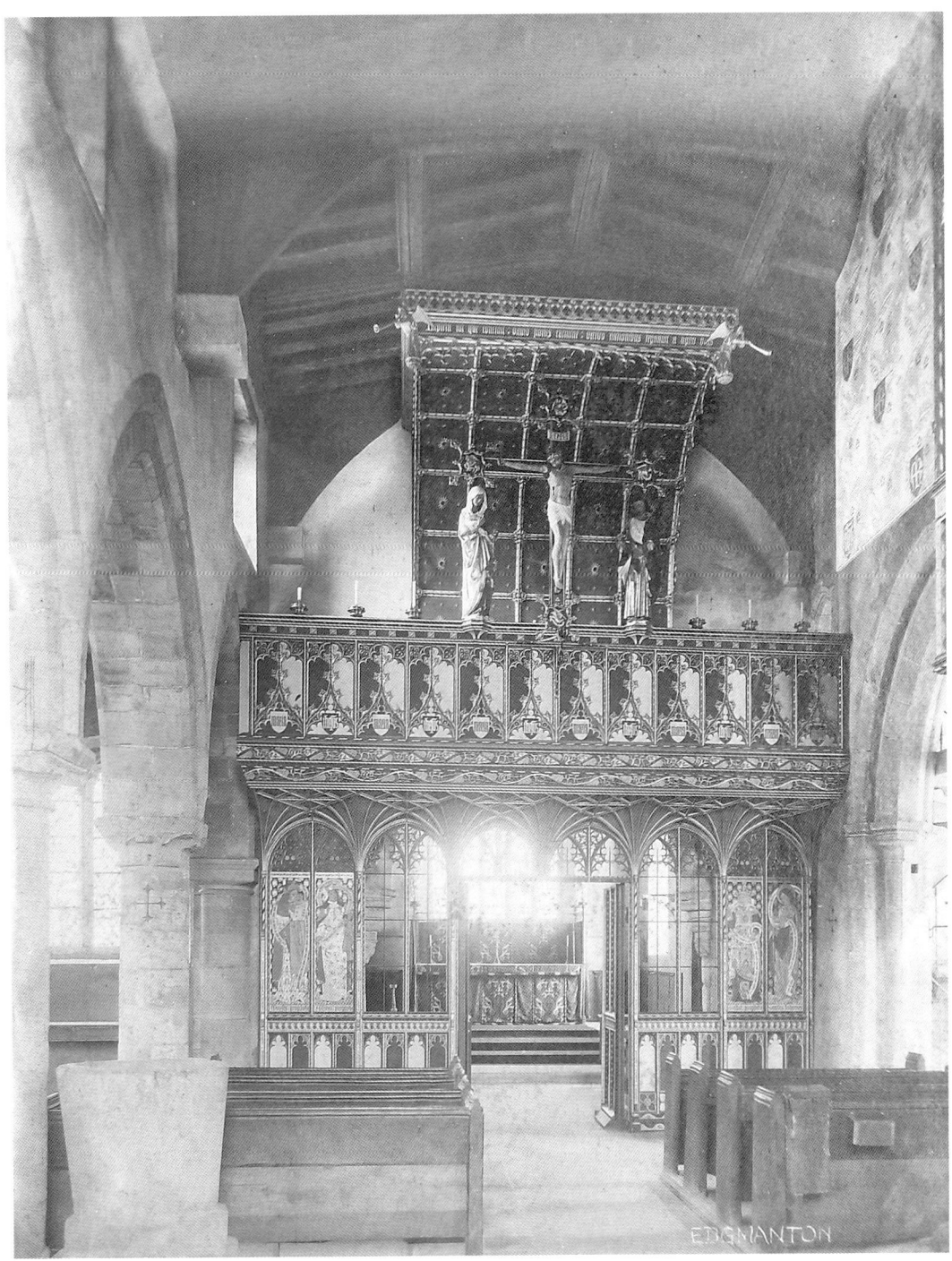

St John the Baptist, East Markham, Nottinghamshire. Design for a screen and organ, 1897. Comper's client at this church was the Duke of Newcastle, who was also his client at Egmanton. The work was not executed due to a disagreement between Comper and the Duke. Drawing by William Bucknall.

ST BARNABAS, PIMLICO, LONDON

Chantry chapel and furnishings including altar, 1889–1901

St Barnabas, Pimlico, had great significance for Comper. It was not only a centre of medievalist ceremonial and plainchant with an Anglo-Catholic tradition dating from the consecration in 1850, but the Vicar, the Revd Alfred Gurney, a priest-poet and Wagnerian, was one of his earliest patrons and took a kindly interest in him during his pupillage. It was at St Barnabas that Comper was married to Grace Bucknall in 1890, and his elder children were baptised there.

St Barnabas was designed by Thomas Cundy, possibly assisted by William Butterfield, in 1847. Built of Kentish ragstone it is part of a group comprising a vicarage and school set behind a stone wall. Pugin designed the altar plate, a cross and candlesticks for the high altar, and a massive *corona lucis*, given by A. J. Beresford Hope. Butterfield designed the lectern. The interior presents a synthesis of decoration unmatched by any other church of the Gothic Revival. The nave has low, open seats; Latin texts are painted round the nave arcade and there is polychromatic decoration on the pillars surviving from the earliest scheme of decoration; the chancel has returned stalls. The altar is raised on three steps of Purbeck marble and the sanctuary is lined with wall arcades and a sedilia. The east and west windows have triple lancets, the latter finished by a rose window. Originally the glass was by William Wailes and cast a filtered blue light on the interior.

Alfred Gurney was appointed Vicar in 1879. He attracted a rich and influential congregation and turned St Barnabas into one of the most fashionable churches in London. He received the world in style at the vicarage. Comper remembered a visit in 1882 when he was eighteen and still working with Kempe. Here he first encountered the hypersensitivity of the extravagant cult of the beautiful that characterised the Aesthetic Movement in late-nineteenth century England. 'It was in response to an invitation from Alfred Gurney to "one who combined the love of Cowley with the love of art". A fear I held that evening dress might be out of place was reversed when the Parsonage door was flung open by two footmen. Rossetti had just died and the conversation of a select company at dinner was devoted to descriptions of his last hours, and of his habitual fear of being alone; he would keep a friend with him to the small hours of the morning and rise before noon to stretch out his brush from his couch to touch his canvas. To everything the guests murmured "How beautiful!". That was the aesthetic fashion of the day.'

Gurney should not, however, be dismissed as a fashionable clergyman and aesthete with few pastoral priorities. 'The Vicar of St Barnabas was a devoted priest,' Comper remembered, 'and the truest of friends, who wore himself out in his parochial work and in his social kindnesses. I have known him so tired as to go to sleep during Wagner conducted by Richter, and yet he put in an appearance at an aesthetic supper party afterwards before we got home, although he had left word with his servant to call him in time to say the

The Crypt Chapel at St Barnabas, Pimlico, London. In 1889 Comper was given one of his first commissions, for a rood beam and sanctuary lamp of wrought iron for Bodley's crypt chapel, the first of a series of works at the church carried out over the following decade. Photograph: Gordon Barnes.

six o'clock Mass the next morning. But the Parsonage knew guests like A. H. Stanton, and Fr Congreve was more frequently there and would give short retreats, as for Advent Sunday. Gurney's own sermons attracted some to St Barnabas and the plainsong under G. H. Palmer perhaps attracted more. W. J. Birkbeck was a well-known figure there.'

At his own expense Gurney defrayed much of the cost of the internal decoration that makes St Barnabas one of the most beautiful churches in London. He enthused Comper with a love of Wagner and it was in the vicarage that, at a Sunday afternoon At Home, he introduced him to Aubrey Beardsley, another of his protégés, to whom he also introduced Wagner.

Together they attended *Tristan and Isolde* at Covent Garden where Comper was impressed by Beardsley's enthusiasm for all that was medieval. It was in 1893 when the illustrations for *Morte D'Arthur* were coming out. But Beardsley's medievalism, dependent upon Burne-Jones, Morris and Aestheticism, was entirely different from Comper's and he had little regard for the drawings. Dismissively Comper judged Beardsley an amateur 'with a wonderful gift for line, but none for colour'.

Gurney's main gift to St Barnabas was the reredos, designed by Bodley, and installed in 1892, in a newly-paved sanctuary of black and white marble. On Christmas day in that same year Comper had gone to Matins and the Missa Cantata. In a letter to his mother he wrote: 'They were singularly beautiful

St Barnabas, Pimlico, London. High altar by Bodley, with Comper's sacrament house and painted decoration (1890–96), flanked by angels in shallow relief, with a figure of St Barnabas over. Photograph: Cyril Ellis.

St Barnabas, Pimlico, London. Figure of the Virgin and Child on the south wall next to the sedilia, flanked by tapers, 1890–96. Photograph: Cyril Ellis.

services – that is to say as far as music was concerned for they kept throughout to the unspeakably lovely old English music and hymns. Mr Bodley's reredos which I saw for the first time seemed to me to belong to an entirely different order of things. Splendid as it is (it cost £1,000 or more) and from the aesthetic (only too aesthetic in the abused sense of the word) point of view, faultless; it has not the old Gothic ring about it, nor has it the grave and real character of the Tractarian church of which St Barnabas was the example and is no longer.'

In 1889 Gurney gave Comper one of his first commissions, for a rood beam and sanctuary lamp of wrought iron for Bodley's crypt chapel where the Blessed Sacrament was reserved. Between 1890 and 1896 Comper decorated the arcades and lower walls of St Barnabas' sanctuary with flowing diapering in a deep tone of green and gold. He designed a sacrament house, flanked by censing angels in shallow relief, surmounted by a figure of St Barnabas, bordered by taper brackets emerging from fleurs-de-lys. He added images of the four Evangelists in the arcading of the east wall, a figure of the Virgin and Child on the south wall next to the sedilia flanked by tapers, and exquisite groups of winged angels in song high in the chancel immediately below the ceilure, and above the high altar.

This work points an informative contrast between Comper's early work and that of his master. Bodley's mature altars followed late-Gothic German and Spanish precedents and were informed by the rubrical demands, based on the *Pontificale Romanum*, of the second edition of the *Directorium Anglicanum*,

St Barnabas, Pimlico, London. Design for Chapel of the Blessed Virgin Mary (Gurney chantry), built in 1901. Drawing by William Bucknall.

revised and edited by F. G. Lee in 1865. An altar should have a gradine, or shelf, upon which stood the ornaments. There should be a high reredos. In Bodley's later altars a false tabernacle was sometimes inserted in the middle of the gradine. His reredoses became ever more powerful and were modelled on continental precedents that were incorrectly assumed to have a continuous medieval development. In their disposition they owed more to the liturgical models of the Counter-Reformation.

Comper's reconstruction of the authentic Gothic altar reversed Bodley's influence and led to an understanding of the altar itself, rather than the reredos, as the point of real consequence. The delicacy of Comper's perfected medievalism in the carving and colouring of the imagery and diapered walls points to a greater refinement of detail than is found in Bodley's reredos and Pugin's altar ornaments, however splendid.

Gurney died in 1896 and in 1901 a chantry chapel designed by Comper was thrown out from the east end of the south aisle, dedicated to the Blessed Virgin Mary. It is one of the most complete and delicate examples of his early work, in which flowed the cumulative influences of his passion for English and Flemish late-Gothic art and architecture, and it marks the culmination of his achievement on a small scale.

Surrounded on north and west by parclose screens with coved cornices crowned by brattishing, it has delicately diapered walls, and a low reredos representing a *pietà* of such finesse of execution that it equals a Flemish original. The east window has a standing figure of Mary, bordered by standing images representing the Visitation. The south wall is entirely filled with a window of the Coronation of the Virgin, set in white glass with quarries in yellow stain surrounding the main subjects, which include the bearded figure of Gurney, vested in a flowing surplice, kneeling towards the altar on which he fixes his gaze.

Gurney was succeeded by the Revd and Hon. Alfred Hanbury-Tracy who continued to furnish St Barnabas under other hands. Comper had also designed monumental brasses and vestments and had prepared designs for a rood screen; but in 1906 they were discarded for a design by Bodley. Kempe and his nephew, Walter Tower, were brought in to undertake stained glass, heavy Germanic imagery for the rood and flanking walls of the screen, chapels, an imposing statue of St Barnabas at the west end, and ponderous diapering in the upper walls of the chancel. It is a little ironic that Comper was succeeded by his early masters whose work lacked his delicacy and originality. This points to the suspicion with which his work was regarded by received taste.

But in 1932 Comper designed a heraldic monument in the north aisle to Hanbury-Tracy, gleaming with burnished gold, and in 1953 he made a new east window, with a figure of the Pantokrator in the centre, to replace Wailes's glass which had been destroyed during the Second World War.

ST MARY, KEMSING, KENT

Restoration, completed 1909

The restoration of St Mary's, Kemsing, was commissioned by the Revd T. C. Skarratt, a clergyman of assumed refinement and culture, and completed in 1909. Previously semi-ruinous, it is the best of a group of early restorations in Kent. Skarratt was appointed in 1890 and spent his fortune on the church, starting a restoration by Sir Thomas Graham Jackson and W. F. Unsworth soon after he arrived. But Comper believed, on the evidence of a photograph of the beautiful unrestored, if semi-ruinous, interior that it 'betrays the too frequent story of zeal outrunning discretion'.

Robert Hugh Benson was a curate here from 1897 until 1901. He praised the exquisite taste of Comper's work, commended the dignified, careful ceremonial and beautiful music, enjoyed life in the big, comfortable, vicarage and admired Skarratt's unworldly, if relatively luxurious, medievalism. 'Skarratt and his house and church!' he told a friend, 'They are too beautiful! And he is exactly like Napoleon Bonaparte, painted red; and the Wooden Man of Boulak. He also has an Italian garden, and a choir that sing like seraphim.' Comper's monumental brass to Skarratt in the chancel bears out Benson's description. Skarratt and Kemsing vicarage summed up the clerical and lay patronage of Comper's early work; it was a congenial setting in which he was at ease. 'When I visited it,' recalled Fr Cyril Martindale SJ in his biography of Mgr Benson, 'the late summer had stripped the grounds of their best glories. Still, round many lawns, on the terraces, and in the Italian garden, roses and

St Mary, Kemsing, Kent. The church in 1870, before restoration. It had been 'restored' before Comper's began work here, with what he believed was 'zeal outrunning discretion'.

Kemsing Church looking East before Restoration. 1870.

St Mary, Kemsing, Kent. Comper 'at his most rarefied'. Left: The altar, c.1900. Photograph: Cyril Ellis. Above: Interior looking east, showing the screen, with Comper's rood and Royal Arms of 1908. Photograph: Cyril Ellis.

purple clematis and huge tufts of sweet peas and smoke-blue flowers looked gorgeous against yew hedges, clipped into fantastic forms, and in the tiny ponds crimson water-lilies burned.'

Kemsing shows Comper at his most rarefied. If anything it is over-delicate with painted panels replacing carving on the reredos and a narrative window of Christ in Glory contained in a nimbus which anticipates his later discovery of the Pantokrator. The Blessed Virgin and St John the Baptist are also represented above a choir of priests and kings and the Visitation of Our Lady. Comper was not happy about the small scale of the powderings on the walls but admitted their effect. The splays of the windows are treated in gold and diaper and those on the north and south sides in blue and gold. The heraldic tester is gilded and gold predominates in the reredos. The panelling was given by the Skarratt family in memory of their parents and bears squirrels in reference to their coat of arms. The altar frontal was composed of panels of rose-red silk damask, alternating with parti-coloured panels of red, black and

The Holy Innocents, Wrotham, Kent. Reredos of 1907, with the Virgin and Child surrounded by blue-robed angels. Comper regarded this as among his best work of the early twentieth century. Photograph: Cyril Ellis.

gold tapestry, with a frontlet of blue silk embroidered with the opening words of the *Magnificat*. The textiles are to Comper's design and the combination of colour was taken from medieval illuminations. In 1908 a rood and figures of seraphim were added to the loft and the coat of arms of King Edward VII in a lozenge. A memorial window, to Skarratt, of the Annunciation was erected in the west wall and a lectern by Comper given in 1914.

Comper regarded his work at Kemsing among the best specimens of his work from 1901 to 1911, and included in this category a reredos designed at the same time for the neighbouring church at Wrotham. Designed in 1907, the Wrotham reredos in the south aisle is composed of a canopied panel representing the Virgin and Child surrounded by blue-robed, rose-chapleted angels of the Wilton Diptych enclosed in an arcade of twisted lily stems.

ST JOHN THE EVANGELIST, NEW HINKSEY, OXFORD
New church (nave only built), 1898–1900

Comper had long wanted to build a new parish church that would represent his liturgical ideals. The closest he had come to doing so was at St Margaret's, Braemar, in 1895–1907, where Dr Wickham Legg was responsible for

St John the Evangelist, New Hinksey, Oxford. Design, partially carried out 1898–1900. East Anglian perpendicular in form, with the figures on brackets showing German influence. Drawing by William Bucknall.

commissioning the design, primarily for summer use for English visitors, and to exemplify his own liturgical ambitions. Legg considered it the best of Comper's churches.

St John's, New Hinksey, was not completed due to shortage of money and the opposition of John Oldrid Scott, the Oxford Diocesan Architect, who objected to the Gothic altar and Comper's desire to start building with the chancel. In its fragmentary form it is a noble work of architecture, with a tall arcade composed of quatrefoil piers and broad, flowing aisle windows glazed with bottle-end glass. The roofs are handsomely painted. Comper had undertaken extensive visits to East Anglia in 1895, 1897 and 1898, and the church is East Anglican Perpendicular in form, with little influence from Germany apart from the figures on brackets and the glazing of the windows. The rood is high above the screen, set against solid panelling. The present high altar is a commercial copy of an English Altar, acquired independently from Dearmer's Warham Guild.

St John's anticipates St Cyprian's, Clarence Gate.

St John the Evangelist, New Hinksey, Oxford. Exterior design, partly carried out 1898–1900. Drawing by William Bucknall.

St John the Evangelist, New Hinksey, Oxford. The north arcade.

ST CYPRIAN, CLARENCE GATE, MARYLEBONE, LONDON
New church, built 1902–3

St Cyprian's provided the opportunity Comper was seeking to build a parish church in London. 'Its design in 1902 was in truth the expression and summing up of all one had so far learnt.' It is a memorial to the Revd Charles Gutch, the founder of the parish. The promoters – the Revd G. F. Forbes, Sir Cyril Cobb and Dr Wickham Legg – wanted to build a quintessential Anglican church for the twentieth century in which the principles of the Oxford Movement would be realised in an English form, free from continental influence The wool churches of East Anglia, notably Attleborough, Norfolk, informed the plan, furniture and form; indeed, it became a personal vision of East Anglia. But St Cyprian's was also influenced by the small basilican churches in Rome – notably by S. Sabina (AD 422–32) – which Comper had seen in 1900, translated into late-Gothic terms. If it were classicised it would become a primitive basilica. St Cyprian's opened a new understanding of liturgical worship from being designed as a consistent whole on rational principles.

In a note, *On the Significance of the Building*, published for the consecration in 1903, Comper wrote that 'The new St Cyprian's follows the fully developed type of the English parish church which the middle ages produced and later times have continued and handed down to us by a tradition never entirely broken.' Its function was 'to make the high altar public to the whole body of worshippers … and to do this in such a manner that shall not grossly violate the earlier tradition of the Christian Church which veiled the altar from view.' He explained that

> the open chancel screen, the transparency of which is completed by the great windows behind it, the low-down east window and those which light the altar from the sides [make] the whole church a lantern and the altar is the flame within it.
>
> It is not by the lightness of its screens and the largeness of its windows only that the altar is brought into prominence and made the principal object of the church. Care is taken to keep the levels as low as the vicissitudes of the site will allow … the steps are concentrated upon the altar itself without the sacrifice of their real dignity, which is spaciousness and not height, and the table does not lose the prominence due to that most important part of the altar by being raised above the level of the eye. … By the richness of its coverings, no less than by its size and austere isolation, it expresses its supreme and august importance. … To repeat what most needs repeating to-day: it is the emphasis of the table of the altar which is of real consequence; and the reredos and curtains round it and the canopy over it are solely for the purpose of giving dignity to this.

Comper concluded by saying that St Cyprian's was designed to represent an ideal of worship contained in *The Book of Common Prayer* and defended it against a charge of antiquarianism. 'Its design neither seeks nor avoids originality, still less does it reproduce any period of the past, but only to fulfil these and the other needs which are ours to-day, and to do so in the last manner of English architecture which for us in England is the most beautiful manner of all.' The sanctuary levels were kept low, the altar at eye level, visible to the whole body of worshippers, and the single row of choir stalls on either side of the chancel left a wide space for ceremonial and an unobstructed view. The figures on the rood were executed with wonderful majesty; they followed the Classical dignity and structure of Graeco-Roman and early-Christian sculpture by representing triumph rather than suffering. And the same Classical influence informed the images of Our Lady and St Cyprian.

St Cyprian's came as a shock to an older generation of churchmen. They were wary of the novelty of Comper's liturgical innovations which were entirely different from the Roman models that had been popularised since 1865 by Dr F. G. Lee in his revision of the *Directorium Anglicanum*. These principles had been widely applied in Anglo-Catholic church planning and

St Cyprian, Clarence Gate, Marylebone, London, 1902–3, an early design. Comper said that 'Its design neither seeks nor avoids originality.' Nevertheless, the building came as a shock to an older generation of churchmen. Drawing by William Bucknall.

St Cyprian, Clarence Gate, Marylebone, London. The high altar in 1903, as it appeared when the church was consecrated. Photograph: Cyril Ellis.

arrangement and in the work of Comper's masters. They were also startled by the impact of the cool white interior, its spaciousness, restraint and the dazzling effect of the gilded screens and altar. It was worlds removed from the constructional polychromy of Butterfield's All Saints, Margaret Street, Street's St Mary Magdalene's, Paddington, and other mid-Victorian churches, and the faultless aestheticism of Bodley & Garner. Comper sought the 'old Gothic ring'.

T. Francis Bumpus, the author of *London Churches Ancient and Modern* (1904), is a useful test of opinion. He had criticised the Gurney chantry in St Barnabas, Pimlico, 'furnished under what that gentleman [Comper] considers the true English mediaeval style'. And of Comper's claim that the English Perpendicular style was 'the most beautiful manner of all' he wrote, 'Whether all my readers will concur in these sentiments I will not undertake to say, but one thing is very certain, and that is, that Mr Comper's diligent researches into the history and significance of our old English Uses have enabled him, both architecturally and ritually, to produce one of the most beautiful, harmonious and correctly arranged churches that has been built in London for a long time.'

At the consecration the rite was based upon the pontifical of Egbert, Archbishop of York (d. A.D. 766), because it embodied the 'real, true cere-monial of the old Church of England'. The musicians, supplemented by the nuns' choir of St Katharine's Convent, Queen Square, Holborn, sang plainchant in 'voices of exceptional sweetness', under the direction of the Revd G. H. Palmer, the plainsong scholar and choirmaster of St Barnabas, Pimlico, in the rood loft where they were heard but not seen. The nave was strewn with branches of pine, box and rose petals, and the chancel with crimson roses and white lilies. Bishop Winnington-Ingram wore Comper's magnificent cope of Russian cloth of gold which the Bishop of Norwich wore at the coronation of King Edward VII, and a jewelled mitre. Gold copes for the cantors, embroidered by the Sisters of Bethany, were lent from St Mark's, Philadelphia, and All Souls, Brighton, and the red silk tunicles from St Mary Magdalene's, Paddington. Candles were lit before the twelve consecration crosses on the pillars of the nave to represent the twelve apostles. Yet St Cyprian's was barely furnished apart from the long high altar beneath the low cill of the east window with the hangings of gilded and painted leather and the partly completed rood screen.

St Cyprian's had a powerful influence upon contemporary ecclesiastical taste and was quickly copied. Percy Dearmer had been appointed to St Mary's, Primrose Hill, in 1901, two years before St Cyprian's was consecrated and the design exhibited in the Royal Academy. In a short time Dearmer had applied Comper's aesthetic by whitening the mid-Victorian red brick walls of St Mary's, making a foil for brightly coloured textiles and Arts & Crafts church furniture designed in a medievalist style. After the Great War this solution and the English altar were applied as a formula to many churches by the Central

St Cyprian, Clarence Gate, Marylebone, London. The arrangement of the east end after completion of the screens and the east window, with a glimpse of the altar furniture added by Comper in 1924.

Council for the Care of Churches under the influence of F. C. Eeles and the originality of St Cyprian's and Comper's early experiments were quickly lost in the mediocrity and imitation that followed. This caused Comper pain and annoyance. The Warham Guild had premises above A. R. Mowbray & Co., the church bookseller, at 28 Margaret Street, Marylebone. 'On my way to All Saints, Margaret Street, this morning,' he wrote to a correspondent, 'I noticed a reredos in a shop window which was a poor but unmistakeable copy of one of mine. … Afterwards, my nephew went into the shop and they shewed him an album of photographs amongst which he recognised bad and weak copies of almost every reredos I have designed. … Thus it is not only the main ideas but the details which they all take from my work.' Now that that era is over, and many English altars have been swept away, the freshness and innovation of what Comper had achieved can once more be recognised. It established his primacy as the most influential English church architect of his generation.

A simple red brick exterior gives no impression of the beauty and surprise of the interior. It is a fusion of controlled austerity and splendour. Austerity: created by the wide spacing and severe detail of the arcades, the simple unworked mouldings, white walls and wide windows with web-like tracery, filled, in the aisles, with bottle-end glass. Splendour: in the gilded and painted

St Cyprian, Clarence Gate, Marylebone, London. The rood and screen, with the chancel beyond. Above the high altar can be seen the tester. One critic commented on 'a remarkable feeling of space and clarity of planning'.

St Cyprian, Clarence Gate, Marylebone, London, looking east. The photograph was taken under Comper's direction in May 1939. Photograph: Dell & Wainwright, 1939.

delicacy of the screens, stretching for the entire width of the church, with a loft, rood and figures of St Mary and St John and winged seraphim. The plan of the west end with a vaulted narthex and double arches supporting a choir gallery is taken from St Agnes', Kennington, and George Gilbert Scott Junior's influence was also shown in Comper's original design for the double choir screen with the three arches in front of it, subsequently modified in its present form. Stephen Dykes Bower described St Cyprian's in 1933 as a 'beautiful and individualistic interpretation of Gothic, an inevitably right expression of Anglican propriety and, liturgically, the most satisfactory church in London'.

The furniture and painted glass took many years to complete and continued until the end of Comper's life. During this time Comper radically changed his mind about medievalism and the exclusive claims of Northern Gothic. The Mediterranean scheme of colour: the pale lemon tone of the gilding, the star-spangled, grey toned blue in the screens and imagery, the masses of blue, softer and purpler, in the tester, the emerald green, are taken from the sixteenth-century coffered ceilings of the Roman basilicas and the broad masses of colour in the eleventh-century mosaic churches of Palermo. The splendour of the completed screen made the altar look 'flat and dull' and in 1924 Comper provided a foil by adding six slender candlesticks of pewter, two tall standard candlesticks, and a polygonal tabernacle of bronze gilt.

It is mistaken to regard St Cyprian's in purely late-medieval terms. Nor should it be seen exclusively within rational premises. Comper designed his buildings to 'present an organic whole from which nothing can be taken and nothing added. Function and suitability to its purpose must, it is true, be there; but they have no more to do with architecture than the lilies of the field.'

Yet the clear and rational planning appealed to promoters of the Modern Movement. In 1938 it was visited by Hubert de Cronin Hastings and J. M. Richards, the proprietor and editor of the *Architectural Review*. Hastings later wrote to Betjeman: 'I quite forgot, when writing to you before, to tell you that Marx [Richards] and I went together to Comper's church in Baker Street to make sure that you were mad. To our surprise – to our inexpressible surprise – we discovered it was absolutely lovely. Not everyone's cup of vodka, perhaps, but indubitably the work of an architect – with a remarkable feeling of space and clarity of planning; qualities which, you and I know so well, are practically non-existent today under whatever disguise the pseudo architect presents himself. I confess that I was much astonished and so too, strangely enough, was Marx who was immediately converted. You have scored again brother.'

The diagonal photograph shown here was taken, after a good lunch at the St Ermin's Hotel, under Comper's direction in 1939, accompanied by John Betjeman and John Samuel Bucknall, between 3.00 and 3.30 on a May afternoon – an hour and from a point which Comper regarded as the best time for light and the best position to see it. At that time, continuing until the late Fifties, the chairs were removed when the church was empty. This

St Cyprian, Clarence Gate, Marylebone, London, looking west, showing the gallery and font. Until the late Fifties, the chairs were removed when the church was empty. Photograph: Dell & Wainwright, 1939.

contributed to the spacial and architectural distinction of the building but the idea was Comper's and was indebted to the Continent. 'The nave floor should be cleared of all chairs which are not actually in use as a concession to physical frailty,' Comper wrote in 1950 in *Of the Christian Altar and the Buildings which Contains It*. 'This is the universal practice of the Orthodox Church, the Roman basilicas, and most continental churches, and it has been followed with noted success in a London church in which the congregation themselves stack the chairs at the west end after a service. They are brought out singly as wanted for private prayer particularly just before dark when many come, as they do in France, to say their evening prayers before the church is closed at 9 o'clock. It is a church, too, of silence and its Vicar's example recalls that of Disraeli at Hughenden when showing visitors the church, who would not speak until he led his questioner to the porch.' St Cyprian's in those days had a palpable atmosphere of prayer, now lost, that was all-enveloping.

ST JOHN'S HOME & HOSPITAL, COWLEY, OXFORD
Chapel, completed 1907

Comper had established an association with the Society of All Saints Sisters of the Poor in 1889 when Fr Congreve introduced him to St John's Home & Hospital, Cowley, Oxford. It was run by the order as a nursing home for chronic sick ladies and Congreve was their chaplain. The home had been given to the Community by Fr Richard Meux Benson SSJE, the founder of the Cowley Fathers and a friend of Comper's father. Comper designed furniture for the temporary chapel, a room twenty feet wide, including a Gothic altar and screen.

In 1902 he was given the commission for a wing of the hospital, a mortuary and a permanent chapel of stone, and the building was completed in 1907. St John's Chapel was the last work designed in partnership with Bucknall and was the cause of the dissolution of the practice. Bucknall had already designed the vicarage, schools and parish hall of St Mary and St John, Cowley, and Comper was to restore the Bartlemas Chapel in the Cowley Road. They were well known to the Order.

Alone among non-collegiate Oxford chapels – until Pusey House Chapel, designed by Temple Moore in 1911–14, followed it – the stone screen divides the building in two. The plan is composed of an enclosed nuns' choir, separated from the nave by an elaborately carved stone screen containing an altar, and there is a narrow south aisle with arcades to give access to a small chapel and the hospital. The nave was intended for patients. A hammer-beam roof with pendants runs from east to west with no division. The finely detailed, panelled stalls are in dark oak and provide a foil to the white walls and

Chapel of St John's Home and Hospital, Cowley, Oxford, completed 1907. The Mother Superior of the Order running the home described the chapel as 'simple, severe, majestic' and 'holy in the extreme'.

Left: The east end, used by the nuns for their offices, emphasising the scale of the building.

Below: The high altar.

Chapel of St John's Home and Hospital, Cowley, Oxford, completed 1907. The chapel in relation to Comper's hospital wing. Early photograph.

pale glass. The altar from the temporary chapel was moved into the completed building in 1907 and became the high altar.

The chapel made a profound impression on Sister Mary Teresa of All Saints, the Mother Superior. It was her vision that had enabled it to grow from a modest start to its final form. She was a Suckling, a descendent of Lord Nelson, and had been born at Barsham, Suffolk. She had known the East Anglian wool churches all her life and recognised how profoundly they had influenced Comper's work. Writing on the Feast of the Assumption, 1907, she told him of the first Mass and compared St John's Chapel with the Suffolk churches.

> Today we had our first Mass in our new church & Fr Congreve came down from town on purpose to say it & we had the proper Assumption office at his dear hands & all went without a hitch. We had a humble service of blessing yesterday evening, & drove away evil spirits with holy water, incense & the choir boys sang in the rood loft. For my own part having just returned from Southwold, Walberswick, Blythborough, Covehithe and Dunwich & having seen what *had* been exceeding magnifical, sitting in sackcloth & ashes, when I

ST JOHN'S HOSPITAL CHAPEL, OXFORD.
DESIGN FOR THE PATIENTS ALTAR AND CHOIR SCREEN OF STONE WITH OAK DOORS.

Screen of the Chapel of St John's Home and Hospital, Cowley, Oxford, completed 1907. The screen separated the enclosed nuns' choir from the nave, used by patients, and contains a central altar. It allows views of the high altar.

Left: drawing by William Bucknall, c.1907.

Right: the chapel in use c.1960.

beheld our church I had a vision of those old churches in all their former glory; the spirit in ours recalls all that, & Fr Congreve I think was intensely happy in it all, and proud of *you*!

Eight days later she wrote again and developed this theme but also made a comparison between the chapel and the mid-Victorian churches in which she had previously worked. The letter discloses the mind of those who admired and commissioned Comper's work by setting it in the spiritual aspirations of the time.

Today is the octave of the Assumption, one week since we worshipped in our new church. To me to whom the coolness of the evening of life has begun, I will tell you on the threshold of the sorrow of middle life, what this church is to one who has reached the three score span. I have all my life mourned that it has been my lot to worship in a *new* church. All this octave my heart has been near bursting with gratitude at the great mercy & benediction of our wonderful church & I will describe it to you. It is venerable & holy in the extreme, it is simple, severe, majestic. When in Blythborough I could have wept at the recollection of John Mason & Katherina his wife who builded the font & the porch, & who begged that their bodies might be in the doorway, so that those who passed over them might remember & pray for them. *Now* I think their freed spirits must see this *church*, unmutilated and spotless, in her bridal glory, & their grief must be healed, & they must know that once again poor fallen Zion is renewing her youth & beauty. No modern church is she, the moment you enter her walls you are in the atmosphere of centuries of adoration, prayer, praise. You kneel & hide your face & distant echoes resound & multiply, in what *seem to be* far off aisles, & pillars, & chapels. You lift your puny voice, & it too is glorified. Spirits catch it up, & whisper again & again in a mystery. Silence falls, you are alone – no need of book, for in the window before you all things divine & beautiful plead to shut out the empty world & its sordidness. And so, refreshed & beatified, you go forth to meet the dull routine of common day.

For some time difficulties had arisen between Comper and Bucknall and in 1903 Bucknall had proposed a dissolution of the partnership after the consecration of St Cyprian's, Clarence Gate. They came to a head in 1904 when it was discovered that Bucknall's supervision of the structure of St John's was inefficient. He was discovered drunk on site and this exposed a problem that had long put the partnership under strain. In that same year it was dissolved and a division of work made. After the Great War structural problems in St John's Chapel were discovered and investigated by W. A. Forsyth but they did not prevent the community from commissioning Comper to design their conventual church of All Saints, London Colney, Hertfordshire, in 1921.

NORWICH CATHEDRAL

Cope, mitre, morse for the Dean's cope, etc., 1900

W. J. Birkbeck was the squire of Stratton Strawless, Norfolk. He was an Anglo-Catholic with strong medievalist sympathies and his friend, Dr Salisbury Price, had taken charge of the parish. It was Price who introduced Comper to Birkbeck and a simple restoration of the church was undertaken in 1898–1902.

Birkbeck was a keen student of the Russian Orthodox Church and had spent some time in Russia, during which he had acquired precious stones from the Ural Mountains, and some magnificent cloth of gold, with a green ground, woven for the Coronation of the Czar.

These were made into a cope worn by the Bishop of Norwich, with scarlet silk gloves with jewelled mounts, at the Coronation of King Edward VII in 1902. The Sisters of Bethany embroidered the Annunciation of the hood, divided by an upright of silver-gilt. The St George of the morse, garlanded in rose briars, is solid gold, with a large topaz as a pendant, and it contains chrism from the consecrated brow of the King (see illustration on back cover). A precious mitre, jewelled and crocketted, that Comper had designed on the top of a horse omnibus, was also made and the vestments were bequeathed by Birkbeck to Norwich Cathedral. Comper also designed the bindings of red leather of the Coronation Prayer Books. It gave him great pleasure at an

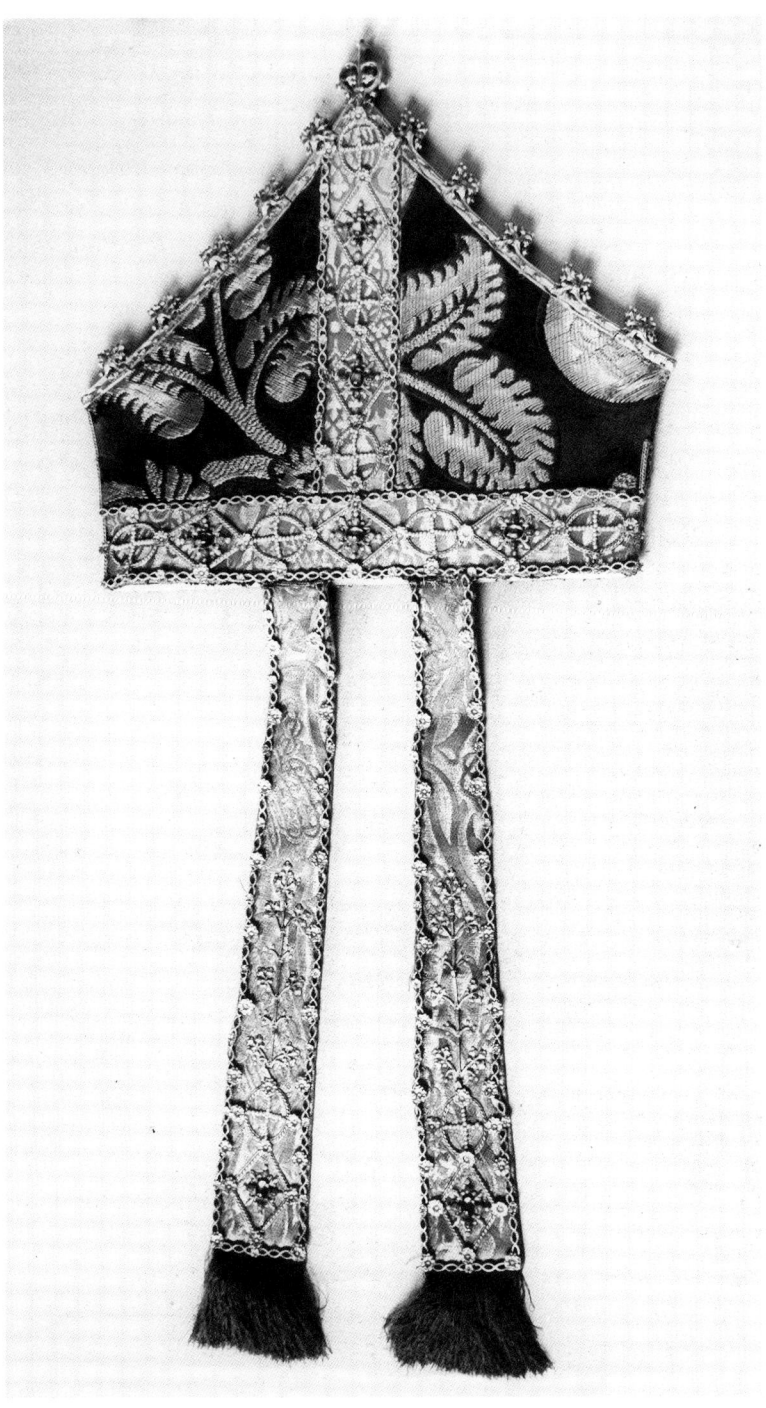

Mitre, Norwich Cathedral, 1900. Comper excelled in all the ecclesiastical arts. Bishop Wand said of Comper that 'he knows exactly how every stitch of the embroidery should go' (seee page 188). Photograph: E. C. Le Grice.

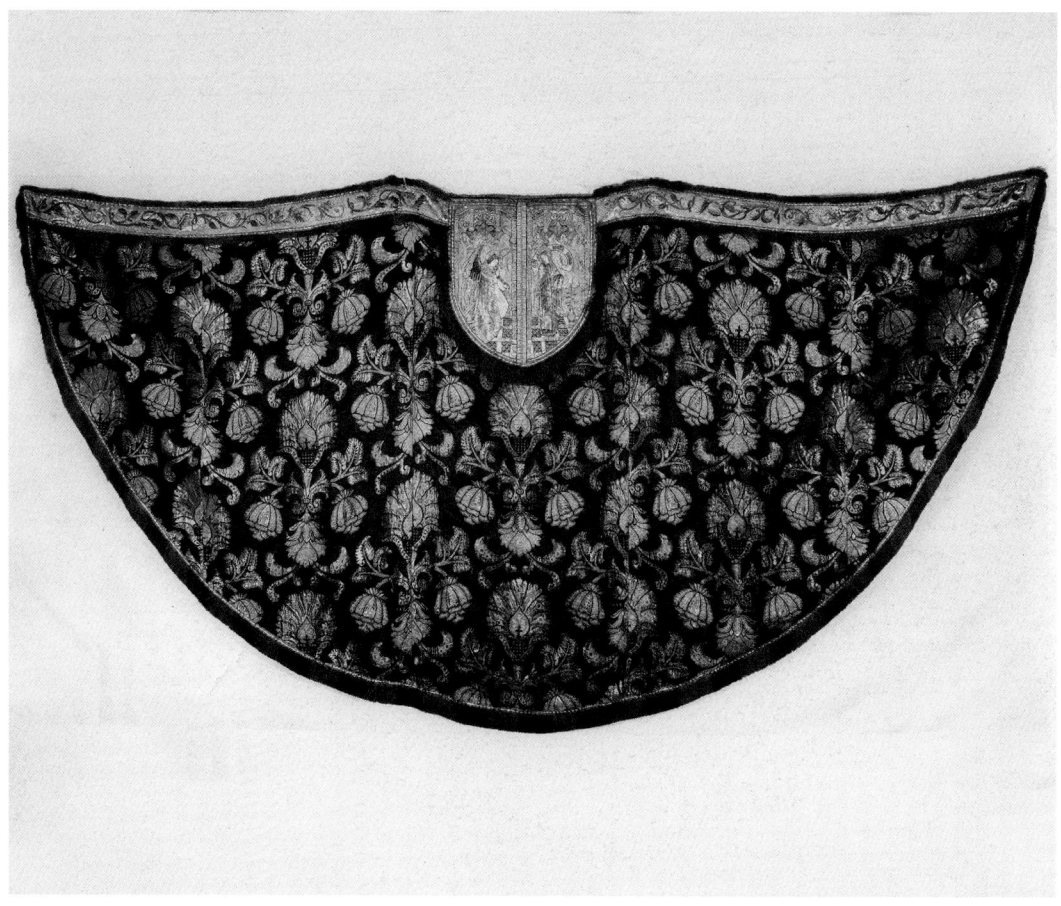

Cope, Norwich Cathedral, of Russian cloth of gold, 1900. On the hood, the Annunciation, embroidered by the Sisters of Bethany. Photograph: E. C. Le Grice.

investiture at Buckingham Palace in 1950, when he was knighted, that he 'saw the large picture of the Coronation of King Edward VII painted by order of Queen Alexandra who was very particular that the scarlet jewelled gloves which we had made for the Bishop of Norwich, who waited on her, should be shown – the only Bishop, she once remarked to me, who wore his gloves.'

The Dean's morse is of silver-gilt set with precious stones and was also Birkbeck's gift. It is in the form of a conventionalised rose with lobes pierced by tracery and was executed, with the Bishop's morse, by Barkentin and Krall. It belongs to a cope of scarlet cloth of gold, embroidered with heraldry and a Dove, that was not designed by Comper. There is also a mitre because the Dean of Norwich, as the legal descendent of the medieval Abbot, is the only Dean in the Church of England entitled to wear one.

Morse for the Dean's Cope, Norwich Cathedral, 1900. Silver-gilt set with precious stones, executed by Barkentin & Krall; a reminder of Comper's range of artistry. Photograph: E. C. Le Grice.

UNITY BY INCLUSION

IN 1900 TWO EVENTS OCCURRED that challenged Comper's conviction of the supremacy of English and Northern European late-Gothic art. The first was the purchase of *An Essay on the History of English Church Architecture Prior to the Separation of England from the Roman Obedience*, by George Gilbert Scott Junior. The second occasion was a reluctant first visit to Rome.

Scott's thesis was that the architecture of Christendom was 'part of the great fact of Christianity', that English church architecture is 'but a portion of a great whole', and he displayed 'the essential solidity of the history of Christian art in England with that of Christian art in general, and of Christianity itself'. Liturgy predetermined church architecture. Scott started with the Constantinian basilicas of Rome because 'our ancestors, on their conversion, but took up the threads of ... a tradition already venerable for its years'. And he concluded that 'this distinction in the ecclesiological and ritual tradition, existed side by side with identity of faith, complete inter-communion, hierarchical subordination, and organic unity.' This had a determining influence in the evolution of Comper's theory of 'unity by inclusion' and he came to regard Scott's *Essay* as 'the best book on architecture written'. It was a stimulating preparation for Rome.

What impressed him in Rome, and influenced his evolution as an artist, were the Graeco-Roman remains, Classical sculpture and the primitive basilican churches. But he was also taken by the compartments of bright, deep-coloured blue set in the solidly gilded coffered ceilings of St John Lateran, juxtaposed with the cathedral's rose-red hangings, and the gilded pillars of the ciborium in the Blessed Sacrament Chapel. On the final day he visited the National Museum and it was there that he discovered in Classical figure sculpture 'the same forms of folds in the draperies of the statues and the identical lines of decoration as in East Anglia'.

It was not only the fusion of styles that influenced Comper. There was a change in iconography. It was the half-length figure of the Pantokrator, the Almighty, the Creator, the sovereign Ruler of all, executed in mosaic above the altars of the Palermitan churches that transformed his thought. He changed the Pantokrator from an overwhelmingly severe representation of Christ as Judge, heavily bearded and long-haired, to a hellenized Risen Saviour, beardless and golden-haired, forever young, taken from the fourth-century Roman carvings of the Good Shepherd. At Cefalù, in Sicily, the Pantokrator is noticeably less severe and it is the Classical representation that Comper followed. But he also paid attention to the Romanesque transformation of the Pantokrator into the Majestas where the full-length figure of Christ enthroned is usually accompanied by saints and angels.

In later life he described these effects in dramatic terms. 'It was ... a lesson like that of St Peter on the house-top at Joppa: "What God hath cleansed, that call not thou common" [Acts 10:15]. All beauty inspired by the Creator Spirit is one, as all goodness is one and all truth is one. It is this which Dante and the spirit of the Renaissance and the Schoolmen saw when they claimed Greece for Christ.' These impressions prepared the ground and sowed the seed for an aesthetic revision. Comper's earliest love of all as a boy was for Fra Angelico, Botticelli and Dante as interpreted by Ruskin. He had first visited Italy in the mid-winter of 1887–8 and only touched the Mediterranean at Genoa and the Adriatic at Ravenna. Oxford, Kempe and Bodley produced a reaction which made Germany and Belgium the goal of architectural journeys, but no turning point was greater that his visit to Rome in 1900. His early medievalist vision, inspired by Nuremberg, was transformed by the light and colour of the south and took him to fresh ideals of diverse and far-ranging influence.

The sway of Rome came to fruition on a visit to Sicily in 1905. It followed the dissolution of Comper's partnership with Bucknall and he was accompanied by Bucknall's nephew, Arthur. They went to see the mosaic churches of Palermo: the Cappella Palatina, Monreale Cathedral and the Martorana. The

Virgin and Child, 1903, made for the chapel of the Sisters of Bethany, Lloyd Square, Finsbury, London. The influence of Classical sculpture is apparent (compare the Virgin and Child at St Wilfrid, Cantley, page 34).

DESIGN FOR THE CHVRCH OF ST ANDREW & ST GEORGE : ROSYTH
PERSPECTIVE VIEW OF INTERIOR

Design for St Andrew and St George, Rosyth, Fife, c.1920. Only the east part was built. The church is now demolished. Drawing by F. J. Lucas.

Sicilian amalgam of disparate architectural styles was the cultural legacy of the Hautville dynasty. Between 1130–90 their policy of tolerance towards their subjects, Latin, Orthodox and Muslim, encouraged a cosmopolitan civilization composed of heterogeneous elements which reached its fullest expression in art and architecture. In the royal palaces and churches, architectural styles were combined to produce a composite form, embracing mosaic, sculpture and woodwork, harmonious and altogether attractive. 'The Court of Palermo,' Comper wrote in *Further Thoughts*, 'embraced not only Western Christendom but the Eastern Church and even stretched out hands to Persia and the highest culture of Islam; and of all of these its churches bear the impress.'

After Comper's final visit to Palermo in 1924 he wrote: 'They are more beautiful these three churches and nowhere have I seen anything like them, or their equal in effect of colour. Nor is it colour only; for, in spite of much strangeness and even barbarism, they remain a model, too, for proportion and a, to me, inexplicable quality of spaciousness.'

Comper's conversion to unity by inclusion was not simply confined to a synthesis of style. He was profoundly concerned with the planning of a modern church and the right position of the altar. In 1912 at the Grosvenor Chapel, Mayfair, the altar was brought forward to the heart of the church with the intention of placing it beneath a ciborium in front of a Classical screen. Whether Comper was aware of the radicalism of what he proposed in terms of the future is unclear but this was the first instance in the twentieth century of an altar brought into direct visual relationship with the congregation; the emphasis of the sanctuary was defined by dark panelling and pews contained within white walls. And the altar was informed by the liturgiological investigations into the form of the primitive altar carried out by Edmund Bishop and published in 1905 in a paper, 'On the history of the Christian altar', which set out the necessity of the ciborium. The proposed ciborium was disqualified at a consistory court hearing.

In 1919 Comper made plans for the church of St Andrew and St George to meet the needs of the naval base at Rosyth, Fifeshire. The plan was roughly a square of nine equal bays, with an extra central bay which terminated into an apse and was designed to form a Lady Chapel behind the high altar. The altar was to stand beneath a ciborium in the third bay and within an open rood screen of three arches. The design for the screen, defined by columns of the Tuscan order, was later executed in St Ninian's Cathedral, Perth. There was also to be a low aisle-less nave with a plain barrel ceiling and a tall, spire-topped tower. The plan was suggested by Bressuire, near Nantes, which Comper had paced out in 1913. St Andrew and St George was not finished and never realised Comper's plan.

The first part of Rosyth was completed in 1924 and it was in that same year that Comper discovered the primitive ideal on his second visit to French North Africa, now known as Algeria. He wanted to trace the developments

The Basilica Eufrasiana, Parenzo, A.D. 550. One example of early church planning which greatly influenced Comper's development. Photograph: Alinari.

from the Greek temple, and the scale which was found suitable for worship, to the adoption of the same principles by the Constantinian church. It was only in the Mediterranean countries that patterns from antiquity remained, and in North Africa that the evidence could be found of churches which had not been changed by subsequent alteration. Comper recognised that they were of value in the planning of a modern church.

It was at Theveste, now known as Tébessa, in the south-east corner of Algeria bordering on Tunisia, that his search ended. It was there in the then little known ruins of the church complex that he noticed the parallels with the Roman basilicas and the Adriatic cathedrals in the placing of the high altar (see plan page 213), and it was this and their liturgical implications that sealed the precedent. 'What the earliest churches, then, establish in the position of the altar in the nave is direct contact with the people. The celebrant and clergy face east towards the doors and the people are facing west. This is still the use of the great basilicas of Rome ....'

Although Comper only once visited Dalmatia, in 1925, on a journey that did not include Parenzo, he knew of the Basilica Eufrasiana in that city from photographs and plans. The Basilica is one of the most ancient, singular and interesting cathedrals on the north shore of the Adriatic surviving from primitive times. It has preserved the complete layout of a major bishop's church, including a tiny atrium, a baptistery opposite the cathedral, a triconch martyr's chapel attached to the north aisle, and the lavish two-storeyed episcopal audience hall, the salutatorium. It has also preserved the marble shafts of Proconnesian marble of the columns in the nave, the stucco decoration of the soffits in the north arcade, the columns of the ciborium, the sanctuary plaques of marble, the mosaics between the windows and in the vault of the apse, and even an encrustation of marble and mother-of-pearl below the windows. They show the fragmentary use of Eastern architectural elements in Western churches of the sixth century. There is a fine altar frontal of silver beneath the marble ciborium, enclosed in *cancelli* screens decorated with arabesque patterns. As an unaltered specimen of the time of Justinian, in form and planning, it is the best of a group of Adriatic cathedrals, and the ancient custom of celebrating Mass, with the celebrant turned towards the east behind the altar, as in the Roman basilicas, was maintained through history.

Comper saw the liturgical necessity of an unencumbered altar. He was deeply impressed when Cardinal Verdier, the Archbishop of Paris between 1921–31, pontificating at Notre Dame, set up an altar at the crossing and his throne in front of the high altar, in order that he might be among his people. This ideal was realised in the plan for London Colney, Hertfordshire, which was the first attempt to apply what he had learnt at Theveste. 'This intimacy was still further realised,' Comper recalled in *Of the Christian Altar and the Buildings which Contain It*, 'at the consecration of the Chapel of the mother-house of the All Saints Sisters at London Colney by the Bishop of St Albans in 1927, when an equal part of the worshippers was facing each of the four sides of the altar.'

In this way Comper's liturgical experiments led to their ultimate conclusion, by way of an unexecuted plan for Aberdeen Cathedral in 1928, in the building of St Philip's, Cosham, in 1937. These experiments anticipated the evolution of church planning and the centralised eucharistic space that became normal in the Roman Catholic Church and the Anglican Communion as a result of the liturgical movement after the Second Vatican Council, 1962–5. Comper was never part of this movement and independently established his planning theories from first principles and a direct response to the primitive plans. Unlike most who followed the movement by embracing Modernism, he sought in the Christian architectural tradition spiritual values and organic growth which he applied to the liturgical needs of his own time.

Plato once more provided the philosophical foundations of Comper's mature understanding of architectural unity. The second dictum of Socrates's speech in the *Symposium* is that man 'should … recognize the beauty which resides in one as the sister of that which dwells in another. It is right to seek for beauty generally, a man must have little sense who does not look upon the beauty of all bodies as one and the same thing.' Beauty, Comper believed, must be conceded by the eye, as truth by the mind and goodness by the heart. He conceived the application of Platonist influence in stylistic terms:

> And this result arrives from a combination of styles and forms into what is enduring of the two perfected styles of Greek and Gothic. It can be shewn, I think, that this is not new in architecture. … And I do not know that the combination of pointed vault and classic pillar in my work is any less natural and harmonious than the Martorana at Palermo and the great church of Monreale, and any less than the expression of its time. Sicily had, I suppose, an exceptionally wide field for those days in which to gather, and it used its opportunity to the full. So did the Emperor Frederic II, and so did Avignon under the Popes. Today we have an even wider field and it would be unnatural not to use it.

The fruit of Rome and the Sicilian churches ripened in a natural progression that took Comper on further travels and indebted his work to ancient and modern Greece, Italy, France, Spain and England, North Africa and the Mediterranean, accomplished with fastidious artistry in the pursuit of a consistent ideal.

ST GILES, WIMBORNE ST GILES, DORSET
Restoration and refurbishment after fire, consecrated 1910

In 1732 the fourth Earl of Shaftesbury built a church at Wimborne St Giles. In 1887 the interior was recast by Bodley in the Decorated Gothic style for Harriet, Countess of Shaftesbury, as a memorial to her husband, the eighth Earl. At midnight on 30 September 1908 the interior of the church was destroyed by fire. Comper was commissioned by the ninth Earl to rebuild and enlarge it. Comper owed his introduction to Lord Shaftesbury to Fr Philip Waggett SSJE, a Cowley Father who moved in Society.

Wimborne St Giles came at a decisive time in Comper's development. New influences took time to germinate in his mind.

But it was not only new influences but new assistants that helped the second period of Comper's work to come into being. Bucknall and Comper's later drawing office at 35 Old Queen Street, Westminster, was given up and a study established at 228 Knight's Hill, Norwood. William Bucknall would have found it difficult to adapt to Comper's development. His place was taken by Arthur Bucknall and E. T. Jago, chief draughtsman in J. F. Bentley's drawing office who had worked on Westminster Cathedral. Jago possessed accomplished structural skills and much of the success of the buildings erected between 1906 and 1914 is attributable to him. He married an American opera singer and emigrated to America in 1914 to work for Cram, Goodhue and Ferguson. There were also three improvers: T. W. Inwood,

Martin Travers and W. Ellery Anderson. Four articled pupils were accepted: Christopher Webb (who became a glass-painter), W. H. Randoll Blacking, the Hon. Hubert Adderley and Sebastian Comper. Of those in the study it was only Ellery Anderson who came close to Comper's standards in his own work; he went into partnership with E. A. Roiser and had an ecclesiastical practice in Gloucestershire. There was also Geoffrey Webb, brother of Christopher, who, though not a pupil or an assistant, worked in Comper's style with some success. The Webbs were nephews of Sir Aston Webb.

Comper's only serious professional rival was F. C. Eden (1864–1944), a contemporary for a brief time in Bodley & Garner's drawing office, with whom he had a guarded acquaintance. They had a mutual friend in Edward Brook, the squire of Ufford, Suffolk, who had in 1919 commissioned a war memorial chapel from Comper in the church. '"Brookie" as his friends called him,' Comper remembered,

> had an Italian valet who burnt incense in the library before we withdrew there after dinner. He had a great friend in F. C. Eden the architect, but he justly complained that English architects never spoke well of each other's work, although he acquitted me seeing that I was a sincere admirer of Eden's work. Maybe it was a little 'precious', like the work of Pater, the good qualities of which it shared; but John Betjeman is a witness to its first-rate and original qualities at Blisland in Cornwall. One thing I owe to him in particular. He was, I believe, the first to use burnish gilding in church decoration here in England and it was only by threats of going elsewhere that Gibbs, Bernard Smith's foremost painter, consented to employ it. Nor was burnish gilding the only thing I owed to Eden whose whole work was of a very superior order to the Powell's whom Bodley employed; but the furnishing in the libraries of Exeter Cathedral and in the Lady Chapel at All Saints, Clifton, are possibly Eden's best works on such a large scale.

The first application of the theory of 'unity by inclusion', at Wimborne St Giles, is a subtle fusion of Classic and Gothic which retains a Northern European and national expression. The complete destruction of Bodley's Gothic interior and the need to start afresh, coupled with the preservation of the eighteenth-century work, led to the new departure. The north wall of the original church was taken down and a spacious north aisle and Lady Chapel were added beneath a flat timber roof. The walls were pierced by windows whose mullions and tracery were taken from the hall of Oriel College, Oxford, where Comper was designing the heraldic glass and a new screen and panelling.

The south aisle is confined to a narrow passage to give width to the nave. Circular piers rise to Renaissance capitals decorated with the shields of the two sides of the family, Ashley and Cooper, supporting three broad arcades. There is a timber-framed roof borne on the outspread wings of angels and the organ is in a choir gallery at the west end.

St Giles, Wimborne St Giles, Dorset, 1908–10. Rebuilt after a fire, this is Comper's first application of 'unity by inclusion'. Photograph, 1910.

The screen crosses the entire width of the church and incorporates the Shaftesbury family pew which is entered from a south door. The front of the loft is decorated with figures of the apostles and the rood is flanked by St Mary and St John standing on Greek dragons, discovered in Mistra. There are two figures of seraphim and a row of red lamps lines the cornice of the loft. The wood is unpainted and of a dark tone which acts as a deliberate foil to the richness of the chancel. The detail and form are taken from the seventeenth-century wood screens in the chapel of St John's College, Oxford.

The alabaster reredos is painted blue and gold and marks a departure from Comper's panelled reredoses. It is composed of a single panel with a large crucifix flanked by St Mary and St John in the centre and a row of saints on either side. The altar had a frontal and hangings of rose-red silk with orphreys of blue, black and gold Lily tapestry. The splays of the east windows are gilded and decorated with the shields of the eight Earls of Shaftesbury in relief and the mullions have canopied figures of the four Evangelists. The window has in the centre an early figure of the Risen Christ surrounded by angels, represented as a beardless youth. The tester above the altar has the Dove enclosed in carved rays between painted scrolls on which are inscribed the gifts of the Holy Spirit, on a gold ground, powdered with tongues of fire.

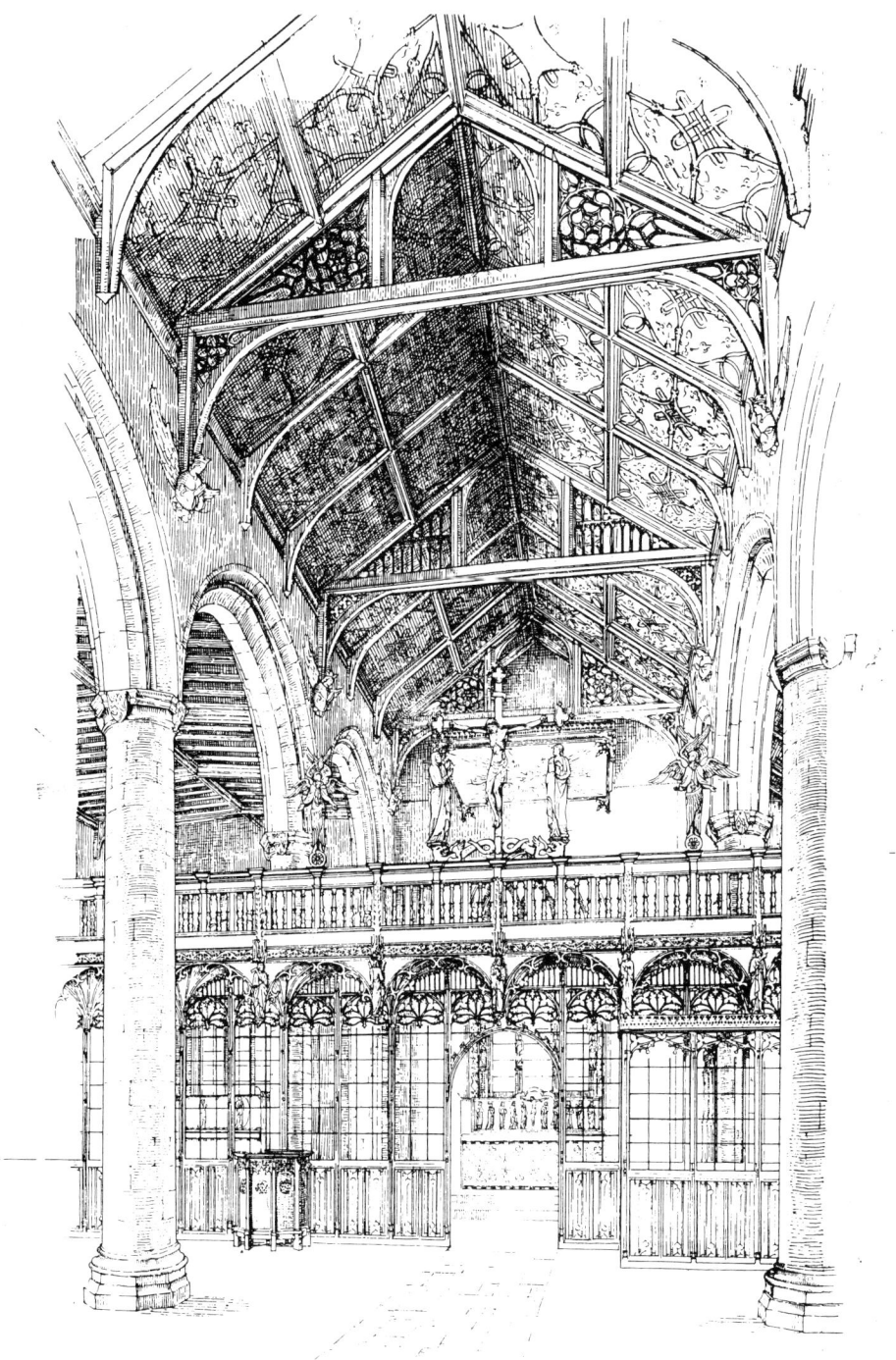

St Giles, Wimborne St Giles, Dorset, 1908–10. Design for rebuilding, 1908. Note the Greek dragons under the feet of St Mary and St John. Drawing by E. T. Jago.

St Giles, Wimborne St Giles, Dorset. The high altar, 1908–10. The reredos is of alabaster, and painted blue and gold. Photograph: Cyril Ellis, 1910.

In other ways Comper's restoration was accretive. The font is eighteenth-century and stands on a new plinth. The gilded cover was not added until 1940. The windows contain some of Comper's finest painted glass and also carefully integrated panels of old glass in the south aisle. Comper restored some of the monuments, notably a fine example of artisan mannerism to Sir Anthony Ashley in the Lady Chapel. On the south wall he rearranged a series of fine eighteenth-century marble monuments with considerable success.

The result looks like a church that has naturally developed through time. It retains a quintessential English quality but one that is far from insular. Comper became impatient with a sterile promotion of Englishness because he knew it was historically false. Writing in old age he said: 'Shallow and narrow is the cry: study and copy what is only English. Why, the best and most characteristic of what is English was brought from abroad by just such English travellers and crusaders, not to mention the Italians and Frenchmen who took up their abode with us. It is the way in which it is used and made one with the England of God's creation that matters. Mere imitation … is worthless. It must be vitalised and made distinctive of the country of its adoption.'

Lord Shaftesbury had been startled by the east window, when George Wyndham had appeared and blessed everything that had been done. At the consecration of St Giles in 1910 Comper met Wyndham, a member of the Conservative Government and one of a small aristocratic *élite* known as the Souls who were in polite revolt against the Victorians. He was about to take up an appointment as Rector of Edinburgh University and was preparing a lecture, *The Springs of Romance in the Literature of Europe*, to be given as his inaugural address.

Wyndham proposed that Romantic literature was composed of syncretistic strands and was one with architecture and politics. He was as interested in the literary and philosophical syncretism of Palermitan civilization as Comper was in the architecture. 'Literature is transfigured into Romance by the twilight of the West, the mirage of the East and the uncouth strength of the North, in direct proportion to the commingling of East and West and North in the politics of the eleventh and twelfth centuries.' Furthermore, 'Romance revives and, extending her welcome to the strange, discovers in it something which has always been latent in men's minds, although starved by convention.'

In 1906 Comper had spent a month in Greece and in the spring of 1910 he had visited Central and Southern Spain. These visits added further strength to his theory that all beauty was one. The idea of unity by inclusion was analogous to Wyndham's theory of literature and captivated Comper. Conversation with Wyndham helped Comper to put his ideas in order and elucidate the principles of his theory, the application of which governed his work for the rest of his life.

In 1928 Lord Shaftesbury wrote to Comper to congratulate him on the commission for Aberdeen Cathedral and to tell him of the impact St Giles' had on visitors.

> I am so pleased to hear of this new Cathedral at Aberdeen and that the construction of it is in your hands. What could be better! I told the Queen about it when she was staying with us at St Giles's as having seen your church which she admired immensely. She was quite pleased at the news – the church has been so much appreciated and admired and hundreds of visitors are constantly coming to see it. We keep a visitors' book there now and it is an interesting record of people from all parts of the world! The glass is so much admired.

ST JOHN, STOCKCROSS, BERKSHIRE

Furnishings, 1905–7

The Sutton family were the richest commoners in England. They lived at Benham House, designed by Henry Holland in 1772–5 for Lord Craven, with a park laid out by Capability Brown. They originated in Nottinghamshire and bought the estate in 1862. Sir Richard Francis Sutton, son of the Baronet who had acquired Benham, died suddenly in 1891, leaving a widow and heir, Sir Richard Vincent Sutton, who was born two months after the death of his father. Lady Sutton let Benham but returned, with her young son, in 1899.

St John's, Stockross, is a plain church, built of hard brick in the Early English style in 1838–9; the architect is unknown. In 1905 a restoration was undertaken by Lady Sutton as a memorial to her husband but it was far from straightforward. She had been introduced to Comper's work in the restoration of Moreton Corbet, Shropshire, undertaken by her brother, Sir Walter Corbet, in 1904. Lady Sutton wanted to build a new church, encouraged by the enthusiasm of her fourteen year old son, and Comper prepared plans for a building that would tantalizingly have been a larger and more sumptuous church than St Mary's, Wellingborough. The furniture and glass which were executed at Stockcross were intended for the permanent church. 'They have been so designed,' he wrote, 'as to fit a more worthy building should the present church ever be replaced.'

The high altar is the richest and most original of the decorated alabaster reredoses of that date and it is infused with Renaissance feeling. It demonstrates an original use of precedent that shows Comper as a master of architectural language. The rose briars that enclose the figures are carved in deep relief and are taken from a cope of gold tissue at Stonyhurst College, Lancashire, which formed part of the vestments bequeathed by King Henry VII in 1509 to Westminster Abbey. The structure of the woven design is in the form of sinuous briars enclosing the Tudor badge and portcullis. These winding briars formed a conspicuous feature of Comper's design for embroidery and he translated them into painted decoration, painted glass and, as here for the first time at Stockcross, into sculpture.

St John, Stockcross, Berkshire. High altar, 1905–7. The alabaster reredos is highly original in design, yet springs naturally from earlier precedent. Photograph: W. I. Croome.

St John, Stockcross, Berkshire. The east end, 1905–7, with a reja *(wrought-iron screen) of 1933. Comper had been fascinated by Spanish* rejas *since the days of his pupillage. Photograph: W. I. Croome.*

At the centre is a figure of the Crucifixion beneath a crocketted canopy; the cross is in the form of a tree from which the branches of the briars grow. It is flanked by figures of St Mary and St John but at the base, enclosed in their own compartments, is a group of the Annunciation. The saints all have significance. St Richard and St Francis from whom Sir Richard's names were taken; St Hugh of Lincoln (the bishop of the diocese from which the Sutton family originated) and St Vincent, the second name of Sir Richard's son and heir. He is portrayed with a raven, which forms part of the armorial bearings of the Corbet family. The posts are decorated with the quarterings of Sutton and carry four bronze gilt angels of original design. Originally, the Sutton quarterings were also stained on a canvas carpet before the altar and a mermaid scandalised the Bishop of Oxford, 'who had the strange fear that she might distract communicants'.

The east window was designed for one of the clerestory windows of the new church. It contains figures of four British saints: St Edward the Confessor, St Margaret of Scotland, St Bridget of Ireland and St David of Wales, and there is more glass by Comper in the smaller chancel windows. St John's was re-pewed, and a new pulpit and a finely carved font of Portland stone were added.

Sir Richard Vincent Sutton attained his majority in 1912. The new church was not started due to the intervention of his family trustees. He served in France and Flanders in the First World War and was decorated with the Military Cross. But in 1918 he fell victim to the Spanish influenza epidemic which swept Europe at the end of the war. Lady Sutton had married the Revd Hubert Astley and they lived at Brinsop Court, Herefordshire, a moated house with a dining hall of King Edward III, which contained work by A. Randall Wells. The church was restored by Comper, and in 1928 a replica of the Stockcross reredos was erected.

Comper's later work at Stockcross is a war memorial chapel in the south transept, executed in 1921–2, and a chancel screen of black iron in 1933. The *rejas* of Spanish cathedrals and churches had exercised an appeal for Comper ever since he had seen one for the first time in Pamplona Cathedral on a tour of Southern France with fellow pupils from Bodley's drawing office in 1882. In 1925–31 he had designed the Warriors' Chapel in Westminster Abbey and provided a towering *reja* with a cresting of conventionalised dolphins, mercurially gilt.

He proposed a similar screen for Stockcross and defended his decision in a letter to the Revd and Hon. L. D. Campbell-Douglas, the Vicar. 'A wrought-iron screen in this position in an English Parish Church is possibly somewhat unusual, but so is this particular church, and the unusually costly ornaments in it which were designed in the hope of their being transferred to a new church … [the screen] will not hide nor detract from the effect of what is already in the Church but on the contrary will enrich it.'

ST JOHN THE BAPTIST, LOUND, SUFFOLK

Organ case, screen, and other work, 1909–14

Some of Comper's restorations were privately undertaken by rectors of the parish, rather than patrons and benefactors. An example is the Revd Booth Lines, who discreetly spent the greater part of his fortune on the church at Lound. He had met Comper while he was Vicar of St John the Divine, Balham, and had moved from there to Lound in 1908. Comper's description of medieval churches as sometimes being little more than barns applied at Lound. It is a small church, confined to an aisleless nave and chancel, with a round tower at the west end. It retained a fourteenth-century screen but the loft and rood had long disappeared.

Lines wanted to return the church to its medieval arrangement and, under Comper's direction, it became far richer than it was in the Middle Ages. Some object to an extravagant treatment in a simple country church, but they are only known in their present stripped form and very little coloured decoration has survived. The spire of the Ufford font cover, in Suffolk, which rivals the contemporary fifteenth-century work of Adam Kraft in Nuremberg, provides sufficient evidence of the scale of English work destroyed by iconoclasm.

Comper's furniture is more developed than it would have been ten years earlier and shows how ingenious and complex the application of unity by inclusion had become in a medieval setting. He believed that proportion is of infinitely greater importance than decoration. The organ, built by Harrison, occupied the west wall and the gilded and painted case rose to the roof. Comper regarded this case as the most successful he had designed. Before the organ stands the fine medieval font in its original position, for which he provided an elaborate cover in the form of a spire of radiating boards in the form of crocketted buttresses in a diminishing proportion. It is an elaboration of the fifteenth-century font cover at Salle, Norfolk. Such font covers were a feature of many late-medieval English parish churches and reflect the widespread medieval convention of using elaborate canopies to identify important objects within a church interior. The lower part of the west wall is lined by benches of dark oak.

Lound gained a popular vogue for its decoration and it remains a church which many identify as their favourite work by Comper. Comper himself considered the west end to be more complete and successful than the east. He was dissatisfied with the screen and considered it to be a failure. He added the loft, with a rood and reredos panels and an altar on the south side, a detail taken from the Ranworth screen. In execution the loft was lowered from the position shown in the original design. This was because the existing exit from the rood stair seemed to confirm Lines's strong wish that the loft should be level with it. But it is too low for the proportions of the church and Comper believed that he should have raised it and gained access by steps concealed in the vaulting of the screen.

St John the Baptist, Lound, Suffolk. Font cover and organ case, 1909–14. In a small aisleless church, this beautifully demonstrates the attention that Comper paid to proportion. Photograph: F. E. Howard, c.1925.

St John the Baptist, Lound, Suffolk. Screen, 1909–14. Photographs: F. E. Howard, c.1925.

Left: The south altar, a detail taken from the medieval screen at Ranworth.

Below: The screen with the rood above. Comper was dissatisfied with the screen, believing the loft to be too low for the proportions of the church.

The Chapel of St Martin, Chailey Heritage Crafts School, Sussex, 1913. Exterior, of Sussex sandstone with a red-tiled roof and oak-shingled spire. It is deliberately built to dominate the landscape.

Lines moved on to be Vicar of Sneinton, Nottinghamshire, in 1917 just before the east window and chancel was generally taken in hand and that further explains the greater success of the west end, as his successors did not have the means to complete the restoration as Comper intended. The furniture shines with gilding and Mediterranean colour. By the north door Comper painted a large figure of St Christopher and he insisted on a motor car, then still something of a novelty, racing up hill in addition to the miller on his horse.

CHAILEY HERITAGE CRAFTS SCHOOL, SUSSEX

Chapel of St Martin, and Song School, 1913–22

The Chailey Heritage Crafts School for crippled boys was established in the Sussex Weald by Dame Grace Kimmins in 1903. The School had grown from the Guild of the Poor Brave Things, founded in London by Dame Grace in 1894. The name of the guild was taken from Julia Horatia Ewing's novel about a cripple, *The Story of a Short Life*. Residential accommodation was provided and the school was run on patriotic and Arts and Crafts principles. The boys were taught useful trades which would enable them to follow an occupation in

The Chapel of St Martin, Chailey Heritage Crafts School, Sussex, 1913. Interior, emphasising the richly-decorated ceiling and and plain wood screen and loft. Photograph: Sebastian Comper.

adult life. During the First and Second World Wars they were joined by wounded soldiers who themselves were taught trades. The Chailey Heritage attracted powerful royal and aristocratic support and Geoffrey Dawson, the editor of *The Times*, described it as 'the public school of crippledom'. Dame Grace had been introduced to Comper by Adeline, Duchess of Bedford, who had come to know his work at the Grosvenor Chapel, Mayfair.

Comper's chapel is built of Sussex sandstone, with a red-tiled roof, and the lofty spire is covered with oak shingles. At the suggestion of Rudyard Kipling, a supporter of the school and an acquaintance of Comper, it was built to dominate the landscape. The interior consists of a nave and a short north aisle containing the organ gallery. The panelled, star-spangled ceiling is richly decorated with heraldic bosses and carved angels. There is a plain wood rood screen and loft, an altar with a gilded reredos and much painted glass.

To the south-west stands the Song School, built in half-timber on an open stone arcade connected to the chapel by a double door. It is modelled on the Psallette at Tours where St Martin is buried. On the evidence of the Song School, it is easy to understand why John Betjeman later recognised an affinity between Comper and M. H. Baillie Scott. In 1932 Sebastian Comper designed St George's, a residential block, and the Seymour Obermer block which contained a remedial gymnasium, printing shop and leather workshop. In company with St Michael's, Newquay, Cornwall, (1909–11) Comper considered St Martin's, Chailey, to be the last example of unity by exclusion.

ST MARY, WARDLEWORTH, ROCHDALE, LANCASHIRE

Church, 1908–12

St Mary's, Rochdale, followed St Mary's, Wellingborough, in 1908. Comper regarded them as sister churches although their origin and traditions were entirely different. Built of red Runcorn stone, it took the place of a mean eighteenth-century building, whose dumpy pillars and windows were corrected, heightened and incorporated in the new church. They form the starting point of the synthesis of Classic and Gothic. The difficulties of the site dictated a plan composed of a nave with a double north aisle. The large and small aisle, which Comper considered a 'rather flattering memory of the very poor original church', was purposely planned in order to bring the east window into the only open space between high cotton mills. The aisle containing the Classical elements was sufficiently low to allow a clerestory above it.

Comper had visited Greece in 1906. The balustrade without and the soffits of the arches within have the fine, lozengy coffering measured by him in the temple of Bassae near Phygalia, 4,000 feet above the sea in Arcadia, said by Pausanias to have been designed by Ictinus, and were invented to carry off the synthesis of style. The main arcade followed Wellingborough, except for some differences in detail. While Rochdale has more obvious Greek detail than Wellingborough, it has a more normally English rood loft, lined with figures

St Mary, Wardleworth, Rochdale, Lancashire, 1908–12. The site was difficult, and the plan is a nave with a double north aisle. Comper fused a number of styles into a unified whole. Photograph: Derek Allen.

of saints in tabernacles. In this, and the window traceries, it resembles the rebuilding of the much finer church at Wimborne St Giles. The dark pews and pulpit are Classical but the parclose screens in the further north aisle enclose a chapel and are Gothic. Above the rood, carved in shallow relief, is the first representation designed on a significant scale of the Pantokrator, placed on a beam, flanked by kneeling angels, delicately coloured, like the chancel ceiling, in blue and gold.

While St Mary's, Rochdale, lacks the spectacular qualities of St Mary's, Wellingborough, architecturally it is a more interesting church. The site made Comper think hard about the plan. The drawings went before the Incorporated Church Building Society for a grant and Comper believed that they gave a hint to Sir Walter Tapper in his plan for the church of the Annunciation, Bryanston Street, Marble Arch (1912–14) which also has a broad nave and double north aisle, though there the furthest is reduced to a passage aisle. The Annunciation is a synthesis of secondary Gothic Revival sources and, with its vaulted west end, curved rood, screens, battering buttresses and external massing, includes elements of George Gilbert Scott Junior's work at St Agnes', Kennington, and All Hallows, Southwark, as well as a dependency

St Mary, Wardleworth, Rochdale, Lancashire, 1908–12. The screen, lined with figures of saints, and with the Pantokrator above the rood.

St Mary, Wardleworth, Rochdale, Lancashire, 1908–12. Early design for the screen, which underwent changes of detail, particularly in its lower elements. Drawing by E. T. Jago.

on Comper for the plan. But, given a good proportion, monolithic clustered piers of Purbeck marble, and a vaulted ceiling, it achieves an imposing result and it acts as an instructive foil to St Cyprian's, Clarence Gate.

By an irony the interior effect of Rochdale came closer to what Dr Price and the Revd T. J. Watts wanted, and failed to achieve, at Wellingborough. Not only is the screen English in character, there was also a long Gothic altar, hung with rose-red silk. A close examination will disclose a difference from other altars of this kind designed by Comper. To north and south there is a wide division between the riddel curtains and the altar. This was insisted upon by Edmund Arbuthnott Knox, the Evangelical Bishop of Manchester, who stipulated that provision should be made for celebrating the Eucharist from the north end of the altar.

Comper continued to work at Rochdale until 1937 but he was surprisingly cool in his enthusiasm for it. The reason was its conventional Anglican life and

the resistance this presented to his religious convictions and development. But, after Wellingborough, it is the most ingenious church of Comper's maturity, coming between the initial formulation of the theory of unity by inclusion and his discovery of the North African church plans after the Great War. Peter Fleetwood-Hesketh believed that it demonstrated 'how far modern Gothic has freed itself from the pedantic imitation of medieval work by the early revivalists'.

WYMONDHAM ABBEY, NORFOLK

Restoration and screen, 1913–34

When Comper visited the East Anglican churches they were unrestored and in a Cotman state of decay. Few had been touched since the Reformation had stripped them of imagery. 'The gloriously beautiful East Anglian churches,' Comper wrote, 'have suffered terribly in post-war (1914–18) years from bad internal restorations and vulgar English altars under the auspices of the Advisory Committees. To those who knew their exquisite beauty and refinement in their sad but untouched condition it is a grief.'

Comper worked widely in East Anglia, starting with a restoration of the tower and sanctuary levels of St Peter Mancroft, Norwich, in 1897. It was the restoration of St Leonard's, Mundford, near Brandon, that led to Comper's altar screen at Wymondham Abbey. In 1907–12 he replaced the Mundford heraldic traceries, including the Annunciation and the crests and shields of F. J. O. Montague, on the fourteenth-century screen. Montague had come to live there from High Melton, near Doncaster, Yorkshire, where in 1904 Comper had added a reredos and a screen with the royal arms beneath the rood. At Mundford he added a rood loft to carry a new Harrison organ with heraldic shades and a covered spiral staircase leading to it. As at Wimborne St Giles, Comper applied an accretive hand. The organ is flanked by two old hatchments on the wall of the chancel arch which he regarded as 'a most important recovery historically, and a beautiful decoration of our old churches'.

The rood, with St Mary and St John and also St Peter, St Paul, St Andrew and St James, are on the front row of the loft itself. In contrast to Lound, the whole was left in dark oak, unified with the simple row of returned stalls and high desks for the chancel, all richly carved, with a low front seat and moveable stools for boys. The new open timber roof of the chancel is richly decorated in gold and blue and gained for Mundford the popular name of the 'blue grotto of Norfolk'. The lancets of the east window were filled with painted glass, and its splays and the alabaster reredos were also decorated in gold and colour.

Sir William St John Hope, of the Society of Antiquaries, had advised Comper on the heraldry at Mundford, and he had also advised him at St Peter Mancroft. He was influential in recommending Comper for the altar screen at Wymondham in 1913. But Comper was a little wary of Hope and thought him, on the strength of his choice of Christopher Whall for the glass of the

Lady Chapel of Gloucester Cathedral, 'strangely devoid of taste for so great an antiquary'. Only the nave and aisles of the abbey church remained and the blank east wall presented a forlorn termination to the Romanesque nave. A stone screen had been proposed in 1901 by Hicks & Charlewood, of Newcastle, but had not been executed.

Comper designed a great screen of tabernacle work in decorated wood which was, in materials, consistent with East Anglian tradition. The inspiration was the high altar of Westminster Abbey as depicted in the fifteenth-century funerary roll of Abbot Islip. There is a large canopy over the screen, decorated with trumpeting angels and the gifts of the Holy Spirit radiating from a Dove. The screen has two tiers of nine tabernacles and three of those in the upper tier are over a central figure of the Majestas, which, on a considerably larger scale than the other figures, occupies the middle of the tiers of statuary. Over that, upon a beam one bay of the clerestory westwards, are the rood and winged cherubim. The symbolism represents Christ in judgement as described in the Apocalypse: 'Behold, a door was opened in heaven: and the first voice which I heard was as it were of a trumpet talking with me; which said, Come up hither, and I will shew thee things which must be hereafter. And immediately I was in the Spirit, and behold, a throne was set in heaven and one sat on the throne' [Revelation 4:1–2].

The design is subordinate to the Majestas, which dominates the nave as the focal point and centre of the church. Here at Wymondham it is translated from mosaic to carved wood in the same way that in 1927 it was turned into painted glass, on an even greater scale, in the east window of All Saints conventual church, London Colney, Hertfordshire. The screen was dedicated in 1921 but the decoration of the tabernacle work in burnished gold and Mediterranean colour, using the same masses of blue and gold as at La Martorana, was not completed until 1934.

In 1923 the young John Summerson went on a sketching tour of East Anglia with a fellow student at the Bartlett School of Architecture. They visited Wymondham.

> We found the reredos breath-taking. It was still comparatively new and I had no idea that such lovely work could be created in the 20th century. About the same time I got to know Pugin's work. … Pugin, Bodley and Comper have always had for me the same sort of magic – a genius for making late English Gothic come alive. … I must confess I have never been much attracted to Comper's Renaissance work. It was the Pugin – Bodley – Comper resurrection of Gothic which has always exercised the strongest appeal. Neither Giles Scott nor Tapper quite have it. Pugin, of course, was something like a saint. Beside him Comper was a bit of a prig, Bodley an amiable school-master, Tapper a bore and Scott a thoroughly nice man who, next to designing churches, enjoyed a round of golf.

The Wymondham altar screen is the largest and most beautiful English screen erected in the twentieth century, surpassing all others. And looking to

Wymondham Abbey, Norfolk. The altar screen, 1919–34. The young John Summerson found it 'breath-taking'. Photograph, 1947.

Wymondham Abbey, Norfolk. Detail of the altar screen, 1919–34. Photograph, 1947.

the future, the iconography anticipated Sir Graham Sutherland's monumental tapestry at the east end of Coventry Cathedral. But it is unfinished and does not fully represent Comper's intentions. A bad Edwardian pavement contradicted the medieval sanctuary levels and raised the altar too high and it was not possible to carry out the alabaster reredos proper which was an integral part of the design. From the soffit of the tester Comper desired the suspension of a pyx for reservation of the Blessed Sacrament.

Comper wanted to create a vision of heaven. The screen illustrates the density of sculptural richness and colour, the finesse of workmanship, the Classical structure of the tall images, their elusive movement, the elegantly disposed drapery of the figures in flowing but restrained folds, and the play of light on the gilded surfaces. In company with the Majestas and the Classical shell-heads to the upper tabernacles the superficial impression of fifteenth-century precedent is transmuted into a developed expression of the theory of unity by inclusion.

ST ALBAN, HOLBORN, LONDON

The Stanton chantry, completed 1917

During the years of Comper's pupillage to Bodley and Garner, 1883–7, he lived in rooms on the attic storey of 4 Doughty Street, Holborn. Bodley & Garner's drawing office was in South Square, Gray's Inn, nearby. The Revd A. H. Mackonochie, the grave and severe Vicar, was a friend of Comper's parents and a regular visitor to St Margaret's, Aberdeen. St Alban's was the most advanced Anglo-Catholic church in London and was designed by William Butterfield (1861–2).

There were many more dimensions to St Alban's than ritualism, not least the influence the church exercised on architects of the Gothic Revival. Bodley & Garner were members of the congregation and Garner designed a great triptych for the high altar painted blue and gold. Some of their pupils worshipped there. Bodley considered the enormous arch opening into the nave beneath a western saddle-back tower to be the finest arch of the Revival. J. D. Sedding was a churchwarden and, through his influence on the Revd E. F. Russell, a well-connected curate, many Arts and Crafts artists worked for and attended St Alban's.

The best known curate was the Revd A. H. Stanton, one of the most popular and outstanding preachers of the nineteenth century. He treated his preaching as a fine art, had taken lessons in elocution from Henry Irvine, and

St Alban, Holborn, London. Comper's font cover, 1909, some thirty feet tall, soaring beneath Butterfield's western arch. Photograph: Dell & Wainwright.

St Alban, Holborn, London. One of Comper's Stations of the Cross (1914–29) that filled the lunettes of Butterfield's arcaded panelling of the aisle walls. Photograph: Sebastian Comper.

C. H. Spurgeon, the Baptist preacher, was his model. He could draw multitudes. At first Comper was put off by Stanton's studied acting, theatrical attitudes, dramatic pauses and repetitions, his turn of the head in profile, and self-conscious gestures. Sweeping his biretta from the ledge of the pulpit, he startled his hearers by leaning over and asking, "My good lady please hand me back my cap." 'The fervour, the charm, the persuasiveness of his eloquence,' wrote Russell, 'was not simply the overflow of a richly-endowed nature, but sprang, from deep roots, out of the noble character of one of the most sensitive and sympathetic of men.' Stanton was one of the most attractive figures of the Anglo-Catholic movement. Many thought he showed in his life something of the largeness, force and fire of the canonised saints. A champion of the underdog, he had a magnetic influence on the young. To Mother Kate of St Saviour's Priory, Haggerston, he always appeared as a second Lacordaire, 'with his warm heart for his friends, and his special gift for dealing with, and winning, the hearts of young men'. Stanton soon became a friend, and Comper used him as his confessor.

Although he was an unremitting Romanist, Stanton greatly liked Comper's work and encouraged him. 'Perhaps few of those who knew the power of his evangelical preaching and his Catholic orthodoxy,' Comper recalled, 'realised the width of his sympathy and knowledge; and still fewer were aware that he was an ecclesiologist and intense lover of architecture and of all that it includes. He was not an aesthete in art like his friend and colleague,

St Alban, Holborn, London. 'Adoramus te', a memorial panel by Comper filling one of the lunettes of the blind arcading in the aisle walls. Photograph: Sebastian Comper.

E. F. Russell, whom I recall him describing as "full of taste, but all of it wrong". Like Bishop King, Stanton spent his holiday in Catholic countries on the continent, but it was in mufti, mainly for the sake of the architecture, and he knew Spain and Sicily.' 'Fr Stanton's love and admiration of your work in every detail,' wrote Sister Mary Teresa of All Saints in 1908 after he had visited St John's Hospital Chapel, Cowley, 'was as if he was a proud father with an honoured son, & "Ninian is *never* satisfied with what he does!"'

At Mackonochie's invitation, Comper had designed vestments, embroidery and a little minor work for St Alban's from the start of his practice. In 1904 he was appointed Bodley's successor as consulting architect to the church by the Revd Robert Suckling, the second Vicar and brother of Sister Mary Teresa of All Saints. In 1909 the congregation presented Suckling with a subscription of seven hundred pounds. Comper's first major commission followed, for the polychromatic spiral font cover of wood, decorated with panels of the seven sacraments, that soared for thirty feet beneath Butterfield's noble saddle-back tower, adding scale to the arch and emphasising its dignity. It was presented by Fr Suckling with his gift. Often confused with the work of Bodley, in the opinion of John Betjeman it gave majesty to the west end of the church. It was Comper's tallest font cover, probably the highest in the country, and one of his most elaborate works. As beautiful were the Stations of the Cross that were organic with the building and filled the lunettes of Butterfield's arcaded panelling of the aisle walls. These were Renaissance and owed a great deal to

Fra Angelico, Mantegna and, to a less extent, Tiepolo. None of the precedents were directly copied but all were tested by a direct appeal to life, and all redrawn from photographs in the same pose. At the same time the life-size statue of St Alban was added, resplendent with gilded hair, clad in golden armour as a Roman centurion, standing on a slender pillar decorated with chevrons.

Butterfield did not provide side chapels in his churches. Fr Stanton, with F. E. Sidney, the churchwarden, consulted Comper on how an altar could be got in, dedicated to Our Lady, with a *pietà* for its reredos. It took shape in 1917, after Stanton's death on 28 March 1913, in the chapel containing his tomb, known as the Stanton chantry. This was situated at the east end of the south aisle of the church. It was a fusion of architecture with the fine and applied arts. The first proposal was for a separate chantry chapel, similar to one built in 1890 by C. H. M. Mileham for Fr Mackonochie, but funds were insufficient. £7,347 was raised and the entire work cost £6,731 16s. 8d. The Stanton chantry was enclosed on two sides by a stone altar screen and the tomb canopy, decorated with pendant vaulting; and on the west by an iron grille, the lower part of which was extended to protect the tomb on the north side. The double vaulted tabernacles of Nailsworth stone were cut out of a single block of stone, the finials and pinnacles of the outside niches alone being added, and there was very skilful cutting of the alabaster of the tomb itself.

The altar was of black Derbyshire marble, and had lower and upper frontals of blue silk, richly embroidered by the School of Embroidery of the Sisters of Bethany. The altar and screen stood under a wooden tester, or canopy, bearing in the soffit a relief of the Coronation of the Virgin. The silver candlesticks and cross, in the *cinquecento* style, were inlaid with lapis lazuli and malachite. St Alban's was too Roman for a hanging pyx; instead it had a tabernacle with a *cinquecento* door, decorated with the head of the Saviour surrounded by cherubs in low relief, an early work executed in bronze gilt by Frank Knight.

The bronze effigy of Fr Stanton, and an equestrian group of St George, were modelled from Comper's cartoons by Alfred Drury RA. Drury had previously modelled a low relief of Burke for the tablet to him designed in 1897 by Comper for Beaconsfield church, in Buckinghamshire. Small alabaster figures and the tabernacle work were executed by carvers employed by W. D. Gough, and the decoration in gold and colour was executed by the *atelier* of H. A. Bernard Smith. 'The large figures in the chantry owe much to Drury's great skill in modelling,' Comper recalled. 'He was not, however, so happy in the likeness of Stanton's head, and the effigy generally was not sufficiently finely modelled, or cast, to allow of the mercurial gilding promised for it.' This proved disappointing for Comper: 'It is forgotten that the gilding of bronze effigies was a universal tradition and that in so recent an instance as the Wellington monument it was one of the tragedies to Alfred Stevens that for lack of fine chiselling he could not have it gilded.' Of all modern sculptors, Comper had the highest admiration for Stevens.

St Alban, Holborn, London, showing the tomb canopy of the Stanton chantry, 1913–17, made of Nailsworth stone. Photograph: Dell & Wainwright.

St Alban, Holborn, London, the Stanton Chantry, 1913–17. Looking east from the south aisle, through the iron grille at the entrance to the chapel, to the reredos, a finely-carved pietà.

St Alban, Holborn, London, the Stanton Chantry, 1913–17. The tabernacle door, by Frank Knight, in bronze gilt. Photograph: Frank Knight.

The effigy rested upon a stone tomb-chest decorated with the Stanton arms in *champlevé* enamel. The altar had a reredos and screen of painted and gilded alabaster with a *pietà* in the centre surrounded by angels and flanked by large figures of the Annunciation, executed by Drury to Comper's design. When it was completed it was received with unqualified praise, expressed in terms that demonstrate the unequivocal admiration that Comper's work inspired. 'Our church,' wrote Russell in *St Alban's Magazine*,

> is permanently enriched by one of the most superb monuments of modern times, erected to perpetuate one of the worthiest of the men who have been God's gift to us. The honour of the beauty is due, of course, to Mr Comper, who was chosen as architect of the memorial because Fr Stanton admired

St Alban, Holborn, London, the effigy (1913–17) of Fr Stanton. Modelled by Alfred Drury.

and loved his work beyond that of any living architect. In the beauty and refinement of its structure as a whole, in its wealth of imagery, of niche, canopy, and pinnacle, in the delicacy and finish of its detail as well as in the subordinated splendour of its decoration, Mr Comper has given us a monument unsurpassed amongst the monuments of our time.

Forty years later the tester was reproduced by J. S. Bucknall and William Butchart in the Holy House of the Anglican Shrine of Our Lady of Walsingham, Norfolk. There was no other chantry as sumptuous in England to an unbeneficed Anglican priest, and Roman Catholics as well as Nonconformists subscribed towards it.

In 1920 Comper resigned from St Alban's because he was not given the commission for Suckling's memorial. He was replaced by Sir Giles Gilbert Scott. 'I need hardly add,' he wrote to F. E. Sidney, 'how deeply I feel the severance of an association begun in earliest childhood when Mr Mackonochie used to visit my father's house in Scotland and to which was added in later years a professional connexion which I valued more than any other.'

The Stanton chantry had an almost symbolic place in Comper's development. Not only did it embody his spiritual aspirations, and those of his generation of Anglo-Catholics, in a tribute to one of the foremost leaders of

St Alban, London, Holborn. Comper's design (1946–8) for a post-war restoration of the badly damaged church. It was not executed. The ciborium was first designed for Downside Abbey in 1925. Drawing by F. J. Lucas.

the movement, it marked the end of the luxuriant scale of commissions that
had been given to him until the start of the Great War. Its execution during the
war had added pathos as many of the young men who had come under
Fr Stanton's sway fell in battle.

Comper's best work was done between 1904 and 1914. After the war,
architects had to face reduced economic circumstances and there were fewer
opportunities to work with the same scope. The majority of Comper's lavish
post-war commissions had been given before the war and were, with
a handful of notable exceptions, the completion of existing work. By a
strange irony, although three of Comper's sons and all his young assistants
and workmen fought in the war, none died, and the same standard of
workmanship was continued in his post-war work.

St Alban's was badly bombed in 1941 and most of Comper's furniture was
destroyed. The ruin of the Stanton Chantry was the major loss of Comper's
entire achievement as its design, workmanship and splendour were without
parallel. St Alban's, in company with Scott's St Agnes', Kennington, and
Pearson's St John's, Red Lion Square, was one of the most serious church
casualties of the Second World War. Comper made a design, faithful to
Butterfield, for the restoration but it was rejected. It was too expensive, too
elaborate for the severer post-war restrictions after 1945. Comper was then
eighty-one and he had no qualified architect working with him who would
enable it to be executed.

In 1945 Sir Giles Gilbert Scott and his brother, Adrian, prepared two
schemes: one for doing what was absolutely necessary, and the other for
restoring the church to its original form. St Alban's was not faithfully restored,
there is more of the Scotts than Butterfield, but Stanton's tomb-chest
survives; a little glass by Comper; and the figure of St Alban, regilded
and coloured by Butchart, designed for the original church, was replaced.
The tabernacle door from the Stanton chantry was refurbished by Knight
in red enamel and mercurial gilding and replaced in the east wall of the
sanctuary.

SOUTHWARK CATHEDRAL, LONDON

Various major works, especially 1923–31

The Augustinian priory church of St Mary Overie, London Bridge, Southwark, became the Cathedral of the newly-formed Diocese of Southwark in
1905 and was rededicated to St Saviour. It has had a long, complicated,
destructive building history and what is seen today is largely indebted to the
nineteenth century. Sir Arthur Blomfield restored and enlarged the church in
1890–97 by adding the nave, modelled as far as possible on the Early English
original, and furnishing the choir. In 1898 embroidered stoles, burses and
veils were commissioned from Comper, some of which survive, executed by
the Sisters of Bethany, and a white frontal for the altar in the retro-choir,
elaborately embroidered with angels. In 1907 Blomfield built the Harvard

Chapel opening from the north transept. From the crossing proceeding east Southwark Cathedral is medieval, dating from the thirteenth century, and includes the transepts and the retrochoir of four bays.

The Cathedral was run as a collegiate church before a Provost and Chapter was constituted in 1937. In 1905 Comper's brother, Leonard, was appointed a member of the college and remained until 1911. There was little money for furniture but Bodley had designed the font with a towering cover, and the bishop's throne. Most of the glass was by Kempe, bar the west window by Henry Holiday, and in 1905 the empty niches of Bishop Fox's sixteenth-century altar screen were filled with statues by Nicholls of Kennington.

Cyril Forster Garbett was appointed in 1919 and as well as being Bishop was also Dean. Southwark was one of the poorest dioceses and the Cathedral the poorest cathedral in the kingdom. The total amount available for the payment of the Cathedral clergy was £200 and the Canons were all honorary and part-time. The Precentor, Canon Haldane, who put in more time than anybody else, was also Rector of St Peter's, Sumner Street, and Chaplain to Guy's Hospital. There was practically no endowment; collections and donations were barely sufficient to pay for the music and the wages of the staff; there was no money for repairs. But to Garbett, the Cathedral was an interest as well as an anxiety.

It was in 1921 that F. C. Eeles recommended Comper, initially against Garbett's wishes, for the design of the war memorial in the retrochoir, and the war memorial in St Peter's, Sumner Street. This established a friendship with John Haldane, later the first Provost, who was one of Garbett's first appointments as Canon in 1919. Haldane's quiet, unfaltering work and sympathy for Comper's design enabled much to be accomplished in the next ten years. It was Garbett who became his strongest supporter, against much opposition from the Chapter and the Diocesan Advisory Committee, but this was forgotten when the work was completed.

The war memorial at Southwark is in the form of a roundel of St George and the dragon, gleaming in silver armour and a diapered surtout, seated on a gold horse with a red harness, fighting a green and gold dragon, contained within a large wreath tied with gold ribbon.

In 1922 the memorial led to the commission for a new Lady Chapel in the retrochoir. This brought an element of conflict with W. A. Forsyth, the Cathedral architect, to whom Eeles, as secretary of the Diocesan Advisory Committee, insisted that all designs should be submitted. Forsyth was a pedestrian architect with whom Comper had collaborated on the structure of St Andrew and St George, Rosyth. But it was an uneasy relationship and the interference from Eeles led to Comper's running battle with the system Eeles had established of advisory committees co-ordinated by the Central Council for the Care of Churches. Garbett and Haldane supported Comper and enabled the retrochoir to assume its present form.

Comper considered that the thirteenth-century retrochoir was the most beautiful part of the Cathedral and all that remained of the original fabric that had not been spoilt by Blomfield's restoration. The Lady Chapel and three other chapels, separated by screens, were apportioned to diocesan guilds and designed over the next ten years. They were dedicated to Jesus (for missionaries), the Good Samaritan (for social workers) and St Christopher (for children). The screens are simple, of dark oak, but they have high crestings, or brattishings, containing scenes from the Gospels, carved in flat relief and are sensitively decorated in burnished gold and colour.

A problem of scale emerged. Scale was essential for Comper. 'There is no more subtle beauty than proportion both in form and colour. It is the hardest to obtain and the last to be recognised as a fact of infinite importance; and one moreover which may not lightly be interfered with by the less skilled and experienced.' In the seventeenth century the floor had been raised because of flooding, and in 1930 Comper, in association with Forsyth, lowered it by eight inches to bring it back to the original proportion and re-laid the original stones. The walls and masonry were lime-washed. 'The obvious way is to whiten i.e. lime-wash it all over,' Comper wrote to Garbett in 1929. 'There is nothing that will bring out so well the beauty of the lines of architecture and, as St John Hope the great antiquary proved, it was the universal custom to

Southwark Cathedral. The floor of the retrochoir being lowered in 1930. Drawing by Hanslip Fletcher.

Southwark Cathedral. The Lady Chapel and other chapels in the retrochoir, reordered 1923–c.1931. Comper thought this the most beautiful part of the Cathedral.

lime-wash and re-lime-wash our churches in England in medieval times, as also it was abroad where the beauty of a few unscraped churches may still be seen.' The lime-wash was continued in the choir aisles. The choir and transepts were left as they were until they could be done together but they remain unwhitened to this day.

The scheme for the retrochoir culminated in an appeal to the diocese launched in 1930 when Garbett organised a Diocesan Festival Week to mark the twenty-fifth anniversary of the foundation of the Diocese. He wanted to raise £3000 for the adornment of the Cathedral and in fact raised slightly more. In preparation, during the previous year Comper was consulted about the choir and sanctuary. He had returned from a visit to Portugal and Spain, fired with enthusiasm for the hangings of rose-red, dating from the fifteenth century, that adorned the cathedrals, juxtaposed with the gilded furniture and the *rejas* of black iron. 'It is the concentration of effect,' he told Garbett, 'where each thing is related to the other that makes these churches so satisfying. Spain (I suppose alone) has an unbroken tradition, at least where the "restorer" has not destroyed it.' With the Spanish cathedrals in mind Comper applied what he had seen to Southwark.

Southwark Cathedral. The choir and sanctuary, which Comper remodelled and integrated over the course of two decades, finishing with the window of the Pantokrator over the east end in 1947.

Superficially, Comper's work in the Cathedral appears medievalist, a reversion to his early style. But he brought to it his accruing understanding of unity by inclusion. First and foremost he recommended solidly gilding the figures and their tabernacles of the lower part of the altar screen as if they were old bronzes, an effect solemn and impressive. This was done in order to give width to the cathedral as a whole, seen most clearly from the west of the nave.

He designed a Gothic altar with decorated riddel posts and casts of the Stockcross angels; but the reredos of gilded mahogany is modelled on the Pala d'Oro, the reredos behind the high altar of St Mark's, Venice, which Comper regarded as the ideal silver-gilt reredos. The design had first been proposed in 1903 for St Patrick's church, Carnalway, Co. Kildare, in Ireland but was rejected. It is composed of a central figure of the Risen Christ surrounded by emblems of the Evangelists. Figures, representing the four Latin and Greek Doctors and the four Evangelists, enclosed in panels formed by moulded ribs in the manner of the metal reredoses, flank the central subject painted flat on a gesso ground of pale gold. The intention was to provide an unaggressive background to the silver cross and candlesticks.

Other earlier work contributed to the design. In 1909 Comper had provided new panels for William Dyce's east wall at All Saints, Margaret Street, Marylebone. Details of figures he had drawn in Mistra and elsewhere in Greece contributed to their design and the All Saints figures, reduced to a small size, were repeated in the Southwark reredos. For the inscriptions for the Greek Doctors Comper sought the help of F. E. Brightman, a Fellow of Magdalen College, Oxford, a scholar and liturgiologist who had published *Liturgies Eastern and Western* in 1896, based on extended research and several journeys to monasteries in the East.

Comper decorated the carved cresting of Bodley's bishop's throne in burnished gold, and added hangings of rose-red silk embroidered with the Bishop's arms, cushions, and antependia to the three desks. But the most dramatic addition were the rose-red hangings of Van der Weyden tapestry that were hung by hooks, as in Spain, from the capitals of the choir pillars, that entirely surrounded their girth and brought them level to the line of gold of the altar screen. 'Too much stress cannot be laid on the desirability of a continuously level line of the gold and the red of the three sides of the Presbytery. It is absolutely necessary to give the full sense of space, repose and dignity that is necessary.' A striking contrast was obtained in Lent by a similar uniformity in the use of white linen. Besides the altar and the vestments, the gilded altar screen was covered by a linen veil on which a calvary cross with the instruments of the Passion were painted. An Axminster carpet of rose-red was laid before the altar. Banners by Comper of St Saviour, Our Lady, and the Child Jesus, executed by the Royal School of Needlework, decorated the choir at festivals. As a unifying element, the stone of the canopy of Bishop Lancelot Andrewes's tomb on the south side of the sanctuary was decorated in gold and colour in order to wed its original decoration with the new decorations of the altar screen.

Comper's final proposal was to take up the line of decoration in the nave. 'The eye asks that there should be something to lead up to the rightly concentrated richness of the high altar, or, expressing it another way, to bring this richness down into the church so that it may not appear too abrupt and isolated from it. And also to give it further length and breadth. There is no lack of precedent in old churches which have not been despoiled of their ornaments.' Nothing, he believed, would meet this better than two altars placed against the west side of the two western piers of the crossing. 'But the reredoses must necessarily, for such a position, be costly and, pending the realisation of the reredoses, the altars might be set there with red tapestry above them, or even the red tapestry without the altars. There would be no waste of material to either plan as there is abundant scope for using the tapestry elsewhere in the church.' This would be unified by a good oriental carpet in the crossing. These proposals were beyond the appeal's resources but they would have added significantly to the unity of the interior.

Haldane, before his death, had supplied five sets of frontals, executed by the Sisters of Bethany, for the principal altars and three for the others, besides complete sets of High Mass vestments, including one of Italian *lama d'oro* (cloth of gold) procured with great difficulty from Rome, that included a mitre. 'It is extremely beautiful for vestments because of the play of light as the wearer moves and the orphreys need only be marked out by laces say in red and gold, with red tassels and fringe and my blue linen lining.' A frontal for the high altar, given by Henry Lloyd, was the first to be made from a new textile designed by Comper, the Strawberry cloth of gold, which he was in process of preparing for the looms in 1928.

Southwark Cathedral embodied Bishop Garbett's English liturgical ideals. A naturally reserved man not given to superlatives, some thought him inhuman and aloof, but it was he who consolidated the Diocese. 'I was celebrating at the Cathedral this morning,' he tersely wrote to Comper in the autumn of 1929, 'and saw for the first time the reredos. It exceeds my expectations. I am delighted with the general effect. It gives an impression of real magnificence in colour.' Praise was lavished on Comper's work, by Canon T. P. Stevens. 'The work gives gaiety and heavenly splendour to a church which stands in as dismal a place as the mind of man can imagine. Those who dislike its new glory would disapprove God's colour scheme on the Italian lakes and his sunset on a September evening. Such people need our prayers.' The beauty of the interior of Southwark Cathedral as it survived until the early Seventies remained a memorial to Bishop Garbett's taste, restless energy, and pastoral care. It summed up his character: simple, tranquil, dignified, reverent, and completely Anglican, with all the essentials and no frills.

Southwark also fulfilled Comper's own liturgical standards and he admired the careful way that Haldane ran the Cathedral in contrast to the barren ritualism of other cathedrals and Westminster Abbey under the influence of Jocelyn Perkins, the Sacrist, and Chairman of the Warham Guild.

> Needless to say there were no ritualistic processions at Southwark. First things were put first, and with the restoration of the full ceremonial of the Eucharist, in everything but incense, there was no need for fancy ritual. The Low Mass, as faithful to the Prayer Book, and in every rubric, as the Tractarians, had every adjunct of correct ceremonial that they used, and may be more. And it was always the same, whether the Bishop, Provost or the young priests whom he imbued with his spirit celebrated. In the more spacious days of motoring, when indeed we have reached Wellingborough for the Sung Mass on a Sunday, it was an easy matter to get to Southwark before breakfast, and nowhere else within reach was found greater reverence.

In 1945 Comper proposed the formation of a new sanctuary in the crossing which would have an altar standing beneath a ciborium of burnished gold. This would have given the Cathedral a liturgical focus consistent with advanced liturgical thinking, but it was too radical for the Provost and Chapter who were content with the earlier arrangements. It would have anticipated the liturgical reforms following the Second Vatican Council which have now been applied throughout the Roman Catholic Church and the Anglican Communion. Comper's proposals would have made the destructive work of George Pace and Ronald Sims that started in 1970 unnecessary and would have maintained the aesthetic integrity of the interior.

Southwark Cathedral should not be seen solely as a furnishing scheme but as the last of Comper's church restorations. He brought the Cathedral into unity as far as he was able, subtly indebting it to a broad European influence that went beyond narrow English precedents. His final significant addition was the east window, erected in 1947, to replace Kempe's glass which had been destroyed during the war. It represents the Pantokrator, the all-sovereign Ruler and Creator of all, surrounded by doves, executed in broad masses of Mediterranean blue and white, touched by yellow, majestically reigning over the cool grey interior.

SOCIETY OF ALL SAINTS, LONDON COLNEY, HERTFORDSHIRE
Conventual chapel, 1921–8; completed by Sebastian Comper 1960–64

Comper's conception of church planning was developed by two visits to French North Africa in 1922 and 1924, recommended by Sir Cyril Cobb, the churchwarden of St Cyprian's, Clarence Gate. His early experiments with the central eucharistic space at the Grosvenor Chapel in 1912 and St Andrew and St George, Rosyth, in 1919, were developed after the strong impetus received from his discovery of the fourth-century church complex at Theveste (see plan page 213). The church dates from *c.*A.D. 400 and is imbued with Constantinian concepts. It is one of the most valuable survivals of the time.

All Saints, London Colney, Hertfordshire, the conventual chapel, 1921–8. Early photograph.

'A broad flight of steps ascend from a forecourt (it is of a later date) towards a colonnaded propylaeum,' wrote Richard Krautheimer.

> From these, three doors lead into the church. All this recalls, if anything, Tyre, or the basilica of the Holy Sepulchre, or the first H. Sophia in Constantinople and its propylaeum. In the nave the piers … carried arches above which appeared the openings of a gallery level by the projection of a cornice. This cornice in turn supported a second or third order of columns ascending to the roof beams. Mosaics covered the floors in nave and aisles. The sculptured ornament is – an exception in North Africa – remarkably fine. From the right aisle, a broad staircase descended to the trefoil martyrium built about thirty years before the main church and replacing a yet earlier memorial. A chancel barrier in the last bays of the nave enclosed the altar, and a second "chancel" was laid out near the entrance. The slightly raised apse is flanked by side chambers, both of which communicate through doors with the aisles as well as the apse.

Comper wrote of Theveste, 'It is, by a long way, the most complete and most magnificent church of the 4th century which we have seen.' And later he described his mature conclusions:

> The plans of the churches which we measured of the fourth century, untouched as some of them are, and none since the seventh century, completed the lesson that it is from these examples of earlier times that we should draw for our parochially-used churches today, rather than from the plans of the middle ages when the larger parish churches were influenced by the examples of the monastic choirs. Also fresh impetus was given to the love of Greek architecture by such exquisitely small temples in Sbéïtla and

Dougga which were evidently the models for the church of the fourth century at Tébessa.

These he had seen on his first visit to North Africa in 1922.

It was in 1924 that these principles were realised in the conventual church of All Saints, London Colney, near St Albans in Hertfordshire. Comper had built the chapel for St John's Home, Cowley, Oxford, for the Society of All Saints in 1902–7. In 1899 they had commissioned the Roman Catholic Arts and Crafts architect, Leonard Stokes (1858– 1925), to design their mother house at London Colney. It is the most outstanding of Stokes's conventual buildings, described by Sir Albert Richardson as a 'modernistic version of the Cambridge college gateway with cornices based on the Greek ovulo moulding'. Another observer contrasted the free style of the design with a more pedantic approach: 'Mr Stokes has chosen to work in Gothic, not the prim, copybook Gothic of the 'seventies, but a plastic, frankly modern type of Gothic, which in his hands is instinct with grace and life.' The building displays Stokes's favourite motifs: it is broadly symmetrical with bay windows, with horizontal brick bands that tie in the window heads and cills, balance the Tudor windows, and the wide low arches with hollow archivolts of the cloister garth, round which the convent is built. The entrance tower has a frieze of figures carved by Henry Wilson.

Stokes was a man of 'paradoxically impulsive temperament' with a violent temper, given to swearing. He had made designs for a chapel but lost the commission because he called the Mother Superior a 'damned woman' to her face; Comper referred to her as the 'saintly Mother Mary Emily'. She was a niece of J. Wickham Legg and a learned religious in her own right. Her erudition and understanding of liturgical principle enabled Comper to make radical planning experiments.

In 1919 the building of a church was seriously considered and she turned to Comper for the design. He was supported by W. A. Forsyth, the architect with whom he had collaborated at Rosyth, and who assisted him with structural problems after Jago had left for America. In 1923 Forsyth wrote to Mother Mary Emily that there were 'a number of architects who are well qualified to carry out your Chapel, but none his equal in producing such excellent design nor in offering such charm of idea or in planning so interesting a building, so complete for its spiritual purpose.'

All Saints convent had an orphanage and hospital designed by Smith and Brewer and Ernest Willmott. Comper's church of pale brick with tall pointed windows in which Perpendicular and Early English motifs are mixed is defined externally by pinnacles set square on the buttresses, and makes a marked contrast to Stokes's work and no effort to stay in keeping. It has an aisleless nave, twenty-six feet wide, with a concrete vault. The church was designed to be strictly conventual, primarily to give privacy to a large choir; but it was also planned to meet the need of visual participation in the worship at the high altar of the other residents of the convent, besides the nuns and

All Saints, London Colney, Hertfordshire, the conventual chapel, 1921–8. The ciborium, and east end. The plan allowed all worshipppers to have complete visbility of the high altar, whilst giving privacy to a large conventual choir.

their visitors and, in particular, of children. An ante-chapel was, Comper decided, quite unsuited to such a purpose, not least because it involved the need of seculars passing through the choir to receive Holy Communion.

Low transepts, or chapels, were provided. The south transept was connected with an ante-chapel by a small cloister, opening upon a fountain in the chapel of St John Baptist. One of the alternate traceries of the cloister's unglazed windows has an interlocking wheel taken from the Dominican convent at Dubrovnik, and the plain pointed vaulting was carried out in stone. The high altar was placed at the crossing beneath a gilded ciborium, the pillars decorated with flowers, and a crocketted ogee crown of eight arches; it is the all-dominating element, enclosed within white walls. The plan enabled worshippers on all sides to have complete visibility. At the consecration of the first three bays by the Bishop of St Albans in 1927 those in the Lady Chapel faced west, so that all present were able to join with him in the elevation of the Host. It was to a fuller extent the realization of the aim of Cardinal Verdier at Notre Dame in Paris. These principles were developed in 1928 in the unexecuted plan for Aberdeen Cathedral, and in 1937 in the design for St Philip's, Cosham, Portsmouth.

While North Africa contributed to the plan, the Chartreuse du Val de Bénédiction, at Villeneuve-les-Avignon, Provence, inspired the whole building, although it is completely English in character. All Saints is 'of that essence of Gothic in the blending of France, England and Italy in the Avignon of the papal captivity'. Avignon seemed to Comper, after many visits, to be 'a culmination of Gothic architecture, like that of Greek under Pericles, in which all mannerism of style and nationality are purged and the fine gold of pure form remains'. The Charterhouse gave an ideal of what a conventual church should be. The dimensions of All Saints are roughly those of the nave of the Charterhouse, though a little higher. In 1926, when the transverse vaulting ribs were ready for their mouldings, Comper, dissatisfied with what he had drawn, went again to Avignon and measured the vaults that were accessible. He arrived closely at other vaults which were out of reach and which were most wanted as a test of scale, though the details differ.

The east window of seven lights is filled with a Jesse tree and was the first to be designed to contain in the tracery a more than life-size figure of the Majestas in painted glass, dominating the building in the manner of the Palermitan mosaic churches. It was executed in three stages, the upper part first, then the centre lights, then the side lights. Different tones of green distinguish the evolution and it was completed in 1957. A pyx was suspended from a crook over the Lady altar immediately against the east window, in the French manner, like that of the Grosvenor Chapel. The choir stalls of oak, stained dark, were executed by Rattee & Kett. Like the ciborium they are Classical with slim Tuscan columns and small buttresses, and, unlike the stalls in the Oxford chapel, they are extremely simple. Comper designed everything, down to the candle sconces on the walls, the candlesticks on the altar, and even specified the size and type of the tapering candles. His control was absolute and he sometimes complained that the candlesticks did not shine as he intended them to shine, and blamed the lay sisters for neglecting to clean them properly.

For years the church remained unfinished, due to lack of funds, but it was eventually completed by Sebastian Comper in 1964. Comper himself had designed a new hospital for old people to the south of the chapel, St Anne's Home, the first portion of which was finished in 1929 at the same time as the church. Both were intended to be one and, on completion, the wards were designed to open into an ante-chapel, in the form of a vaulted narthex providing an organ gallery above. They could be shut off by sliding doors and were inspired by the arrangement of medieval hospitals. The Mass and choir offices could be heard, and seen, through the central opening of the choir screen, but the altars flanking it on both sides were provided for the use of patients. These proposals were forgotten by the time Sebastian Comper was commissioned to complete the church. He added the (liturgical) western bays – the church is not orientated – creating an unhappy void in the ante-chapel, terminated by a solid wall, broken at the top by a round window in Venetian Gothic.

The Society of All Saints gave up the convent in 1974 and moved their mother house to Cowley. The buildings were bought by Cardinal Heenan for the Archdiocese of Westminster and are now the All Saints Pastoral Centre.

THE WELSH NATIONAL WAR MEMORIAL, CARDIFF, GLAMORGAN
Unveiled 1928

The most prolific years of Comper's practice were 1919–23 when he undertook an immense number of war memorials that took the form of painted glass, stone churchyard crosses, calvaries, wall monuments, sanctuary furniture and side chapels. So occupied was he that he abandoned his diary, but for foreign travel. During this time Comper was given two major commissions: the Welsh National War Memorial, Cardiff, in 1923, and the Warriors' Chapel, Westminster Abbey, in 1925. With the addition of the heraldic Parliamentary War Memorial window, Westminster Hall, in 1952, these were his most significant public commissions and put him in the same league as Sir Edwin Lutyens, the designer of the Cenotaph in Whitehall and the Irish National War Memorial, Dublin; and Sir Robert Lorimer, the designer of the Scottish National War Memorial, Edinburgh.

The Welsh National War Memorial was Comper's only secular work. It is also the only invitation to submit a design in competition that he ever accepted. His acceptance was decided by two visits to French North Africa, particularly to Tunisia, where he had been fired by the beauty of Hadrian's Graeco-Roman public works and the colonnades of their theatres. These inspired his conception of a circular colonnade enclosing a sunken court, entered by three porches, focusing the three figures of a soldier, sailor and

The Welsh National War Memorial, Cardiff, Glamorgan, unveiled 1928. Comper's only secular work, and his only competition entry, it caused considerable controversy. Newspaper photograph, 1928.

airman raising wreaths against a central fountain crowned by a nude figure of Victory, holding aloft the cross of his sword hilt and standing between three sporting dolphins.

The figures were modelled by A. Bernard Pegram from a living model, a young naval rating of great personal charm serving in the North Atlantic Fleet, called Fred Barker. In order to find the Greek Ideal Comper had secured permission to review the crews of two battle ships at the Union Jack Club, Waterloo, and Barker was chosen and photographed nude and in uniform. He later wrote to Comper, saying how much he was looking forward to seeing his double in clay. Goscombe John considered the resultant figure of Victory 'Quite Greek' and Sir Hamo Thorneycroft, another Royal Academician, lent his support to Pegram.

On the frieze is inscribed *In hoc signo vinces* (in this sign thou shalt conquer) and upon the inside frieze 'Remember here in peace those who in tumult of war by sea, on land, in air, for us and for our victory endured unto death.' These words were chosen by Comper because it was the first time in history that victory was secured by the meeting of sea, land and air and they were the ruling theme of the model which he submitted under the Greek word, *Triodos*.

The Welsh National War Memorial, Cardiff, Glamorgan. Crowds at the unveiling ceremony, 12 June 1928. Newspaper photograph, 1928.

Comper experienced great frustration in the execution of the Memorial and opposition from the architectural profession. Cardiff has the finest civic centre of any city in Britain. Letters to the city fathers were received from distinguished architects, imploring them not to disfigure such a fine example of town planning by the erection of a bandstand. *The Builder* reported that the President of the Royal Institute of British Architects had shaken his head sorrowfully, saying 'What a pity', and that Professor Charles Reilly, who had come to Cardiff to lecture to the architects of Wales on Liverpool Cathedral, had told them of the monstrosity he had seen rising above the hoarding in the park and was told was their Memorial. 'It would almost appear,' Comper drily commented, 'that the accident of the designer not being a member of the Institute was a condemnation sufficient of itself.'

The Welsh National War Memorial was unveiled by the Prince of Wales on 12 June 1928, but Comper was not presented to him. When the board fence was removed a younger man than his critics told him that, prejudiced by all he had heard against it, he went to see the memorial with a comrade of the war and they remarked to each other that they had instinctively removed their hats as they entered the enclosure. For them, there was an immediate identification and response.

The Warriors' Chapel, commissioned 1925

Comper had close connections with Westminster Abbey that began in 1909 when he was given by Dean Armitage Robinson the first of a series of severe, monumental windows of abbots and kings in the north aisle, strongly influenced by the fifteenth-century glass of York Minster. This was a scheme that was supported by M. R. James, the Provost of Eton, against the harsh criticism of W. R. Lethaby, the Surveyor of the Abbey, who wanted to promote Christopher Whall, and told Comper that in time the windows would be cast out. The series was concluded in 1961, a year after Comper's death. Stephen Dykes Bower thought that the unity of window and wall-surface constituted the greatest glazing achievement in England of the twentieth century.

The commission for the Warriors' Chapel, originally intended to be the chapel of the Holy Cross, was given to Comper in 1925 by Dean Ryle. It was raised to the memory of the million men and women of the Empire who had died in the Great War. The chapel was a complex work, fraught with Abbey politics and a change of Deans and Canons, including the arrival of Canon Dearmer in 1931 against the wishes of Dean Foxley Norris. Dearmer soon made objections to Comper's design but was over-ruled.

At the west end of the south aisle stood an abandoned medieval chapel dating from the time of Abbot Islip which had served as a consistory court and baptistery. It was blocked on the north side by a double monument, the biggest in the Abbey, erected to Captain Cornwall in 1743. This was removed by Dean Foxley Norris to the great benefit of the scheme. There remained a late fifteenth- or early sixteenth-century open stone screen that had traces of Renaissance arabesque painting above the cusps.

The chapel is enclosed in a Spanish Plateresque *reja* of black iron and it acts as a foil to the rose-red and mercurial gilding of the interior. The altar has a finely modelled removable frontal of bronze-gilt with a *pietà* in the centre enclosed in a wreath, surrounded by cherubs enclosed in acanthus arabesques holding the instruments of the Passion, executed in shallow relief. Figures of St Helena and St Margaret of Scotland, stand in tabernacles at either end. They represent British mothers and were chosen because of their associations with the Cross. A red silk frontal to match the upper frontal and hangings was provided as well as a set of white linen for Lent. Comper had discovered a medieval *mensa* which he desired to reuse but he was overruled.

To the entire width of the plain wall of the stone screen, above the openings, were applied a delicate row of alabaster tabernacles and traceries. These were carved by Ernest Smith who had a 'heaven-sent skill' and whose chisel, Comper believed, equalled the Italian Renaissance and produced a result 'as fine as the workmanship in the medieval tabernacles over the entrance to the chapel of Our Lady of the Pew'. Beneath is a rood with gilded figures of St Mary and St John, modelled by Pegram and executed by Frank Knight, and above is a narrow frieze of wrought iron, with arabesques in bronze-gilt that

Westminster Abbey, the Warriors' Chapel, 1925–32. The reja, *or wrought-iron screen, at the entrance to the chapel, with a medallion of St Michael and dragon in the centre. Photograph: W. Clark.*

echo the painted arabesques below, surmounted by a baldachino of red silk with a valance of cloth of gold. And above that is a continuation of the short balusters and cresting of gilded dolphins between the candelabra of the iron screens started on the north side. Inside the chapel the screen incorporates a medallion of St Michael and the Dragon executed in mercurial gilding on a black ground, and facing the nave the Verdun Trophy, given by France to the Lord Mayor of London.

The Warriors' Chapel sums up many influences in Comper's development and also marks a departure in technique. His passion for Spain is expressed in the strong profiles and vertical scale of the balusters of the *reja* with their glimpse of rose-red within. The only other early-twentieth-century

Westminster Abbey, the Warriors' Chapel, 1925–32. Exterior, showing the reja, *or wrought-iron screen, crested by dolphins. Photograph: Dell & Wainwright.*

Westminster Abbey, the Warriors' Chapel, 1925–32. The altar, rood and baldachino. Photograph: Dell & Wainwright.

church architect who was as strongly influenced by Spain was Sir Walter Tapper, Bodley's former office manager and a contemporary of Comper. He designed gilded Spanish screens to enclose his fine regimental chapels in York Minster. But the *rejas* of black iron which Comper had installed in St Mary's, Wellingborough, preceded them by several years. There was also W. Romaine-Walker, a pupil of Street, who had in 1900 designed *rejas* of great delicacy for St Michael and All Angels, Brighton, and the Jesuit church at Farm Street, Mayfair.

The departure in technique lay in the use of mercurial and burnished gilding. From the beginning of his work Comper had used H. A. Bernard Smith, who was a fellow-pupil of Bodley & Garner. Smith had established an *atelier* for church decoration at 5 Staple Inn, Holborn, and had trained a highly finished group of decorators who learnt their trade under Comper's direction. In 1925 a new apprentice was taken, William Butchart. Like Comper, he was an Aberdonian and that forged a strong bond. Comper had been introduced to burnished gold by F. C. Eden but he found it hard to make Smith and his foreman use it. The Warriors' Chapel was Butchart's first job and it was he who finally persuaded Comper to apply mercurial gilding on metal for the first time at Westminster, the only occasion when a workman was independently able to exercise his influence. The result so delighted Comper that he not only said that he wished he could have his time all over again but thereafter also applied burnished gold to wood. Comper thought that Butchart had the same facility with the brush that Smith had with the chisel and was unequalled in his experience. The Warriors' Chapel opened a new chapter and from that time to Comper's death Butchart exclusively executed Comper's painted decoration. It was Butchart's skill that enabled Comper's church furniture to continue for so long. Thereafter, he continued to work at the Abbey under Stephen Dykes Bower, decorating the pulpitum, choir stalls and the artisan mannerist monuments.

ST MARY, BURY ST EDMUNDS, SUFFOLK
Jesus Chancel and Chapel of the Suffolk Regiment, 1935

In 1935 Comper executed a chapel for the Suffolk Regiment that reflected the changed economic circumstances of the time. It showed what he could do simply and he frequently complained that he wished his admirers would notice his plain work instead of being dazzled by gilding and elaboration. He believed that his work was as fully expressed on a simple scale as it was in splendour.

The east end of the Jesus Chancel had a carved and decorated gilded medallion of the Risen Saviour, hung against rose-red silk damask above the altar. In the middle of the altar frontal, powdered with sacred monograms, was the regimental badge, a castle enclosed within a beautiful centre piece of roses and thistles, taken from an eighteenth-century colour in the Regiment's possession.

St Mary, Bury St Edmunds, Suffolk. The Jesus Chancel and Chapel of the Suffolk Regiment, 1935, an example of the powerful effects that Comper could secure with limited means. Photograph: David Cockcroft.

The Battle Honours were inscribed on scrolls on roses in the plaster ceiling beneath the organ at the west end of the chapel, cases for which were designed but not carried out. And beneath the west front of the organ, gates of wrought iron, with the regimental badge, closed the entrance. Instead of scattered memorial tablets, their inscriptions were repeated in a wainscot of dark oak and a beginning was made of a scheme for further memorials in the glass of the windows. The regimental colours were dramatically hung in diagonal groups and one of Comper's distinctive lighting fittings hung in the centre, a simple chandelier of gilded wood and iron with tapers (modelled on some he had measured in the Baroque cathedral of Syracuse, built into a Greek Doric temple, in 1905) from which were suspended clear bulbs of low power.

Comper's work is inextricably associated with rose-red hangings, errone-ously described, to his annoyance, as 'Comper pink'. Purity of colour was an essential element of Comper's aesthetic quest. It was for this reason that he had begun to design his own ecclesiastical textiles which were woven by an old firm of Spitalfields silk weavers, founded in 1813, M. Perkins & Sons. Under the influence of Bodley, the fashion had set in in church work for muted half-tones, olive green, brownish or scarlet reds. Comper saw that they were not true to the colours he had seen in medieval textiles and embroidery, nor to the luminous purity of colour found in Flemish panel paintings and medieval illuminations. Experiments were made but none achieved the pure rose then surviving in the hangings of Central, Southern Italian and Spanish churches.

Comper was helped in his search for the desired rose-red by Geraldine, Countess of Mayo, the director of the Royal Irish School of Art Needle-work, who introduced him to Sir Thomas Wardle, of Leek, in Staffordshire. Wardle's experiments in vegetable and oriental dyeing and art printing on silk, cotton and wool had made him the foremost dyer of the time. He had taught William Morris all he knew about dyeing. Comper had secured a piece of Italian rose-red silk which had been brought back from Sicily by his friend, Mrs Edmund McClure. Wardle was able to reproduce it and other colours, with greater scientific accuracy than the original and to secure its fastness.

From 1901 Wardle's firm dyed Comper's textiles, using Chinese dyes for their purity of colour. The result was surprisingly unecclesiastical in effect. In 1912 a further transformation of colour was achieved by Comper's all-consuming passion for the *ballet Russe* in their second London season, in a conversion to the exquisite oriental colouring of the designs of Léon Bakst. Thereafter he applied Bakst's clear tones in his dyes for textiles.

Few of Comper's textiles, in tapestry, silk-damask or brocatelle, have been woven since the Second World War and what has replaced them in many of his churches and chapels are coarse, crude substitutes that greatly diminish his work. This has happened in recent years in the Chapel of the Suffolk Regiment. What feign to be a contemporary reintroduction of Comper's textiles are invariably of a coarse standard, using bad dyes, that do little to complement his work or enhance his reputation. The loss of Chinese vegetable dyes badly affected the colour of Comper's textiles. 'Today I am told that until the trade is resumed with China,' he wrote in 1941, 'we shall not be able to get the true fast dyes again, including my beautiful rose colour which survives, unfaded, in the vestments and hangings of my churches. All that is now to be had is a poor substitute which cannot be guaranteed not to fade.'

ST PHILIP, COSHAM, PORTSMOUTH, HAMPSHIRE
Church and furnishings, 1935–9

St Philip's, Cosham, was the only new parish church where Comper was able to apply the planning theories with which he had experimented at All Saints, London Colney. It was a modest commission but it enabled him to concentrate upon the essential principles of liturgical planning and construction.

The plan is composed of a nave and two aisles of four bays in which the altar stands beneath a ciborium in the fourth bay in direct axial relationship to the font in the first bay at the west end (see plan on page 207). It shares the breadth rather than the length characteristic of the North African and Spanish churches; and a lesser proportion at the west end provides a gallery for the choir and organ. There is pure intersecting tracery and a floor of composite

St Philip, Cosham, Portsmouth, Hampshire, 1937. The church under construction. Photograph: John Samuel Bucknall.

stone. The plain exterior is also taken from the hard, unornamented surfaces of Spanish churches, and has pinnacles and a small Classical bell-cote.

The ciborium is decorated in burnished gold and complete in its imagery, with the figure of the Risen Saviour surmounting it between four eagles at the corners, from whose beaks lamps are suspended. A small metal tabernacle is provided in one of the pillars facing the high altar, in the hope that eventually it would be replaced by a suspended tabernacle, or pyx, against the ceiling of the ciborium immediately above the altar. The ceiling is painted as a firmament in blue and gold. A silver crucifix with figures of St Mary and St John stands upon the altar between four candlesticks.

Comper himself gave the Majestas in painted glass in the tracery of the east window, and on three sides of the Lady Chapel behind the high altar, beneath the windows, the walls were hung with rose-red silk, now replaced by an inferior substitute. The font cover is decorated in burnished gold and colour and so is the organ case. The walls, Classical columns with their severe and beautiful Corinthian capitals modelled on North African precedents, and plaster vaults, are lime-washed. The sanctuary is surrounded on three sides by oak altar rails. They were a prelude to open, black wrought-iron screens, in the manner of the Spanish *rejas*, which would have enclosed the sanctuary and were never executed. The altar is in every sense the centre and richest part of the church.

St Philip's realised all that Comper advocated in the planning of a modern church. It is his legacy to the future. It was the fulfilment of his quest for beauty and liturgical planning on rational principles; a church that was

St Philip, Cosham, Portsmouth, Hampshire, 1937, looking east. An interior whose purity of form revived interest in Comper's work amongst a wide constituency. Photograph: John Samuel Bucknall.

St Philip, Cosham, Portsmouth, Hampshire, 1937. The ciborium with Lady Chapel behind. Photograph: John Samuel Bucknall.

essentially modern yet indebted to the unfolding development of the Catholic tradition as it had evolved from Constantine to the twentieth century in which the heart and purpose of worship was the gathering of the baptised in the offering of the Mass.

St Philip's led to a revival of interest in Comper's work, especially among the young. Few immediately understood his overriding preoccupation with the setting, position, appearance and significance of the altar but John Betjeman and John Piper were persuaded. One reason for the cult of

St Philip, Cosham, Portsmouth, Hampshire, 1937. Looking west, showing the font and gallery. This was John Betjeman's favourite photograph of the church. Photograph: John Samuel Bucknall.

Comper they started was that his later work, with burnished gold ciboria in an austere and light architectural setting, corresponded with contemporary taste. Another was that his earlier intense and highly decorated medievalism was interpreted as a manifestation of English Romanticism.

A young architect who was profoundly impressed by Cosham was Francis Johnson, one of the leading Classicists of the late twentieth century. He disliked the dull, lifeless, uninteresting work of the late Arts and Crafts architects, notably that of Dr F. C. Eeles's favourite, Sir Charles Nicholson, embodied in St Peter and St Paul, Fareham, Hampshire (1930–31), with its 'usual jumble of ill-digested historical motifs with the usual hesitant details and proportions, silly little gates and things serving no purpose – colour introduced with little reason', and saw it as an 'utter contrast to Comper's approach to the same problem'. Johnson told the Vicar that he 'thought it high time the old boy retired.' In comparison, 'Comper's work has real beauty.'

Johnson visited St Philip's in 1944 while serving with the Royal Engineers in Hampshire. Unlike some, he liked the spare exterior. 'I had a bit of a shock when I saw it,' he wrote to his friend Edward Ingram. 'There it is in brick and a little stone, four square, a church obviously and yet curiously fresh.' He reserved his highest praise for the interior: 'We opened the door ... and we were in another world, a world of bright clean joyous space, elegant, contrasted and colourful ... a small modern church hall, and whether it is "moral" or not to do such things, it is exquisite ... the high altar has a baldachino with solid burnished gold Corinthian columns with Grecian capitals. The details of carving and painting in the superstructure are lovely .... It is a thing of beauty this church and you would be as spellbound as I was.' Johnson did not become an imitator. 'Though impressed by the beauty, clarity and dignity of Comper's work,' wrote John Martin Robinson in a monograph on Johnson, 'Francis was not himself directly inspired to emulate it, except in its more abstract qualities of simplicity, scale, light and controlled colouring.'

'St Philip's is the most complete and most obvious blending of the Greek and Gothic,' Comper wrote. 'And there is no claim of the invention of a new style; for a similar combination was found in past centuries. But, in so far as I am aware, there is nothing exactly like St Philip's; and that is because there is nothing exactly like the age and conditions which produced it.'

PUSEY HOUSE, OXFORD

Ciborium and other furnishings, 1935–9

The Warriors' Chapel in Westminster Abbey, with its Renaissance furniture, and the completion of All Saints, London Colney, in 1927 had fired a new generation with enthusiasm for Comper's work, even before the building of St Philip's, Cosham. It was deepened by the publication in 1932 of his paper, *Further Thoughts on the English Altar, or Practical Considerations on the Planning of a Modern Church*, which showed how far removed he had grown from his youthful medievalism and how dependent he had become on the Western Christian tradition. The Anglo-Catholic movement between the two world wars was dominated by a series of spectacular congresses held in the Royal Albert Hall that demonstrated the force of following the living traditions of the Western Church as opposed to the diluted medievalism that had become associated with a moderate Anglican establishment. Critics of the movement accused it of adopting a modern Roman Catholic standpoint. But Anglo-Catholicism was the strongest religious movement of the time and it would influence the entire Anglican Communion.

Spiritually and theologically Comper was by upbringing and conviction an advanced Anglo-Catholic. The churches in which he worshipped were usually Western in practice and frame of mind, and included some of those he had designed himself or in which he had worked. But his wide travel and research had led to extensive ecclesiological and liturgical knowledge that enabled him to transcend the narrow boundaries defined by being English or Roman. Perhaps he knew too much: his free approach led some to see him as idiosyncratic.

The commission for the chapel of the Resurrection at Pusey House, Oxford, came as a result of a substantial legacy from Lady Powell which had been made to the House for 'an Anglo-Catholic object'. The interpretation of the terms of the will was flexible. Hunger marches from Jarrow and South Wales had recently passed through Oxford on their way to Westminster and had awakened in many Anglo-Catholic undergraduates a strong sense of social justice which they believed should be met by the Church. The decision by Canon Frederic Hood, the Principal, to spend the legacy on decorating the chapel inspired protest and division.

Pusey House chapel was completed in 1914 and is one of the best works of Temple Lushington Moore (1856–1920), a pupil of George Gilbert Scott Junior, and the best church architect of his generation. He was slightly older than Comper and in his work he displayed a subtle reinterpretation and development of Gothic precedent, strong and clear, that made Comper's later work look thin and effete. They shared the same religious convictions and in Moore's adoption of the Gothic altar and the disposition of his rood figures he followed Comper's lead. A weakness in Moore's work was furniture and painted glass and he had approached Comper to suggest that he might undertake the design of glass in his churches. Furniture had also been proposed but Comper declined the invitation. While Moore would probably not have been sympathetic to Comper's syncretistic development, Pusey House shows what they might have achieved if they had worked together.

Despite the conclusions published in *Further Thoughts*, Canon Hood was a little wary of Comper. He thought he was too closely identified with Wickham Legg, and Legg had been a formidable match for a previous Principal, Dr Darwell Stone, a profound and learned scholar who was not a medievalist. Despite the ample legacy, Hood was afraid that Comper would exceed the budget and had considered approaching F. C. Eden, but it was Lord Halifax and Canon H. F. B. Mackay, of Wells, formerly Vicar of All Saints, Margaret Street, who persuaded him to use Comper.

The plan of Pusey House chapel, divided by a stone screen beneath a continuous vault, had been anticipated by Comper in the chapel of St John's Home, Cowley, in 1902–7. The furniture had been arrested by the Great War and Moore's death in 1920. The temporary altar in the chapel of the Resurrection had only a tapestry dorsal and Moore had not left designs for a permanent altar.

Pusey House, Oxford, 1911–14. Ciborium and altar in the Chapel of the Resurrection, 1935, a work of Comper's maturity. Photograph: John Samuel Bucknall.

The Pusey House ciborium is the most finished of those that had preceded it. The inspiration was the Renaissance ciborium designed *c.*1520–22 by Pietro Torrigiano for the chapel of King Henry VII in Westminster Abbey. The Resurrection is the theme of the design. Decorated in burnished gold, it protects a stone altar that has a frontal embossed with a roundel of the Annunciation and dolphin arabesques from which cherubs issue in a pure *quatrocento* style. It was a development of the gilt-bronze frontal designed for the Warriors' Chapel. There is a polygonal tabernacle and a tall crucifix and six candlesticks of bronze, parcel silver and gilt, with tapers. The embroidered inscription on the frontlet is *Resurrexi et adhuc tecum sum* (I am risen, and am with you always). The ceiling of the ciborium has the Dove surrounded by rays and scrolls inscribed with the seven gifts of the Holy Spirit within a wreath of flowers and fruit, painted from life, held by cherubs. Above, a figure of the Risen Saviour is grouped with the soldiers at the tomb, balanced by kneeling angels at the extremities, and the cherubs in the capitals hold eggs as an allusion to the Resurrection. Silver lamps hang from the cornice and a pair of brass chandeliers with tapers is suspended from the chapel vault. There was a hanging of rose-red silk on the wall beneath the windows and a rose-red Persian carpet once lay in front of the altar.

The splays of the east window are gilded and decorated with the Pusey arms and the window is a free rendering of a Jesse tree. It has a figure of the Majestas in the centre, above the Virgin and Child, seated on the perfect circle of a rainbow which can be traced through the five lights of the window; the feet rest on the mystical Thrones which are the third order of angels. At the bottom, next to the middle light, is a small figure of Dr Pusey kneeling at a desk, and in the same position of the opposite light, on the right, is his shield of arms.

The first ciborium executed by Comper was at St Mary's, Wellingborough, in 1914, and its decoration in 1940 owed much to the experience of Pusey House. The second was at St John's, Waterloo, in 1921 (destroyed 1940), and the third at Huddersfield, Yorkshire, in 1923. Then came London Colney; the Waterloo church of St John, Workington, Cumberland, in 1931(though originally proposed as long before as 1915); St John the Baptist, Rothiemurchus, Aviemore, of rose-red silk, in 1931; the church of the Holy Name, Poona, India in 1934–7; the chapel of the House of Prayer, Burnham, in 1935; Cosham in 1937; and the chapel of the Mission House of the Society of St John the Evangelist, Cowley, in 1938. Another was designed in 1939 for Comper's extensions to Derby Cathedral and later executed by Sebastian Comper and, finally, came Aberdeen Cathedral in 1941. Comper unsuccessfully proposed ciboria for many other schemes. The majority of his clients preferred an English altar or a triptych and, despite his change of mind, he continued to design them for the rest of his life. The ciborium was not generally adopted in the Church of England in the same way as the Gothic altar, not simply because it was thought exotic and expensive, but principally because it was associated by Dr Eeles, Dearmer's *protégé* and Secretary to the Central Council for the Care of Churches, with the Continent and therefore discouraged. Yet even he considered the Workington ciborium to be the finest Classical altar in England.

Comper's altar and ciborium, resplendently gleaming within Temple Moore's Blagdon stone walls, made a profound impression upon many. John Betjeman would take people to see it in order to promote Comper's cause. The silver crucifix and candlesticks on Martin Travers's sarcophagus-shaped high altar of Nashdom Abbey, made in 1944–6, were modelled on those at Pusey House and were a result of Betjeman's recommendation. The Pusey House altar and ciborium is the most signal church furnishing scheme of Comper's maturity and equals the scale of his achievement before the Great War.

CUDDESDON COLLEGE, OXFORD

Design for chapel, 1934

Cuddesdon College, Oxford, was founded by Bishop Samuel Wilberforce in 1853 opposite the Bishop of Oxford's palace. The buildings were an early work by G. E. Street assisted by his fellow-pupil in Sir George Gilbert Scott's office, G. F. Bodley. It was a post-Tractarian foundation and by the early part of the twentieth century had become the leading theological college of the Church of England. The majority of the *alumni* went on to high office in the Church.

In 1934 the Revd Eric Graham, the Principal, had organised a competition for a new chapel. He was a cultivated, learned, and restrained Anglo-Catholic, imbued with the spirit of the Caroline Divines and the Tractarians. The tone of Cuddesdon in his time was one of devout Liberal Catholicism. Competitors included H. S. Goodhart-Rendel, J. Harold Gibbons, A. E. Richardson, and the young Stephen Dykes Bower. The assessor was Sir Edward Maufe.

Comper got on well with Graham but he refused to compete. Instead he submitted drawings for an aisleless chapel of three bays with broad windows set above a continuous wall surface and a ribbed vault of plaster. In the sanctuary he proposed an altar with a ciborium, modelled on the one in the Basilica Eufrasiana, set before a screen that enclosed a sacristy and provided a gallery above, separated from the body of the chapel by balusters. A figure of the Virgin and Child was placed above the altar and the Majestas in painted glass, set within a vesica in the tracery of the east window, would have dominated the chapel.

Many who saw the design believed that it embodied the spiritual aspirations of the college at that time and were surprised when Maufe chose an entirely different, in many ways retrogressive, submission from Goodhart-Rendel. It was thought to be a decision influenced by generational discrimination. Comper was seventy at the time; though his mind was fresh, there was a policy

Cuddesdon College, Oxford. Design for a new chapel, 1934. Comper's proposal was not accepted, possibly in an attempt to bring on younger men. Drawing by F. J. Lucas.

to use younger men. Goodhart-Rendel's chapel was not built. Soon after, he was received into the Roman Catholic Church and although an arrangement was made with Sir Charles Nicholson, the outbreak of the Second World War made it impossible to build the chapel.

Comper was bitterly disappointed by being rejected and confirmed in his distrust of competitions. He wrote to Graham saying that this proved to him that his work had never been acceptable to the official Church of England. Despite his connections, influence and many prestigious commissions, Comper was never a member of the Establishment; his Anglo-Catholic convictions ensured that he remained an outsider. The proposals for Cuddesdon were a lost opportunity and nobody will now know what influence they might have had on the future.

ST ANDREW'S CATHEDRAL, ABERDEEN
Major modifications and reordering, completed 1941

In 1928 Comper was invited to undertake the design of a cathedral offered to Aberdeen by the Protestant Episcopal Church of the United States of America as a memorial to Samuel Seabury, the first bishop. The Anglican episcopate in America, and the former English-speaking colonies, dates from the consecration of Bishop Seabury in 1784 in Aberdeen by the bishops of the Scottish Church.

Many thought that Comper should design a cathedral and Aberdeen was his only opportunity. The plan developed its predecessor at London Colney and was substantially based upon Theveste. It had an atrium, nave and presbytery; but was expanded by the inclusion of side chapels and an eastern Lady Chapel. But the choir and presbytery had an entirely different origin and were modelled upon the developed sixteenth-century plan of Segovia Cathedral. The choir was placed west of the nave, eastward of the atrium, with returned stalls against the screen. The high altar was to be in the presbytery to the east, with the congregation seated between them.

All went well until the international economic recession in 1929, started by the Wall Street Crash, brought the plans to an abrupt conclusion and the whole scheme was abandoned. In 1938 Joseph Kennedy, the American Ambassador, laid the stone for the additions to the chancel of St Andrew's, Aberdeen, to which all that remained of the funds was applied to make it worthy of a cathedral. St Andrew's was built in 1816 by Archibald Simpson who had designed many of the finest neo-Classical buildings in the city. It had long been a pro-cathedral though the structure had been dismissively described as 'built in debased Gothic [that] supplied perhaps the plainest and ugliest cathedral in the British Isles. Its pillars are of plaster, the mullions of its windows are of wood, and its proportions bad.'

Street had built a chancel in 1880 and in 1910 Lorimer had removed the galleries, added a screen and a west gallery and porch which Comper considered 'even poorer than Street's chancel'. The removal of the galleries

Design for St Andrew's Cathedral, Aberdeen, 1928–30. The Wall Street Crash brought plans to a halt.

St Andrew's Cathedral, Aberdeen. The high altar, 1937–40. Betjeman said 'You push open the door and your heart gives a leap.' Photograph reproduced from Comper's Of the Atmosphere of a Church, *1947.*

had brought the flat ceilings of the aisles into unsightly prominence and in 1935 Comper met their baldness by fibrous plaster vaulting that followed the admirable curve of the four-centred arches of the nave. They were left in white and were made a field of two heraldic schemes of arabesques and cherubs holding shields representing the arms of the American states, carried out in plaster relief, decorated in burnished gold and colour.

Comper heightened and lengthened Street's chancel; and a south aisle of three bays, with broad windows of Rhyme stone, was added as a Lady Chapel, with arches dying into their piers in the manner of the nave of St Agnes', Kennington. All that remained of the original design for a new cathedral was the high altar and ciborium. It is the last and finest of Comper's ciboria, excelling its predecessor at Pusey House, and he defended its richness by an appeal to Greece. 'When Pericles built the Parthenon, not only did he exhaust all the resources of the State on an unprofitable expenditure, but he spent more on the gold and ivory of its central statue of the Virgin Athene than upon the whole building, and at a time when there was fear of a Persian invasion.'

Like the ciborium at London Colney it is crowned by eight arches, taken from the early sixteenth-century tower of King's College Chapel, Aberdeen, from which rises the figure of the Risen Saviour. The cost of this figure and the four adoring angels at the corners was shared by St Mary's, Wellingborough, through the employment of casts made from the original model. Several of Comper's later altars contributed to each other in this way. The vaulting of the Aberdeen ciborium is slightly elliptical and figures of the four Evangelists and the four Latin Doctors are painted on the severies. From the ceiling was suspended a pyx enclosed within a triple crown of copper, mercurially gilt. Comper intended that copies of the Pusey House crucifix and candlesticks should stand on the altar.

In a paper, *The Bishop Seabury Memorial*, published in 1941 to mark the completion, Comper wrote in *fin de siècle* prose his most poetic account of the significance of the ciborium.

Like the holy city it is of pure gold garnished with the colours of precious stones; the blue of the sapphire and green of the emerald or jade, and the purple of porphyry, and white of the pearl. To these tempered colours the actual decoration of the ciborium is confined, while a more free use of colour is in the painted imagery. It is all water-gilding burnished with an agate. … The four pillars have the Greek entasis, which is a tapering of the pillar in a convex line, scarcely perceptible to the eye: but the eye would miss it if it were not there.

The flash of the metal-like surface of the pillars is broken by fine vertical lines of arabesques. Their capitals are reminiscent of Hadrian's North Africa and the Renaissance of Spain. The larger arabesques on the pilasters above them are an entirely new composition, to which both Nature and the art of Italy have contributed. Their symbolism of corn and grapes, dove and eagle, dolphin or fish and dragon or cockatrice, is not difficult to invent. The dolphin which figures conspicuously in the whole design is chosen as being a symbol of Our Lord and one which is specially appropriate in a church dedicated in honour of St Andrew the fisherman. For the dolphin stands for fish, which is ιχθυς in Greek, and spells the first letters of the title 'Jesus Christ the Son of God the Saviour'. It forms the crockets of the eight arches of the crown, which, like the crown of the old tower of King's College, is the chief feature of the ciborium. These arches terminate in a carved figure of the Risen Saviour, and at their base at the four corners are figures of adoring angels.

In the larger plans for the new Cathedral the Ciborium had carved figures of the Evangelists at the four corners of the pilasters above the pillars. These had to be omitted, but the Evangelists, each paired with the Latin Doctor associated with him, are painted in eight roundels on the severies of the blue-spangled vault of the inverted cup of the ciborium. Between them are four gold seraphs, with peacock's eyes upon their wings surrounding a wreath of flowers and fruit which, like the Holy Dove and rays within it, are carved in relief; and the triple crown of the Tabernacle touches the foot of the Dove.

The best description of St Andrew's Cathedral was given by John Betjeman in a BBC broadcast, 'Aberdeen Granite', in 1947. It gives an impression of what his book on Comper might have been like and also the infectious way in which he furthered Comper's cult.

Aberdeen's best modern building I have left to the last. It is the addition to St Andrew's Episcopal Cathedral by J. N. Comper, an Aberdonian who has already done much distinguished work in the city. You go in by a rather dingy entrance in a flat Perpendicular-style building designed by Simpson in 1816 when he was a man of twenty-six. You push open the door and your heart gives a leap – there stretching away as in an old Dutch oil-painting, is Comper's superb renovation of the interior. White arcades by Simpson in a simple style with big mouldings lead to a great double-aisled East end which Comper has added in a style perfectly blending with the older building. White plaster vaulting diminishes away in perspective adorned with baroque gold and coloured shields. And there, far at the east end, is a great baldachin over the altar in burnished gold with a gold spire rising from its canopy in a manner reminiscent of the spire on King's Chapel. And beyond the gold of this baldachin, intensely gold in this blazing whiteness, you see the deep blue tints, the green and the red of Comper's large East window.

ALL SAINTS, CARSHALTON, SURREY

Furnishings, including organ case, 1920–58

The greater part of All Saints, Carshalton was designed by Sir Arthur Blomfield and his nephew, Reginald, and built in 1893–1914. It is a solid, if commonplace, essay in the Perpendicular style, incorporating part of an earlier church of medieval and eighteenth-century builds. Bodley had added a screen and triptych. In 1920 the Revd W. R. Corbauld was appointed and it was he who commissioned Comper to do some of his best late work

Upper Norwood, where Comper lived in The Priory, Beulah Hill, a stuccoed late-Georgian 'gothick' house, was not far away. 'Some years ago Mr Martin Travers, a former pupil, took me to dinner with Mr Comper,' wrote Betjeman in the *Architectural Review* in 1939 when Comper was working at Carshalton:

> The house was a Georgian gothic building, set among trees in a large garden with a lake and a view over the miles of Surrey from Beulah Hill. There I learned the catholicity of Comper's taste, his admiration for the English Regency, his learning in ecclesiastical art; there I saw those careful note books, full of sketches and photographs, records of his journeys in Italy, Greece, North Africa and Spain and motor-caravan tours of France, with his nephew Mr Arthur Bucknall, who has worked with him since 1891. We went on talking about architecture, literature and people till the lights twinkled out over Croydon in the summer evening. From that conversation, and from many subsequent ones, I realised how the youthfulness, enthusiasm and learning of Comper has given a quality to his work which makes it so outstanding; how his originality has been the source of endless borrowings by church furnishers and fellow architects; how he himself has held so high a reputation for so long.

Comper liked Corbauld (who was a frequent guest at the Priory) and regularly worshipped at All Saints. Corbauld was an advanced Anglo-Catholic, a papalist, and although Comper was impatient with a slavish imitation of Rome that excluded other strands of the Church's historic tradition, and what he dismissively described as the 'cult of the biretta',

All Saints, Carshalton, Surrey. The organ and loft, 1943. After the St Ives organ case (page 38), this is Comper's largest and most complicated design. Photograph: Sydney W. Newbery.

All Saints, Carshalton, Surrey. Comper heightened and coloured the existing rood screen, adding a loft and Majestas (1940–48). Photograph: Sydney W. Newbery.

All Saints represented his own religious position at the end of his life. The ceremonies of the Mass were conducted with fastidious perfection and the music was confined to plainsong, Spanish and Italian polyphony, performed with finished artistry. Above all, Corbauld and Comper shared a desire for the reunion of the Church of England with the Roman Catholic Church.

In 1931 Comper was invited to gild and colour Bodley's triptych and he heightened and coloured the rood screen, adding a loft and a Majestas above the chancel arch. In 1936 he delightfully decorated the eighteenth-century reredos in the Lady Chapel with a Jesse tree and throng of cherubs and burnished gilding. He designed a *reja* between the chapel and the chancel, and a new font cover in 1941, and after the war he improved the pulpit. But his most splendid work at Carshalton is the organ case and gallery at the west end of the church.

Comper was seventy in 1934. During the next ten years his work had something of a new birth. Grace Comper died in 1933: she was his rock. They had had a happy marriage and six children, but Comper put his work before his family and thereafter he was able to apply himself with undivided attention and greater freedom. There were also new patrons, he was sought by the young, and then, in 1937, John Betjeman discovered him and his infectious enthusiasm, extravagant praise and flattery did more than anything to give Comper new confidence. An unrestrained delight in decorative carving and his conversion to burnished gold infused his work with fresh life and vitality.

The Carshalton organ case embodied this new confidence. After the early Gothic organ case at St Ives, Huntingdonshire, fifty years previously, it was Comper's largest and most complicated design. The organ stands in a gallery supported on Tuscan columns that also makes a narthex to the nave. In the spandrels, athletic nude angels, modelled from life, play musical instruments and on the gallery front medallions of saints enclosed in arabesques flank a chair-case which is alive with carved cherubs, volutes and more arabesques. The sumptuously decorated organ case rises to the roof and conceals the west wall.

While the Carshalton case and gallery inspired praise from Corbauld and Comper's admirers it was received with less enthusiasm by organ builders and specialists. Cecil Clutton, for instance, thought highly of Comper's early organ cases but in his book, *The British Organ*, criticised in purist terms a basic error of scale in the Carshalton case, and went on to identify the technical faults. 'Comper has tried to produce a design comparable to large Continental cases in complexity but compressed in scale to fit into an average British church. The result is not unlike the model of a case with the smaller pipes reduced to the thickness of stair rods, the whole being completely unrelated to the instrument that it contains or indeed to a real organ of any kind.' Clutton preferred straightforward, English eighteenth-century organ cases. His practical objections are valid, but the Carshalton case should be seen more as a screen that conceals the instrument.

Corbauld amused Comper. 'His ecclesiastical tastes are rococo as well as his architectural ones,' Comper wrote to Betjeman in 1948, 'he is perfectly satisfied so long as gold leaf is heaped on everywhere.' But while he disliked the Blomfields' building Comper thought that some of his best work was done for Carshalton, although he considered that, overall, the church lacked unity.

ST JOHN OF JERUSALEM, CLERKENWELL, LONDON

Design for reconstruction, 1943

In May, 1941, the medieval priory church of St John of Jerusalem was destroyed in an air raid that wrecked many other buildings in London. It was used as the church of the Order of St John of Jerusalem and Lord Shaftesbury was the Bailiff Grand Cross and Almoner. In 1940 Comper had completed the font cover of St Giles, Wimborne St Giles, and Shaftesbury was aware of his continuing powers. He was appointed chairman of the Church Committee and in 1943 approached Comper, on the eve of his eightieth year, to make plans of reconstruction and a large addition. They were discussed at St Giles House. 'I think they are perfect,' Shaftesbury subsequently wrote to him, 'and that you have excelled yourself in the beauty of their conception. Let us hope that they may be carried out in their entirety and that no insurmountable obstacles may present themselves.'

The design of a circular church within a square marked the most developed expression of Comper's architectural theories and liturgical planning. It was the fruit of a life-time of study and travel in a quest for beauty. The *lierne* vault ran round a circular processional path and the walls were lined with canopied stalls for members of the order. A Lady Chapel was placed east of the sanctuary, creating an axial system. The altar was enclosed within an octagon, composed of a double arcade of two storeys with fluted columns on the scale of St Mary's, Wellingborough, lit from above by a lantern. Within the vesica of the east window was a Majestas. The altar was as much the flame in a lantern as it was forty years previously at St Cyprian's, Clarence Gate.

Shaftesbury persuaded the committee to launch an appeal in 1944. But the scheme was too ambitious, too magnificent to be considered in post-war conditions restricted by planning regulations, building licences, shortages of materials, war damage compensation and little independent money. The Order of St John of Jerusalem was also worried about Comper's age and when a member of the committee asked who there was in his office who could continue the work if he died, Comper rose from the table, picked up his hat and asked icily, as he left the room, 'Did Michelangelo have an office?' The failure to persevere with the proposals was a severe blow for Comper and Shaftesbury. It was a lost opportunity that spelt the death of early twentieth-century Romantic aspiration. St John's was the final gleam of brilliance before the fire of creative genius was put out.

DESIGN FOR THE BUILDING AGAIN OF THE CHURCH OF THE ORDER OF THE HOSPITAL OF ST JOHN OF JERUSALEM IN CLERKENWELL

Design for the church of St John of Jerusalem, Clerkenwell, London, 1943. A circular church within a square, this ground-breaking scheme was too ambitious for the times, and was not accepted. Drawing by J. N. Comper, Arthur and John Samuel Bucknall, and E. J. Lucas.

The design for St John of Jerusalem shows that a centrally planned church need not be ugly and that modern church architecture does not have to compromise the integrity of its principles if the historic language of architecture is used. Comper shows a way forward from the impoverishment that has beset church architecture in recent years. His theories are there to be tested. The liturgical and architectural tradition of the Church, unfolding through history, is embodied in them.

In 1947 Comper went through a profound spiritual crisis. The inauguration of the Church of South India by the union of three religious bodies, the Anglican Church of India, Burma and Ceylon with the South Indian Province of the Methodist Church and the United Church, caused serious alarm to Anglo-Catholics. The union was achieved by the acceptance of ministers ordained in each of these traditions into a united ministry and although an episcopate drawn from the Anglican succession was to be introduced, Comper saw the creation of the Church of South India as a fundamental blow to church order and an obstacle to the reunion of the Church of England with the Roman Catholic Church.

As a young man he had considered becoming a Roman Catholic but was persuaded against doing so by Fr Congreve. Some of his clients and friends became Catholics and he maintained a touchy connection with them. He wearied of English Roman Catholic polemic and the 'barren futility' of the convert mentality. With cradle Catholics he was entirely different and welcomed their acquaintance, especially those he had met on the Continent. He got on well with the Benedictines at Downside and with the Jesuits at St Mary-on-the-Quay, Bristol, Stonyhurst, and the parish priest of St Cuthbert's, South Shore Blackpool, none of whom were proselytisers. Reunion was one of his main preoccupations, that went back to his parents' ecumenical interests and was the foundation of his friendship with Lord Halifax. While publicly maintaining an anti-convert stance, Rome continually nagged at the back of his mind. He had a devotion to St Pius X and liked to think of the Roman Church and the Church of England as invisibly, if not corporately, one.

A friend of later years was Dr Ronald Pilkington, a Canon of Florence Cathedral and one time Professor of Liturgy at the Archiepiscopal Seminary, who lived in the Cathedral Clergy House at Westminster. He was an early ecumenist with an interest in the Oxford Movement and was sympathetic to Comper's plight. Comper also consulted Fr Martin D'Arcy SJ. He sought reception into the Church but was persuaded against it by the Bucknalls who said that they would be ruined as there would be no opportunity to continue the practice. Thereafter Comper maintained a public Anglican face with an uneasy interior reservation and combined worship at All Saints, Carshalton, with the Brompton Oratory. He would tease people by saying that the Oratory was the only church in London where the authentic medieval surplice was worn.

In 1950 Comper, at the age of eighty-six, received a knighthood. It was Betjeman who organised the testimonials. They included commendations from people as diverse as John Piper, Sir Giles Gilbert Scott, Stanley Morison, the typographer and editor of the *Times Literary Supplement*, Bishop Bell of Chichester, T. S. Eliot, Sir Charles Peers, the Surveyor of Westminster Abbey, Eric Milner-White, Dean of York, and the Mother Superior of the Community of the Blessed Virgin Mary, Wantage. Many thought that he should have been knighted earlier, but a proposal was blocked by Cosmo Gordon Lang, Archbishop of Canterbury, and Dean Foxley Norris, of Westminster, in favour of Sir Walter Tapper. Tapper had worked for Norris at York Minster. The post-war years were times of great difficulty, personally and professionally, and Comper was unable to concentrate so single-mindedly on church design. Land was sold to provide capital for the practice. A new generation thought that Comper's work was wearing a little thin and that it represented an ivory tower. There were disappointments and some were worried about his failing powers.

The situation was drawn to Betjeman's attention by Sebastian Comper in 1947. Sebastian had a difficult relationship with his father which was combined with touching personal affection and admiration for his work:

> Your devotion to the cause of 'the Master' is most re-assuring in this dark age: I worked under him from 1911 to 1930 and knew all the 'birth pangs' of Wellingborough etc and the anxiety of drawing a moulding contour! And I think his sense of proportion and colour in design is unrivalled: a natural born instinct which has been cultivated by unremitting study and a wonderful critical appreciation of beauty everywhere. And behind all, the creative imagination. I am often sorrowing that I am no longer at 'the Study' but it would not support us all and I had to learn to paddle my own canoe: I tried to go back and give some sort of practical help two years ago, but he would have none of it and forgets that I was so long with him … and am no longer a boy! But I am anxious because while he is concentrating on the interest of the moment, everything else is sliding: Arthur Bucknall is away ill and probably will never be fit for much now: John is young and not strong or experienced, and there may soon be a financial landslide with unforeseeable results. None of which troubles JNC in the least! – age having mercifully brought a happy and reckless optimism. I tell you my fears because I know you take a real interest in him: and I wish we could meet and have a talk sometime.

Comper's refusal to retain Sebastian marked the death knell of the practice. He was a qualified architect who, although he did not have his father's spark, had a successful practice, and went on to design, rebuild and furnish many Anglican and Roman Catholic churches. He was trained in his principles and together they might have enabled Comper's post-war restorations to have been executed. Sebastian felt keenly his father's rejection and he believed, with his brothers and sisters, that the family had been superseded in Comper's affections by the Bucknalls. The future led only to decline. By a cruel irony, at the end of Comper's life J. S. Bucknall advertised the practice as if it were a commercial firm of church furnishers and glaziers, a course that was inimical to Comper's ideals, but he was too old to notice.

The plans for rebuilding St Alban's, Holborn, and St John the Divine, Kennington, were abandoned. Arthur Bucknall died in 1952 and he was replaced by his son, John Samuel. Many of Comper's workmen died, retired or left soon after. The work deteriorated and became progressively repetitive, based upon cartoons and drawings made many years previously. The most embarrassing example is the Coronation window in Canterbury Cathedral, incompetently executed after the best glaziers had been dismissed. But the furniture still had freshness and enchantment and was of a higher quality than most contemporary church work, as Butchart's burnished gold reredoses in All Saints, Notting Hill, (1952) and St Mark's, Regent's Park, (1957) show. Less successful was the furniture in the Holy House of the Anglican Shrine of Our Lady of Walsingham (1960–61) which was entirely carried out under Bucknall's and Butchart's direction, using a synthesis of old drawings, some dating from the beginning of the century. To the outside world it seemed that the stream of burnished gold altarpieces and painted glass windows would never cease.

In the midst of this an indication of the high esteem in which Comper was still held after the Second World War is given by his friend, William Wand, Bishop of London, in his subtle preface to *Of the Christian Altar and the Buildings Which Contain It*, published in 1950. This tract was originally intended as a contribution to a volume on the Eucharist, edited by F. L. Cross and published by the Society for Promoting Christian Knowledge, but was found to be too unwieldy for inclusion. It is an old man's work – erudite, discursive, quirky, recondite, opaque – and brings together many strands of Comper's auto-biographical writing as well as liturgical and historical considerations which are freely based, as he acknowledged, upon the work of Edmund Bishop as well as wide reading. Peter Anson said that it reflected the themes and limits of Comper's conversation at that stage of his life.

Wand wrote to please, but he reflected the views of Comper's admirers and well-wishers and the affection he inspired. He began by describing Comper as the 'doyen of our ecclesiastical architects' and went on to say:

> I have known the author for many years; and for a good proportion of them I have had the privilege of living in close proximity to some of his work. To me therefore the artist and the man are very much one and the same individual. ... The continual astonishment of his friends is aroused by the amazing versatility of this great ecclesiologist. He can not only lay out the plan of a great cathedral, but if he designs a frontal he knows exactly how every stitch of the embroidery should go. His glass of course is world famous. In this book he reveals himself also as knowledgeable in church music. 'To know him is a liberal education.'
>
> The author has read so much, journeyed so far, met so many people, that his book, which sets out to talk about the altar, becomes a travelogue and almost an autobiography. But where it seems most irrelevant it is often most

charming and illuminating. Like every true scholar Sir Ninian eschews party shibboleths. He has the most individual of minds, and we can learn as much from his prejudices as we can from most men's treatises. We shall certainly feel a quite particular pleasure in remembering that he has recently joined the company of those 'knighted architects' against whom he so regularly tilts.

In 1953 Bishop Wand commissioned a window, as a memorial to his son, for the private chapel at Fulham Palace.

Comper never lost his gift of placing church furniture in a way which made it belong. This was a characteristic admired by Betjeman. 'I believe the genius of your buildings lies in their proportions above everything else. The plan is always clear and the proportions emphasise it – the way you get font covers, screens, columns, baldachins, steps, window-tracery, altars all in perfect relation to one another is what no one else can do. They aren't so good at colour either. Oh, it *is* a privilege to know you, great genius of Aberdeen.' The final years culminated in the design for the Parliamentary War Memorial window in Westminster Hall, consisting entirely of heraldry, unveiled in 1952. But these late works did little for Comper's reputation, saddened those who had known his earlier work, and some thought he had lived too long. As he advanced to extreme old age his world slowly disintegrated.

Yet Comper retained the capacity to charm. Writing in 1957, Gerard Irvine gave an impression of the architect in his final years:

Despite his ninety-three years Sir Ninian gives the appearance of youth. You get the impression that he is very tall; he has the gait and style of a dandy; his trim beard and white hair as silky as an undergraduate's. In conversation too he reminds one of a clever undergraduate. He delights in paradox and epigram; he loves to tease and shock. Until you catch the twinkle in his eye, you never quite know whether he means some preposterous statement, delivered in a wonderful voice which carries with it the overtones of an age now past – an epoch when he used to dine with Beardsley at Alfred Gurney's and heard the announcement of the death of Rossetti, or engaged in sympathetic converse with Swinburne's sister Isabel.

Sir Ninian Comper died on 22 December 1960. His ashes are buried not where he wished, with his wife Grace and Arthur Bucknall, in the Jesus chancel at Wellingborough, but, at Dean Abbott's invitation, in the north aisle of Westminster Abbey, beneath the noble series of windows of abbots and kings which he had progressively executed during the first half of the twentieth century. Nearby lie Sir George Gilbert Scott, George Edmund Street and John Loughborough Pearson. Carried out under J. S. Bucknall's direction, in the following year the last of the Abbey windows was erected.

THE FUFILMENT OF UNITY BY INCLUSION

ST MARY, WELLINGBOROUGH, NORTHAMPTONSHIRE
Church and furnishings, 1904 onwards

'17 APRIL 1904. 2ND SUNDAY AFTER EASTER sat in 177 Knight's Hill garden & designed St Mary's, Wellingborough, & got the chill which ended in pneumonia.' So, cryptically, wrote Comper in his diary after his recovery. He pasted this extract in an album of photographs of St Mary's which he assembled as the church progressed.

St Mary's, Wellingborough, is the most beautiful English parish church, with one of the most inventive interiors, of the twentieth century, unrivalled by any other. It is best described in Comper's own words, in which he identified the startling, varied sources of design, as he gave them in *Further Thoughts*, even though he regarded them as little more than an 'inventory after the event, than of any previous theory, or marshalling from one's treasures from which to pick and choose'.

> The main ceiling has the unbroken fan and pendants of the latest English vault and which, so far as I am aware, have not been combined before. The octagonal pillars (again I believe unlike all medieval examples) have the Greek entasis and they have the same details of flutes as the Parthenon, while the capitals and bases are of new design. A ciborium stands in advance of the east wall and in front of the large window. A high chancel screen has mouldings and acanthus straight from Classic Greece and a general design which is as much Italian as English, or English as Italian. The dragons on the rood loft are borrowed from medieval Greece, while the ironwork owes most to Spain. It may be added that the main part of the eastern plan of the church has its origins in France. Only to its contemporaries does the church owe nothing.

As previously discussed, the year 1900, when Comper visited Rome, was the turning point in the two periods of his development and it was a second visit extended to Naples and Sicily in 1905, and a journey to Greece in the following year, that consolidated a shift of view. The occasion of the second visit was the design for St Mary's, Wellingborough, a commission received scarcely a year later than the consecration of St Cyprian's, Clarence Gate. What drew him to the South? Comper's initial drawings developed the tall, fifteenth-century octagonal piers of the arcade, carrying four-centred arches, of Northleach, Gloucestershire, with their concave fluting, but they seemed hard and to call out for the Greek entasis; hence the excuse for these visits. All Comper's architectural journeys arose from practical necessities.

St Mary's owes its origin to the piety of three maiden ladies, Henrietta, Gertrude and Harriet Sharman, daughters of John Wood Sharman, a Wellingborough solicitor. Of the three it was Henrietta (1841–1926) who was the guiding spirit. Devout Anglo-Catholics, they had come under the influence of the Revd Henry Vivian Broughton, the Tractarian Vicar of

St Mary, Wellingborough, Northamptonshire, 1904–31. Exterior view from the south-east, 1944.

Wellingborough. Cultivated and widely travelled, in London they worshipped at St Alban's, Holborn, and knew Fr Stanton. Henrietta's spiritual director was Fr Congreve SSJE and she knew Dr Price when he was Vicar of St Ives, not far away in Huntingdonshire. It was a small world.

The Sharmans lived at Elsdon Lodge, Midland Road, in the eastern district of Wellingborough. They worshipped at All Saints and in the early years of the twentieth century the parish was expected to develop in that direction. The sisters offered to build a mission church that would cost at the outside £5,000 and a small chapel dedicated to St Thomas of Canterbury was built. The Revd T. J. Watts, a *protégé* of Price, was appointed mission priest. Then, in 1904, Comper, on the recommendation of the sisters' spiritual directors, was given the commission for the permanent church. Foremost among them was Fr Stanton and he is commemorated in a window in St John's chapel.

At it stands today St Mary's is far more ambitious than the foundresses ever expected and it is entirely different from what Watts and Price hoped. Price had long wanted to form a collegiate body of priests and he wished that this might develop in Wellingborough. He also wanted Watts to stipulate that in style Comper should not go beyond the fourteenth and fifteenth centuries. They were confident that St Mary's would become a model Perpendicular church, furnished in the developed medieval style of which Comper was a master, and would become a centre of medievalist liturgy. When designing windows Comper consulted Watts about suitable Latin and Greek inscriptions and details of pontificalia, in company with the learned opinions of the antiquary, M. R. James, Provost of Eton. Nobody expected, or was prepared for, his architectural development, and many were dismayed by it. Watts had, as a result, a strained professional relationship with Comper. He found it difficult to trust him. In view of the building's present form it is instructive to present Comper's side of the argument which he set down in a 'Memorandum of Facts' in 1949.

> T. J. Watts considered that his orders bestowed upon him a superiority of knowledge to a layman in all the arts pertaining to a church – and *that* apparently independently of any training in them; for he had none. It was presumably on this that he opposed everything which I did in the design and decoration of the church, and after it was done claimed that he was the author of it. Everything that he imagined was not medieval he condemned as soon as it was designed. The tracery of the East window of the Jesus chapel was its first offence. But a much more serious offence was the nave ceiling and the Ciborium. I accordingly twice resigned as architect of the church, fully believing that my resignation would be accepted. But it was not. His opposition became a habit; and lasted to the end when he opposed the 'foolish steeple' to the turret at the west end and at the time when he was appointed on a Building Committee of the Fidelity Trust. My relations with T. J. Watts were always very pleasant when we met, but it was the letters which immediately followed that brought the opposition of a most peremptory kind, and which were couched in terms which I should never have dreamt of employing to a tradesman.

The composure of St Mary's in its completed form gives no indication of the strained politics of the building as it gradually progressed through the twentieth century. Comper and Watts behaved like the mothers in the judgement of Solomon, with Henrietta Sharman in the seat of judge, hearing both sides, and the completion of the church in its present unity and repose is amazing. It was Comper's powers of persuasion and their shared delight in foreign travel and European culture that persuaded the sisters to support him.

Built of golden Northamptonshire ironstone, the exterior of St Mary's is a developed study in the Perpendicular style with a monumental tower and well massed chapels and vestries at the east end that owe a great deal to the massing of Bodley & Garner's chapels of the Holy Angels, Hoar Cross, Staffordshire (1872). There is a wide nave of eight bays broken by octagonal piers. The wide aisles flow at their eastern extremities into the Jesus Chancel on the north and the Chapel of St John, contained within solid screens on the south. The *lierne* vault of plaster, with fan pendants that conceal electric light bulbs, is a reworking of the honeycomb vault of the Cappella Palatina in Palermo. The Majestas of Christ Pantokrator dominates the nave above the rood.

St Mary, Wellingborough, Northamptonshire, 1904–31. The church 'glistens and reveals and conceals to one's heart's delight,' said Pevsner. Photograph: Edwin Smith.

St Mary, Wellingborough, Northamptonshire, 1904–31. Looking north-east to the Jesus Chancel, shortly after it was built. Photograph: Cyril Ellis.

St Mary's took twenty-six years to build. The first part was the Jesus Chancel, on the north side of the choir, completed in 1908. The east end and two bays of the nave were completed in 1918. For many years the ciborium and screens were left uncoloured, simply painted in white, as the screens still are on the north and south sides of the chancel. The nave and tower came in 1931 but a spire was never built. Thereafter, between 1931 and 1950, the surfaces of the screen and ciborium were decorated in gold and colour. The first part of an elaborate font cover in the form of a spire was started with an octagonal screen, pierced with panels of gilded dolphin arabesques, that surrounds it. This idea was first suggested in Bucknall & Comper's design for St Crispin's, Yerendawna, India, in 1903. The font cover was not completed and the present one was designed by Sebastian Comper in memory of his father.

At Wellingborough Comper is seen as an architect, not simply as a church furnisher: the church is splendid in form as well as in decoration. The use of local stone shows him as a constructor. Comper was insistent that St Mary's is essentially an English church, within as well as in its exterior. Its plain tower, contrasting with a certain amount of rich masonry in the rest of the building, is characteristic and intentional and continues to favour East Anglia. But it is in the sophisticated plan, taken from France, where the decorative abandonment of the furniture, glass and decoration is contained within a disciplined expression of liturgical space and a masterly synthesis of architectural unity, that gives St Mary's its architectural sophistication.

In the spring of 1901 Comper had visited Rouen with his friends Canon and Mrs Edmund McClure. They went to the early sixteenth-century church of St Patrice to look at the painted glass, representing the Triumph of Religion, executed in 1540 by Jean Cousin. But it was the plan of the church that interested Comper as much as the windows. A square nave, like a vestibule of coloured glass, opens into the choir which is flanked by two wide aisles leading to wider transepts. The choir extends into the first bay of the nave and the tall round piers dividing the aisles gracefully support a finely detailed ribbed vault. The plan of the east end of St Patrice gave Comper the idea of a church with four aisles but the plan that resulted was vetoed by the Bishop of Peterborough who did not want a south chapel.

Comper translated the choir of St Patrice into the basilican choir of S. Clemente, Rome, (*c.*AD 380) by making a chancel of two bays, brought into the body of the church. The enclosure on three sides and the wide aisles emphasise the central position of the high altar which stands forward from the east wall. The Classical screens are more varied here than any others in the church and include *rejas* of black iron crowned by arabesques enclosing cherubs. The chancel screen, with three wide Classical arches in the form of a pulpitum, gives scale to the nave and the high altar, and is designed in a synthesis of styles. On the north side the extensive music galleries connect the rood loft with the organ gallery at the west end of the Jesus Chancel, and open

from a library in the parvis of the north porch which once contained Dr Price's books. The walls were intended to be lined with a dark wainscot which was, once more, taken from St Agnes', Kennington. The pews and elevated pulpit, shaped like a wineglass, with a sounding board, are Classical.

This is no superficial theatrical stage set for spectacular services, like the work of Comper's imitators and his former assistant, Martin Travers. The church is built for the liturgy in its pristine purity, nothing else. For Comper the Mass was the meeting place of earth and heaven. St Mary's is a vessel for the Eucharist and all within and surrounding it take their heightening from it.

Comper's principal antagonist in the second half of the twentieth century was Sir Nikolaus Pevsner who rarely missed an opportunity to dismiss or overlook his work in *The Buildings of England*. It was Pevsner's moralistic condemnation of historicism, of modern architecture conceived in the Classical and Gothic language of architecture, that won the day in his relentless campaign to establish the ideology of the International Modern Style, with its machine and functionalist aesthetic, as the architectural style of all time. He desired a clean break with the past. To do otherwise resulted in architecture that was not only bad, he believed, but also immoral in that it attempted to resist social progress. He achieved lasting damage to Comper's reputation by persuading his readers that his work was artistically and architecturally valueless. The only building that made him melt was St Mary's,

*St Mary, Wellingborough,
Northamptonshire, 1904–31.*

*Opposite: Looking north-east
from the south aisle, to the
screen. Photograph, 1944.*

*Right: Looking north-east
across the nave to the organ.
The partly-completed decoration
of the nearest arch may be seen.
Photograph: Frank Knight,
c.1944.*

Wellingborough. 'It glistens and reveals and conceals to one's heart's delight,' he wrote in the Northamptonshire volume, and recommended his pupils to see it. When asked why, he replied: because the dates are right.

Other Modernists were converted. 'There is no surprise that someone like myself,' wrote J. M. Richards, 'who advocated the fresh look at architecture's social and structural principles represented by the Modern Movement, should admire Comper's buildings, which belonged to their own age. It is not denigrating them to identify them with the last flowering of the Gothic Revival although he was building more in the 20th century than in the 19th. Looking to the future should not blind one to the past.'

Pevsner and the Modernists were more interested in the mid-Victorian phase of the Gothic Revival which sought originality. Comper and his masters were in reaction against this development and their studied avoidance of originality was easily accused of copyism in their own lifetime and since. 'For the twentieth century, the architecture of the 1850s, which strove to be original, must necessarily be more interesting,' wrote Michael Hall in his penetrating paper, 'What do Victorian churches mean?'

> Yet there was also a conscious if more elusive philosophy of design at work in the later Gothic Revival, a philosophy predicated on the creative use of paradigmatic style. As Bishop Forbes observed, there is no past and no future

to the supreme God: an architecture that is designed to reinforce that belief about humanity's relationship with eternity is entitled therefore to reject the idea of historical development or progress in design. In heaven, there are no revivals.

St Mary's, in its serenity and repose, may look as if it was completed at one time but the reality is that the spectacular result that we see today was the fruit of Comper's maturity and old age. He was forty when he made the first design. The furniture was progressively designed, but only half-decorated, between 1904 and 1931. Part of the rood screen had been completed in 1925 but the rest did not follow until 1937, and the same applied to the colouring of the screens of the Jesus Chancel, the roof of the north choir aisle (modelled on the decoration of the nave roof of Salle, Norfolk) and the organ cases.

The ciborium was not completed until 1940. It was then that the figures were added, and a copy of the Pusey House altar frontal. The balance of the lavish decoration, both liturgically and aesthetically, depended upon it; for it made the high altar what it should be, the richest detail of the whole church. The Majestas and cherubim came in 1946 and 'besides Christianising the church, they make the necessary division for the chancel and reveal the proportion of the building.' So, through the rest of the decade until 1954, when Comper attained his ninetieth year, further decoration and ornaments were added. Specimens of decoration were made to guide continuity and much remains to be finished, not least the painting of the vault in blue and gold. Pevsner disliked the Italian influence and what he described as the 'pretty-prettiness' of Comper's late work; it was too decorous and over-refined for him. But at St Mary's the Mediterranean impact that he found so tiresome carried the day.

Other critics delighted in it and were untroubled by the accusation of pastiche which bedevilled Comper's work among some Modernists. One was Lord Clark of Saltwood, who had been introduced to Comper by Betjeman when he was Director of the National Gallery.

> I regard Comper's work as pastiche and I like it. I do not regard these as alternatives. I see no reason why, at certain periods when the consciousness of historical styles is strong and reviving, works of art should not be created in this way. Comper belonged to an age which was deeply conscious of the past and all the better for it. One could think of examples in music (Strauss's *Ariadne*) as well as in poetry and architecture. For that matter the Palladian style in 18th century England is no more than a pastiche, and often a very incompetent one, of Italian styles invented more than 200 years earlier. I particularly like Comper's attempt to unite Gothic and Classical archi-tecture, which was done most beautifully at St Eustache, Paris, and in the 18th century at St Mary's, Warwick. Lutyens, the greatest English architect since Wren, was a pasticheur. I will admit that he would have been greater if he had been able to work in an authentic contemporary style.

St Mary, Wellingborough, Northamptonshire, 1904–31. The Jesus Chancel at the east end of the north aisle, shortly after the installation of the east window in memory of Grace Comper, 1935. Photograph: Frank Knight.

St Mary, Wellingborough, Northamptonshire, 1904–31. Looking west down the south aisle. This church was Comper's favourite work. Photograph: Edwin Smith.

On a less exalted level the effect that St Mary's had on one who had largely spent his life removed from aesthetic stimulus is found in a letter from Osmund Victor, a priest of the Community of the Resurrection, Mirfield. He wrote to Comper in 1934 from St Paul's, Bedford, while on furlough from the African missions, set the church in its social context, and spoke for many who were not associated with architectural criticism but had a direct response to Comper's genius.

> You will perhaps pardon a letter from a complete stranger – calling as it does for no reply – but, home for a short time from S. Africa where the last 25 years of my life have recently been spent, Canon Robins took me over yesterday to S. Mary's, Wellingborough. I had seen it before, but not in its (so far) completed state – so wholly and entirely lovely as it is I thought I must write to say 'thank you' for it. I must say that it gave me a pain in the pit of the stomach to think of so great a glory tucked away in a wilderness of mean streets, and I should fear unappreciated by the great bulk of those who live round it. But for all that it is a very wonderful thing which you have given to the world, and the memory of it will remain with me for life.

Wellingborough understandably was Comper's favourite work because it was there, in a relatively unfettered context, that he was able to achieve all he wanted to do. It was a laboratory for his art in the same way that his early restorations and churches had been. St Mary's represented more than mere stylistic evolution and experiment. Comper was heavenly-minded in a way that has almost become inaccessible to modern thought. He believed that 'a church should pray of itself with its architecture; it is its own prayer and should bring you to your knees when you enter.' He saw St Mary's not solely as a work of art but as an expression of beauty and unity that reflected the beauty and unity of the Holy Trinity and was a foretaste of the eternal beauty of heaven.

'The whole history of the altar throughout all periods reveals the high place given to beauty in the Christian Church. All the arts have been enlisted by her to do honour to her Lord in the Eucharist,' he wrote in *Of the Christian Altar and the Buildings which Contain It*. 'In all the arts the Church took over the best traditions of Jews and Greeks adapting and perfecting them to her use. And the measure of achievement is the degree in which she succeeds in eliminating the sense of time and producing the atmosphere of heavenly worship.' At the heart of Comper's faith lay a fundamental belief in the Real Presence of Christ in the Eucharist. The magnificence of his work was an expression of conviction in the truth of this doctrine. No setting on earth, he believed, could be more beautiful than a church, a place where Christ's abiding Presence with his people is fulfilled.

Historically much endeavour reached fulfilment here. There is the earnest ecclesiology of the Cambridge Camden Society and a resolution of the mid-Victorian battle of the styles. Comper's scales were just: he weighed Gothic with Classic, *cinquecento* with Greek, synthesised into one without

St Mary, Wellingborough, Northamptonshire, 1904–31. The Risen Christ and angels on top of the ciborium. Photograph, 1968.

aesthetic compromise. The historical perception and doctrinal certitude of the Oxford Movement were combined in a commemoration of the triumph of the hard-won battle for the Eucharist that had transformed Anglican worship with lasting effects. The sweetness, light, beauty and refinement that had developed into the late-flowering of the Gothic Revival were applied to an understanding of the Church of England as national, yet international, in what Anglo-Catholics believed was its inherent Catholicism.

Comper was a man of high culture, with a respect for learning, order, hierarchy and tradition and his patronage was almost exclusively religious and aristocratic. He led a thoughtful, literate and civilised life. His work should be seen in the light of the Renaissance approach to human wisdom and tradition,

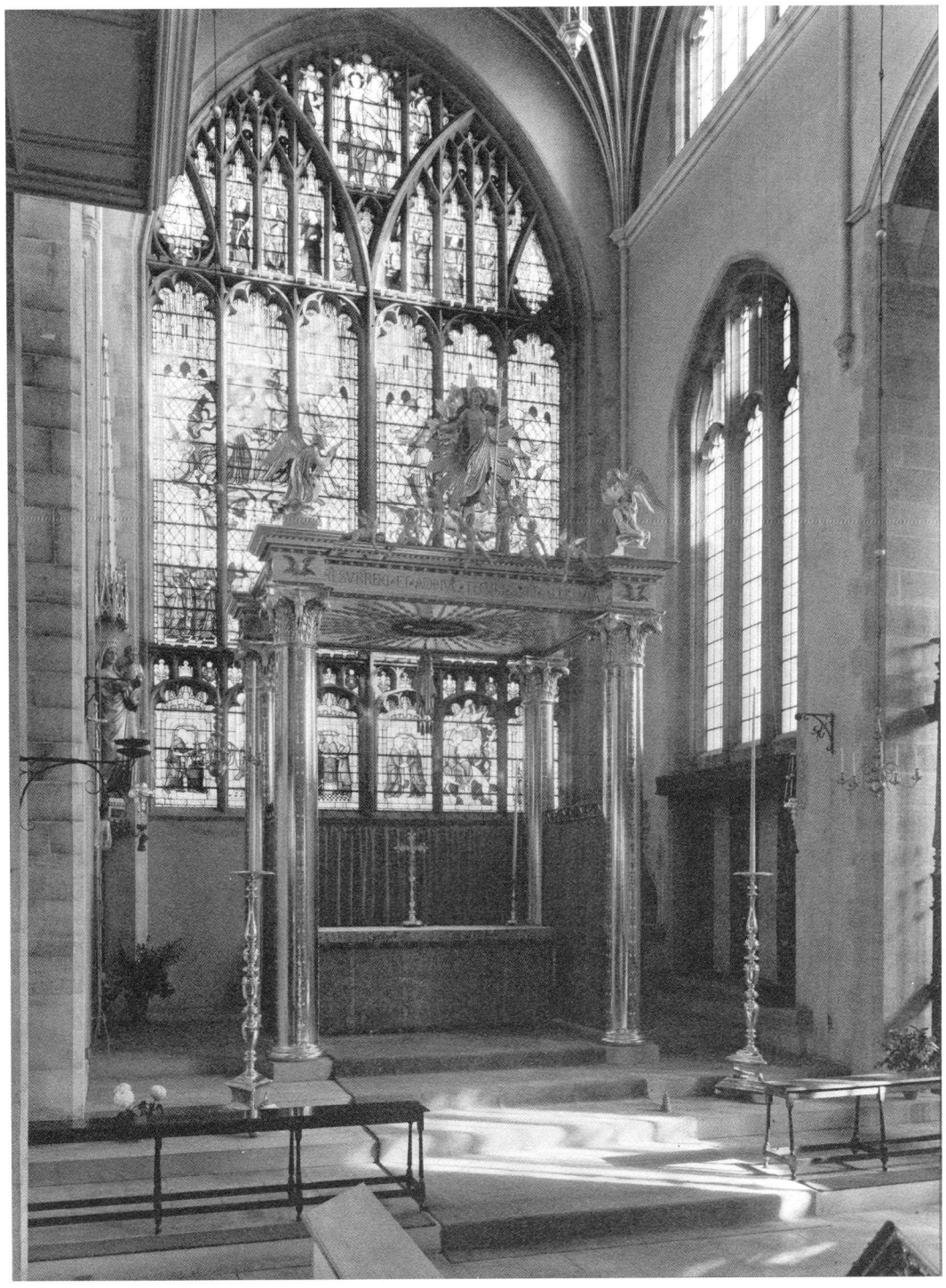

St Mary, Wellingborough, Northamptonshire, 1904–31. The high altar as Comper wanted it, with two candlesticks and a hangying pyx. Photograph: Harry Moore, 1942.

St Mary, Wellingborough, Northamptonshire, 1904–31. The vault and Majestas. Photograph: Edwin Smith.

in which one generation is nourished and sustained by the intellectual and artistic achievements of its predecessors. These qualities are fully embodied in St Mary's, Wellingborough. The social conditions of his generation, the learned and cultivated world of the English upper-classes, the perfectionist expression of their spiritual aspirations in early twentieth-century Anglo-Catholicism are gone forever. They were swept away by the cultural revolutions that followed the Second World War, the Second Vatican Council of 1962–5, and the stealthy metamorphosis of the social, moral and technological environment since 1968. Anglo-Catholicism declined into a hermetic, self-authenticating tradition and, in the light of an unprejudiced study of Anglican history and theology and later developments that broke the apostolic institution, the classic Anglo-Catholic case became indefensible. But beauty and the historic tradition of the Church, as Comper discovered, never dies. Despite the low culture of the modern world, there is always, through the regenerative power of Catholicism, a hope of rebirth. Commanded by a figure of the Pantokrator, the Almighty, the Ruler and Creator of all things, the eternal Christ forever young, at Wellingborough majesty and grace are fused in one.

John Betjeman, John Piper and Sir Ninian Comper: *Of the Atmosphere of a Church* in context

Anthony Symondson SJ

'OF THE ATMOSPHERE OF A CHURCH' is, perhaps, the most persuasive and influential of Sir Ninian Comper's liturgical papers. It has entered the mythology of many who admire his work and when it was published in 1947 quickly came to have an impact upon a new generation of Anglican priests, architects and theorists who had come under the influence of the continental liturgical movement. Foremost among them was Peter Hammond, rector of Bagendon, in Gloucestershire, who had studied art before his ordination and whose radical book, *Liturgy and Architecture*, was published in 1960, the year of Comper's death. Hammond quoted Comper in support of his thesis that functional requirements should determine the liturgical planning of churches:

> As Sir Ninian Comper has written, 'We can learn a lesson from the simplest of our medieval churches whose fabrics were little more than a barn – hardly so fine a barn as barns then were – but which became glorious by beautiful workmanship within. To so low and plain a fabric a worthy altar has only to be added and the white-washed barn will have an atmosphere of prayer and love ....' Far better the white-washed barn which derives its purpose from a worthy altar, set in the right place, than the pretentious structure, lavishly adorned within and without with sculpture, mosaic, painting and stained glass, which ignores its own fundamental *raison d'être* and that of the *ecclesia* whose house it is.[1]

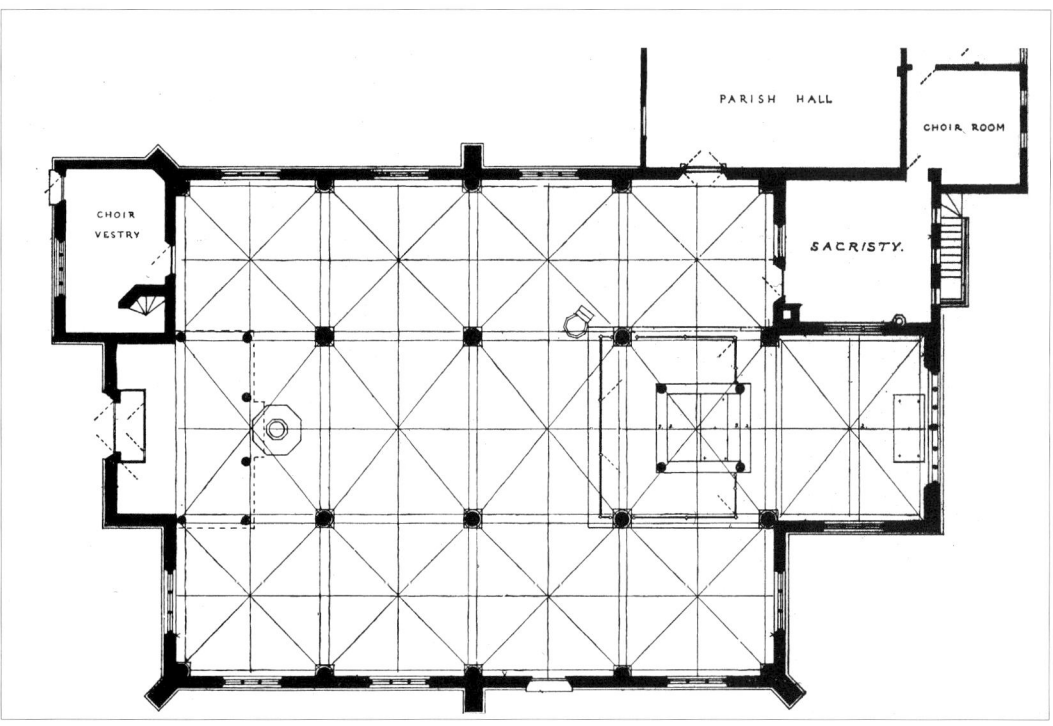

Plan of St Philip, Cosham, 1937. Note the west gallery, for the organ and choir; the free-standing altar, beneath a ciborium, surrounded by altar-rails; and the Lady Chapel at the east end.

Hammond went further and isolated Comper's last church, St Philip's, Cosham, Portsmouth (1937) as one that 'bears little resemblance to anything that the man in the street is likely to associate with functional architecture. Yet there is no church built in this country since the beginning of the century which is so fitted to its purpose.'

He continued by explaining why:

> It is the work of an architect for whom architecture is essentially the hand-maid of the liturgy, and Christian tradition something far more vital than a storehouse of precedents and historic detail. The church functions as the great majority of modern churches – for all their display of contemporary clichés – do not. It is a building for corporate worship: a building to house an altar. From the point of view of plan it is extremely simple – a short rectangle, with the altar free-standing beneath a ciborium, surrounded by cancelli, or altar rails, and a small chapel behind it. There is a west gallery for singers and the organ. The plan embodies the architect's conviction that the type of layout common in the fourth century, with the altar 'in the midst of the worshippers, and not separated from them by any choir but only by a very open screen, or merely by low cancelli … is suited to the needs of today in a way in which the medieval plan, to which we in England still adhere amidst all the vagaries of styles, is not suited, developed as it was for monastic use.'

The church of St Philip provides a conclusive answer to those who assert that to bring the altar forward, into the midst of the people, must involve the sacrifice of mystery. We can well afford to dispense with the false mystery which is dependent upon romantic vistas, Wagnerian gloom and other devices more appropriate to the opera house than to the Christian church. The little church at Cosham scorns such theatrical tricks. It exemplifies the contention that 'knowledge of tradition is the first requisite for the creation of atmosphere in a church', and that this elusive quality 'must be the product of one mind so steeped in tradition as a second nature that … he can receive the inspiration to apply it to the needs which he has to meet.' This is an authentic *domus ecclesiae*, a church of very rare quality, completely subordinated to the demands of the liturgy which is its inspiration and *raison d'être*. The twenty years which have elapsed since its consecration have produced nothing worthy of a comparison with it on this side of the Channel.[2]

There is a reason for quoting Hammond at length. *Liturgy and Architecture* claimed Comper as one of the moderns in much the same way that Peter Anson and John Betjeman had done in their pioneer essays of the late Thirties.[3] Hammond placed St Philip's, Cosham, in the canon of modern church architecture and won for it lasting critical acceptance. He concentrated upon the rational and functional principles of Comper's late architectural theories in a campaign which resulted in the formation of the New Churches Research Group and the foundation of the Institute for the Study of Worship and Religious Architecture at Queen's College, Birmingham. Anson likened Hammond to St John the Baptist for bringing liturgical ideas to an architectural audience,[4] but Hammond's work, and what resulted from it, deliberately led to a dramatic eclipse of all that Comper represented, bar church planning.

Fundamental to Comper's theories – and essential to his liturgical writing – was the necessity of beauty as a divine imperative and the transcendence of worship:

> The purpose of a church is not to express the age in which it was built or the individuality of its designer. Its purpose is to move to worship, to bring a man to his knees, to refresh his soul in a weary land. This would seem to be the Creator's purpose towards man in giving him the beauty of nature, and it should be the purpose of all art. In art man partakes of this purpose of his Maker and objectively he brings the best of all He has given him to create of beauty (in liturgy, poetry, music, ceremonial, architecture, sculpture and painting) to be the expression of his worship. For mankind in the mass the neglect of beauty spells the hardness and narrowness either of a puritan or of a materialist … The note of a church should be, not that of novelty, but of eternity.[5]

Can that be said of the church architecture of the last forty years? With a few notable exceptions, I think not. The churches that grew from *Liturgy and Architecture*, the New Churches Research Group, and the Birmingham Institute are mostly failures for trying to combine two mutually inimical ideologies: the cults of primitivism and Modernism. Like their proponents and architects, Comper returned for inspiration to the fourth century, to the early Constantinian liturgy with its profound sense of the Church as the Body of Christ and the *plebs sancta Dei*, the holy common people of God. But he was not a catacomb romantic because he saw tradition as an accretive process to which all ages of the Christian centuries contributed. The more familiar he became with church art the better grasp he had of tradition. Comper moved from seeing the late Middle Ages as a golden age, in comparison with which other centuries were either immature or decadent, to concluding that the Christian centuries and their Classical inheritance had a valid application to an understanding of tradition as a vital, rather than static, force. He saw no need to abandon the historic styles of architecture but drew together into an artistic unity the most beautiful of all periods subject to the controlling thought of the designer. He conceived churches not merely as rationally designed liturgical spaces but as unified works of art.

Comper repudiated Modernism. He wrote of his masterpiece, St Mary's, Wellingborough, Northamptonshire (1904–31): 'Only to its contemporaries does the church owe nothing.'[6] Why did Comper turn his back on Modernism? The answer is simple: because it is ugly. Modernism meant for him the excesses of what is known as Art Deco, stripped Classicism and the *moderne* reduced to self-expression and the expression of the age. He saw these claims 'used to cover what is merely such incapacity and ugliness as every age has in turn rejected'.[7]

In 1937 Comper met Betjeman. He was seventy-three, Betjeman thirty-one. It was a fateful meeting that led to a friendship of twenty-three years. Comper had a strong influence on Betjeman's thought and understanding of church architecture. In return, Betjeman's sympathetic interest in Comper, coming at a time when age and circumstances might have led Comper to believe that his work was coming to an end, gave him a new lease of life. They were at ease in each other's company and in their letters they expressed themselves with surprising freedom. It was due to Betjeman's encouragement that Comper was stimulated to make the startling and original plan for the rebuilding of St John of Jerusalem, Clerkenwell, in 1943. And from the publication of Betjeman's article, 'A note on J. N. Comper: heir to Butterfield and Bodley', in the *Architectural Review* in 1939, he became Comper's principal advocate. Betjeman continued to praise his work in books, articles, broadcasts and films for the rest of Comper's life and beyond. Writing of Betjeman to Gerard Irvine in 1948, Comper said: 'To no one does my work owe more than to him.'[8] It is impossible to dissociate the influence they had on each other.

But in 1937, the young John Betjeman was half-persuaded by the cause of International Modernism expressed in the ideals of the Modern Architecture Research Group (MARS). Betjeman shared Comper's loathing of the modernistic and recognised in his work the same qualities as Hammond in comparison with what they perceived to be the bland, formulaic church architecture and planning of Sir Edward Maufe and Sir Giles Gilbert Scott and the Expressionism of N. F. Cachemaille-Day. In contrast, Betjeman believed that what C. F. A. Voysey and M. H. Baillie Scott had achieved for the evolution of the small house, Comper had achieved for the church and thus secured a place in what was genuinely Modern. Betjeman was an aesthete and he responded to the beauty of Comper's work; Hammond was a puritan ideologist who believed that Comper's planning theories should be realised in a recognizable Modern form from which all historical and associational references were eliminated.

The ideology of International Modernism was based upon a clean break with the past and governed by social and scientific principles demonstrated in a collective view of society from which religion would slowly be eliminated. It grew from an atheistic principle. When Modernist principles were applied to church architecture the emphasis on planning, while bringing the altar into the heart of a church, became communitarian at the expense of transcendence. Comper saw this tendency, in company with the Modernistic, as a death-blow to his primary understanding of a church whose 'purpose is to move to worship, to bring a man to his knees, to refresh his soul in a weary land'.[9] The mystery that Hammond acknowledged at Cosham was sacrificed, with the exception of rare instances such as St Paul's, Bow Common, Stepney (1958–60), by Robert Maguire and Keith Murray, a building which, despite its ruthless austerity, has a numinous quality created by light and shade and the careful position of the altar in the centre of the church beneath a ciborium of light steel.

II

It was against the background of Modernism in church architecture as it was then understood and the invigorating influence of Comper's burgeoning friendship with Betjeman that *Of the Atmosphere of a Church* came to be written. In 1939 Comper was invited by Canon Gabriel Gillett, the Principal of Chichester Theological College, (whom Betjeman described as 'a most charming and gloomy man')[10] to give a talk on church architecture to the students. Comper was recognised as the leading English church architect, whose work was considered matchless. But it was not an entirely conventional invitation. Chichester was an Anglo-Catholic college and the emphasis was provocatively in a modern Roman or, as it was then euphemistically called, Western direction. It has entertainingly been described by Colin Stephenson in his autobiography, *Merrily on High*.

In contrast, the tone of Chichester Cathedral was unequivocally English, under the Dean, A. S. Duncan-Jones. Duncan-Jones was a supporter of the Sarum, or English Use, a follower of Percy Dearmer whom he had succeeded as Vicar of St Mary's, Primrose Hill, and a strong advocate of the Central Council for the Care of Churches and its secretary, Dearmer's *protégé*, F. C. Eeles. To them the college and what it represented was inflammatory and so was Comper.

In his early work Comper had done more to revive medieval authenticity in support of a purely English interpretation of the Ornaments Rubric of the Book of Common Prayer than any other architect. His scholarly papers, *Practical Considerations on the Gothic or English Altar and Certain Dependent Ornaments* and *The Reasonableness of the Ornaments Rubric Illustrated by a Comparison of the German and English Altars*, given to the St Paul's Ecclesiological Society in 1893 and 1897, set out his principles. Comper's research and conclusions underpinned Dearmer's popularization of the English Use, published in *The Parson's Handbook* in 1899. These were commercially applied by the St Dunstan's Society and Warham Guild which had been founded by Dearmer and were supported by Eeles. Both developments rankled Comper; but so persuasive was his early work in the reconstruction of the Gothic altar, in his church restorations conceived as unified works of art and in his first London church, St Cyprian's, Clarence Gate, St Marylebone (1902–3), that a new understanding of liturgical worship was opened.

It embodied the aspirations of a school of clerics and liturgical scholars who wanted to give English church worship a national expression founded upon the Prayer Book which was also consistent with the gains of the Oxford Movement. Their leader was J. Wickham Legg whose work was channelled through the Henry Bradshaw Society, the Alcuin Club and the Plainsong and Medieval Music Society, in all of which Comper was involved. His work was regularly illustrated from 1899 to 1910 in the *English Churchman's Kalendar*, started and edited by Legg to encourage the accomplishment of their aims. To this school the future was set fair for the implementation of an English genus of Anglo-Catholicism that they hoped would come to permeate the Church of England.

Comper's understanding of art and architecture was founded upon a primary appeal to beauty and reason mediated in eucharistic terms and was not simply confined to the tenets of a faction, however learned. Comper had a fluid architectural mind that was not satisfied with decided views. The results of his early medievalism were seen by those who were persuaded by his arguments to be definitive and in no need of modification or development. Few understood the liturgical motivation behind his experiments and judged the work by its results. Many were, and are, intoxicated by the decorative splendour of Comper's work, its beauty, colour and gilding, and superficially see it in theatrical terms without being aware of the profound thought behind its principles and the ingenuity, integrity and expertise of the design and execution. Comper liked his work to be enjoyed but he was impatient with those who saw it merely in terms of burnished gold and unqualified praise. He had a developed critical faculty and he appreciated the same level of perception in others. An understanding of his work calls for education and taste. Comper's liturgical principles made the altar the deciding feature of church planning. What to some seemed to be retrogressive antiquarianism was essentially a radical attempt to restore to the Church of England a continuity with the medieval past and reunite it with the historic Catholic faith. At the front of his mind were the liturgical demands of the modern age. It was this factor and the way it was realised in his work that later attracted the interest and admiration of proponents of the Modern Movement and gives Comper's work lasting significance.[11]

Comper's liturgical awareness explains the unforeseen consequences of his journeys to Italy in 1900 and 1905 and his later visits to Greece and Spain. He recognised the implications of *respondere natalibus*, of returning to the birthright of Western European civilization. What is interesting is that he had no desire to go to Rome and only did so from filial duty. It was a Holy Year and John Comper, his father, wanted to visit Rome for the last time before he died and invited his eldest son to accompany him. Comper was prepared to be repelled and his expectations were fulfilled by the Baroque churches, a style he then loathed. Until he became conscious of the connections of the Graeco-Roman past, the early basilicas and the seduction of clear Mediterranean colour and light his mind remained exclusively Northern European. If Comper had merely been a ceremonial set dresser he would have been satisfied by his early enthusiasm or might have developed into an architect who applied what was received. If so, his professional life would have been less troublesome. It was his understanding of liturgical principle and the need for the Eucharist to become the heart and centre of worship in which priest and people are united as one at the altar that led to developments that nobody expected and which anticipated the ideals of the twentieth-century liturgical movement. Thereafter Comper sought beauty by inclusion rather than exclusion.[12]

The dramatic change in Comper's work from 1910 onwards when he first applied his new theory in the restoration of Lord Shaftesbury's church at Wimborne St Giles, Dorset, came as an unwelcome surprise to many of his early patrons and those influenced by his work and this was intensified when he repudiated the Gothic altar and substituted for it the primitive altar standing beneath a Classical ciborium which for him became the ideal Christian altar. First realised in St Mary's, Wellingborough, the ciborium became a liturgical feature from which he was reluctant to depart.

In 1924 Comper discovered the primitive ideal in church planning on his second visit to French North Africa, better known today as Algeria. He visited the ruins of the fourth-century church complex at Theveste (modern Tébessa). It is imbued with Constantinian concepts and is one of the most valuable survivals of the time. It was here that he distinguished the plans on which all subsequent developments of church building varied. The basilica, by the interrelation of its composite elements – nave and apse, bishop's *cathedra*, reading desk and altar, with the baptistery by its side – expressed in architectural form the priorities of patristic Christianity in the doctrine of the Church and defined constant liturgical polarities. Inferred from the evidence of architecture, Comper came to realise that the Church is the assembly of the

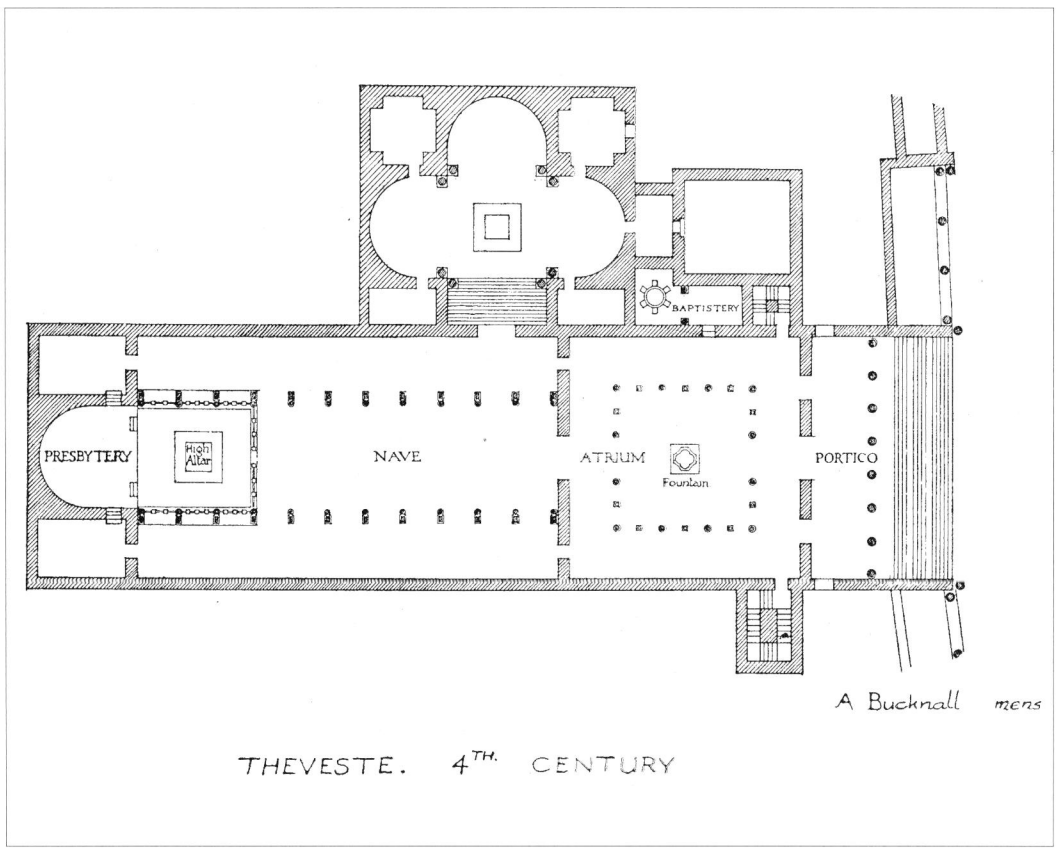

THEVESTE.   4TH.   CENTURY

The fourth-century Constantinian plan at Theveste (modern Tébessa) revolutionised Comper's church planning. This plan was drawn by Arthur Bucknall, Comper's nephew and assistant, and was published in Further Thoughts on the English Altar *and* Of the Atmosphere of a Church *to demonstrate its application to the planning of a modern church.*

faithful who become initiates through baptism; a body taught by the bishop, who expounds the scriptures; and an assembly of worshippers that, as ministers and people, celebrate the Mass as the central act of worship.

At the conventual church of All Saints, London Colney, Hertfordshire (1924–7), in his unexecuted plans for Aberdeen Cathedral (1928), in the chapel of the House of Prayer, Burnham, Buckinghamshire (1932–5) and most fully in St Philip's, Cosham, the implications of what he had measured at Theveste were brought to bear upon his late church planning. St Philip's, as Hammond recognised, 'embodies the architect's conviction that the type of layout common in the fourth century with the altar "in the midst of the worshippers, and not separated from them by any choir but only by a very open screen, or merely by low *cancelli* … is suited to the needs of today in a way in which the medieval plan … is not …."'[13]

Between the two world wars the movement for an English Use was officially adopted by the Central Council for the Care of Churches as the Anglican ideal and diluted medievalism was applied as a formula in cathedrals and parish churches, irrespective of churchmanship, style and suitability, under the influence of the Diocesan Advisory Committees. Eeles tried to involve Comper in this drive, but he steadfastly refused. He no longer believed in the English cause, nor that architects should be restricted by committees; he disliked seeing the commercialization of his work, nor was he willing to be circumscribed by a model that he had outgrown. Comper fought for artistic independence in much the same way that he had opposed the Architects' Registration Act of 1931, believing that architecture was not a profession but an art. By giving Eeles the cold shoulder he isolated himself from the *status quo* and thereby lost many opportunities. Their antagonism developed into an implacable enmity which came to fruition in 1933 when Comper published a paper, *Further Thoughts on the English Altar, or Practical Considerations on the Planning of a Modern Church*, which he had given to the St Paul's Ecclesiological Society in the previous year. It was widely read and in it Comper attacked the Diocesan Advisory Committees in definite terms. Eeles over-reacted, prevented the paper from being reviewed in the *Church Times*, and stepped up his battle to discourage prospective patrons from using Comper; Duncan-Jones was co-opted to answer it in a leader in *The Guardian*, the Broad Church newspaper; letters flew. Undeterred, Comper distributed copies to many of the most influential churchmen he knew, all of whom counted.

Eeles regarded the development of Comper's church planning as idio-syncratic and could not understand its liturgical implications. Duncan-Jones saw in the application of the theory of unity by inclusion nothing more than decadence in comparison with the purity of Comper's early work. Both freely spoke their minds. The mainstream of the Anglo-Catholic party which looked to the liturgical and devotional life of the Catholicism of Western Europe as it had developed since the Reformation had long entertained reservations about Comper because of his identification with medievalism. But his work at All Saints, Margaret Street, St Marylebone (1909–28), St John's, Waterloo Road (1924–8; destroyed 1940), London Colney, Burnham, Cosham and, above all, in the chapel of Pusey House, Oxford (1937) was received with approval because it embodied the main current of liturgical development in the West. On the strength of these works, his scholarship and his known antagonism to Establishment taste Gillett extended his invitation.

III

The nation was bracing itself for war, but Comper's paper was duly published in *The Cicestrian*, the college magazine. In an editorial Kenneth Thompson welcomed it and acknowledged Comper's distinguishing characteristics:

> It is some months since Mr J. N. Comper first consented to write an article for the *Cicestrian*. We were extremely grateful to him then, but we have even more reason to thank him now for having written at this time an article which has

cost him many precious hours. It is refreshing to read of the construction and furnishing of churches from the pen of a man, many of whose works (designed to the glory of God in worship) are being removed to 'places of safety'. That Mr Comper resents (as he does) his works being handled as though they were designed for the museum or dilettante's gallery, shows more plainly than anything he has written, more clearly even than the beauty of the work itself, that here is a man who understands what is meant by Christian Worship: a man who, captivated by the idea, has devoted to it that great art, which endless study and ever youthful enthusiasm have developed in him and brought to such an amazing flower. Mr Comper's more recent convictions – as we see them expressed in his work – his ciboria, his 'degenerate arches', even the number of lights he puts on the altar; these things alone throw the medievalist into an apoplexy; a matter which in itself bears witness to Mr Comper's greatness as a teacher (through his art) of a universal and living Christian Worship. When a man goes into one of Comper's Churches (and for us at Chichester, until the war started, Cosham was close at hand) he is immediately struck by one thing – the self-consciousness of the whole place. The building almost sweats self-consciousness from every stone, from every gilded pillar and painted capital. But the odd thing is that it is self-consciousness of being in a Church for the worshipping of Almighty God (and not of being an admirable contrivance of Mr J. N. Comper) which so strikes the observer, even if he has entered with the set intention of admiring the work of the artist – or being shocked by it.[14]

After *Of the Atmosphere of a Church* had been published the reaction from the Deanery was predictable. 'I hear that the Dean of Chichester, Duncan-Jones, was furious at your article,' wrote Thompson, '& said in a choky voice, "This must be answered," and "Of course, Comper used to be very good – but now his work is very debased." Alas you have declined from Dearmer! It is extraordinary how people are hag ridden by prejudices & *a priori* doctrinaire policies.'[15] Betjeman was overjoyed and encouraged Comper to fight on, 'DUNCAN-JONES IS A MENACE, IT IS AN HONOUR TO HAVE RAISED HIS IRE. I AM DELIGHTED.'[16] The issue quickly sold out: in much the same way that the quarterly, *Pax*, published by the Benedictines of Prinknash Abbey, had sold out two years previously when Anson had published his article, 'The work of John Ninian Comper: a pioneer of the modern liturgical revival'.

It was not only Comper who was opposed to the ossifying influence of Eeles and his associates. Within the Central Council the voice of Sir Eric Maclagan, Director of the Victoria and Albert Museum, a strong Anglo-Catholic and sometime churchwarden of St Mary's, Graham Street, Pimlico, insisted, under the influence of H. S. Goodhart-Rendel, on the encouragement of modern church art. Within Chichester itself there was a reaction led by Bishop George Bell. In 1939 Bell approached Sir Kenneth Clark, the Director of the National Gallery, about getting modern artists to do work in churches in his diocese. Clark saw the secretary of the Society of Mural Painters, on the committee of which sat the young John Piper who had shortly before been introduced to Comper by Betjeman at luncheon in the grille room of the St Ermin's Hotel, which at that time was one of his favourite restaurants.

Betjeman recounted Piper's description of what had happened at a meeting of the committee when the subject was discussed.

> He thought before going to the meeting that it was a pretty dotty idea and just like a business bishop's. He did not like the idea of modern artists disfiguring old churches though let them do what they like with Cachemaille-Day and Maufe. When he got to the meeting he found all the bogus moderns there, and all of them talking about money and how to get money out of the Church and he staggered and infuriated them all by suddenly saying: 'Are any of you believing Christians?' 'Good Lord, no!', they said and thought it very funny. So he said he thought that they had no right to do such a thing as Church work and to take money from the Church, and he left the meeting saying he was going to offer his services *free* to any bishop who might like to use them, and that he would see to it that they were none of them employed.[17]

Despite Piper's threat, the committee approached Bell, and thus was launched the English career of Hans Feibusch and the commission in 1942–3 to paint the walls of Berwick church, Sussex, by Duncan Grant, Vanessa and Quentin Bell.

In reaction to this endeavour and to Eeles, in 1944 Piper mounted a travelling exhibition sponsored by the Council for the Encouragement of Music and the Arts (CEMA) entitled *The Artist and the Church*. Comparison was invited 'between painting by Roualt and ancient stained glass, or between modern stone carvings and the figures on a 12th century font'. Piper was outraged by the staleness and mediocrity of church art, architecture, patronage and design. The same independence of mind he had shown at the meeting of the Society of Mural Painters made him realise that there was no point in trying to work within existing systems, least of all with the Central Council for the Care of Churches whose patronage, he believed, was rooted in the late nineteenth century and had 'separated itself finally from the main and most vital roots of this country to become, on the whole, etiolated, provincial and over-traditional. The artist is partly to blame for this by being uncooperative and indifferent; the Church is partly to blame because of its lack of discrimination and loss of artistic conviction.'[18]

He also attacked the barren cult of craftsmanship that had developed from the late Arts and Crafts Movement and the puritan principles of the Society for the Protection of Ancient Buildings that continued to be encouraged by Eeles and the Central Council:

> It is significant that nowadays when there is a question of furnishing or adorning a church the man who comes first to mind for the job is likely to be a *craftsman*, and not an artist. For the craftsman is likely to be 'traditional', and safe – that is capable of being kept in order; while the artist is likely to be over-personal and over-daring. But a slavish pursuance of tradition defeats its own ends. The 'traditional' becomes in the end imitative and repetitive. The

artist, if he is a good artist, must be a craftsman as well. The craftsman, if he is freshly creative, and only if he is so, will be an artist.[19]

Piper was out to bridge gaps, burn boats and make a fresh start. He was not against tradition, only a frozen interpretation of it. He wanted to encourage serious modern art in English churches, executed from within a context of tradition deeper than convention. Informed by neo-Romanticism, the exhibition was a demonstration of the accretive aesthetic which Piper and Betjeman were to advance in the *Shell Guides*, in Piper's articles in the *Architectural Review* – which opened up an entirely unconventional understanding of the British landscape and the vernacular – and in his topographical painting.

Piper set out his purpose in the foreword to the catalogue:

> The objects in this exhibition have been selected by a painter who is also a churchman and a lover of churches, old and new. It is not intended to be impartial or complete. Nor is it intended to be any kind of survey or conspectus of the work of any period. It reflects the personal taste of the arranger, and does not speak for any other person or body. In this way only can such a small exhibition dealing with a subject of such enormous scope hope to have unity. Where it touches on the art of the present, it shows works that have actually been executed for churches, or the work of artists who by their temperament, might well execute work for churches in the future. Where it deals with the art of the past the bias is in favour of the unfamiliar.
>
>   This is not prejudice, or caprice. By showing comparatively unfamiliar works of the past and present side by side it is hoped that they will be seen in a fresh relationship to the whole tradition of English Church art – which is the only profitable way in which contemporary work by the artist for the Church can be looked at, since in competition with careful 'traditional' work its suitability will always be doubted, and the value of its originality and vitality will always be underrated.[20]

The exhibition was composed of eight sections mounted on twenty portable screens: wall paintings, stained glass, sculpture, textiles, lettering and printing, mosaic work and church restoration, hatchments, and one section was to be entirely devoted to the work of Comper. The difficulty was to persuade him to be included as he shrank from publicity and was opposed to exhibitions. Betjeman set out Piper's ends:

> My friend John Piper writes that he is nervous you may not help in his exhibition of church art. He says his sole object is to have no *Maufe*, no *Sir Giles*, no *Blacking*, no *Eeles* and he has already had a row with Eeles' secretary. You are his hero and next to you Ellery Anderson and F. C. Eden and Etchells and no one else at all – except the great Victorians and the even greater medievals. I really think this exhibition, if it comes off, will be the biggest blow Eeles has suffered. Do see him, if he writes to you. I am sure you will find him a sympathetic friend. He is the only sound man on church matters beside yourself.[21]

Comper needed no more persuasion and his work was represented by nineteen exhibits. They included painted glass from St Mary's, Wellingborough, and London Colney, drawings and photographs of Aberdeen Cathedral, the Heritage Crafts School Chapel at Chailey, Sussex, unexecuted designs for St John's, Stockcross near Newbury, Berkshire, and a new chapel for Cuddesdon College, Oxford, St Philip's, Cosham, and the high altar of St Mary's, Wellingborough, the tabernacle of All Saints, Margaret Street, the font cover of St Alban's, Holborn, and the decoration of the eighteenth-century reredos at All Saints, Carshalton.

Comper's was the only section which had its own introduction in the catalogue:

> 'No English architect is better known in cathedral close or distant rectory than J. N. Comper, few architects are less well-known to what has come to be called "the profession" ', as Mr John Betjeman has written. Comper began as a medievalist and has developed into a creative artist-architect – the finest, as many people believe, now working for the Church. He himself has said: 'English architecture of the fourteenth and fifteenth centuries and one may add the sixteenth is, it is true, the culmination of Gothic in this country, but it is not the rock from which we were hewn, nor yet the end beyond which we cannot go.'[22]

The Artist and the Church was a direct challenge to Eeles and official Anglican taste. 'I regard this exhibition,' wrote Betjeman, 'as a preventative measure; we will otherwise be swamped by Maufe, Sir Giles & Co.'[23]

Piper recognised in Comper's work a natural development of architectural continuity which also conformed to the Modernist canon. Among a handful of modern architects Comper found himself with Ellery Anderson and E. J. A. Roiser, represented by their restoration of the church at Shipton Sollers, Gloucestershire, and Frederick Etchells in his restoration for Edward James, the Surrealist patron, of the church at West Dean, Sussex. And among artists were included the textiles of Phyllis Barron and Dorothy Larcher, the murals by Duncan Grant, Vanessa and Quentin Bell for Berwick, stained glass by Georges Roualt and Evie Hone, sculpture by Henri Gaudier-Breszka and Henry Moore, embroidery by Norah Clutterbuck and Dorothy Allsopp, typography by Bruce Anderson, lettering by Eric Gill and mosaic by Boris Anrep and Eric Newton.

The work of the living was combined with photographs and drawings of medieval wall-paintings, sculpture and stained glass, eighteenth-century monuments, hatchments and embroidery, seventeenth-century memorial tablets, pre-Raphaelite cartoons, specimen sheets of bibles, prayer books and church notices printed by the Oxford and Cambridge University Presses and the Curwen Press, etchings by John Sell Cotman, and photographs of neglected country churches in a state of pleasing decay.

This exhibition did more even than Betjeman's prose to continue Comper's professional life after the war and to introduce it to a new generation. It rescued him from Eeles's policy of dismissal. But, ironically for him, it also secured the sum of Piper's hopes. It attracted the attention of Walter Hussey, a young clergyman who had recently been appointed to St Matthew's, Northampton. As a result, he commissioned in 1944 and 1947 Henry Moore's Virgin and Child and Graham Sutherland's Crucifixion, works which shocked Comper profoundly when he saw them on the way to Welling-borough. Years later, when Hussey had become Dean of Chichester, a statue of St Richard by Comper, gleaming in burnished gold, was surrounded by the work of Piper, Sutherland, Ceri Richards, Cecil Collins, Marc Chagall and others who had by then become Establishment artists. Chichester embodied what Piper had striven to achieve twenty-five years earlier and has resulted in its own detrimental imitations, which themselves have become part of received Anglican taste.

IV

Betjeman's enthusiastic advocacy was decisive, but, in the end, caused a reaction which has severely damaged Comper's reputation. This was in part because of the nature of Betjeman's friendship, in part because of his excessive praise which flowed into his journalism, in part because of his insecurity, and in part, perhaps, because of his delight in unfashionable causes and his desire to mislead through paradox and humour. He could not resist provoking the earnest.

Comper was delighted by Betjeman's attention and friendship; he responded to flattery and few had flattered him as freely as Betjeman. But like Voysey, he was confused by being seen as a Modernist. Comper would not accept Modernism in any form, he believed it to be malignant. This gave an opportunity to Peter Anson, who enjoyed nothing more than teasing correspondence. His surviving letters to Comper of the Thirties and Forties are full of waspish taunts. He plagued him with articles on modern church architecture that would guarantee a rise but he also insisted on reminding him that Betjeman himself was a member of MARS.

In 1939 The Architects' Journal published a poll among public figures who had been invited to choose six new buildings which they considered of greatest merit. Betjeman's own choice included St Philip's, Cosham, in company with W. Crabtree's Peter Jones department store in Sloane Square, Maxwell Fry's Ladbroke (now Kensal) House in Ladbroke Grove, a block of flats built by the Gas, Light and Coke Company for their employees on a narrow strip of land next to a canal, Berthold Lubetkin's Penguin Pool in London Zoo, and David Pleydell-Bouverie's Amusement Park on the foreshore at Folkestone. Comper did not see the article until 1944; Anson had sent him a cutting. At the same time Anson was trying to persuade him, without success, of the merits of Goodhart-Rendel's design for the monastic buildings of Prinknash Abbey.

Comper challenged Betjeman on his choice of modern architecture and received a reply in which emotionally he defended his position in a way that also casts light on the apparent contradiction of including Comper in *The Artist and the Church*. First came a diatribe against Goodhart-Rendel:

> I think Goodhart-Rendel is neither sincere nor conscientious and his design betrays the man – a twittering aesthete with too much money, too great a desire for power of a worldly sort, no sensibility and no aesthetic confidence. His design is commercial ecclesiastical – Giles Gilbert Scott at his worst – not even the wicked old grandfather who was sincere if not conscientious.

He continued by defending his selection of Peter Jones and Ladbroke House against Comper's criticism of their ugliness:

> As for my apparently inexplicable choice of Peter Jones and Ladbroke House: here is the explanation. I was asked to choose six modern buildings. I could not think of six at all easily. Our way of life has so changed – who am I to say whether for better or not? That we have two sorts of life: 1 The commercial, physical, material which is always changing, has no standards because no beliefs. 2 The unchanging and spiritual for which your architecture stands and in which you stand head and shoulders above any other architect. The function of a church does not alter. The function of shops, roads, houses, flats does. In the former I look for a growth in style and arrangement and satisfying beauty which you so ably describe and put into brick and stone. In the latter, I look for planning, standardisation that is convenient and inoffensive, unpretentious and sincere, and necessarily temporary solutions of economic and social and traffic and planning problems.
>
> Architects are not artists today, so I choose buildings which come nearest to engineering. For the flat and the multiple store as for the railway station and the aerodrome and the motor and aeroplane, I regard engineering not architecture as the happiest medium. Indeed to apply the word architecture to such buildings in the sense of Perp architects, of Wren, Gibbs, Soane and yourself, is to misapply it. The result of true architecture, the product of an integrated society and a united personality comes out only in a whole Christian town dominated by a superb Christian church.
>
> We both know that the world is now being ravaged by evil. But from evil comes good. Ladbroke House, for instance, is a sincere attempt to have slum dwellers in as much light and with as much humanity as the wretched site and amount of money will allow. It is an unpretentious and kindly building. Peter Jones is a frank engineering effort, a shop in the Crystal Palace manner, something which can be taken down and put up elsewhere something that is both unpretentious and practical. Art does not come into it. Hence my choice. I would never choose the work of Sir Gilbert, Sir Herbert, Sir Reginald,[24] J. J. Joass because it is insincere stuff, an unthinking attempt to compromise between two worlds and two criteria.
>
> Now I do not think we should say that this steel and glass stuff, this engineering, is only evil, and I am deliberately choosing the less evil from the greater in selecting Peter Jones and Ladbroke House. It is no more evil than eating, drinking, washing and sleeping are evil. It is a necessity. For necessity

we should have necessary, not pretentious, engineering. The evil occurs when self-advertisement, greed and pretentiousness enter.[25]

Timothy Mowl has cast doubt on the sincerity of Betjeman's commitment to Modernism. It was certainly tentative and confused, but this letter, never meant for publication, still less to be carved on tablets of stone, casts light on his thought at a time before he became disillusioned by the ruthless, ideological post-war implementation of Modernist principles encouraged by Sir Nikolaus Pevsner, and cold-blooded town planners.

The letter also shows the disloyal nature of some of Betjeman's friendships. It is hard to forgive him for sneering at Goodhart-Rendel. In later life, he ingratiated himself with him and claimed him as a mentor. Betjeman could be an unreliable friend. Comper himself was not immune from Betjeman's mimicry, shafts and mockery behind his back, as many of his published letters and the recollections of his contemporaries prove. To some he referred to Comper as 'the Master' while A. L. Rowse remembered that to others his sobriquet was 'Sir Niminy Piminy'; it is the second and its implications that has remained in many minds.[27]

Sir John Summerson noticed that whatever Betjeman did for Comper was double-edged. His campaign to obtain a knighthood for him was undertaken as much to annoy the Royal Institute of British Architects as to achieve a belated recognition; Comper was an unregistered architect and his practice was theoretically illegal. Similarly, the splendid dinner given in the Athenaeum for his ninetieth birthday – though sprinkled with a Duke, an Earl, deans, canons, church architects, the *beau monde* and some of Comper's family and pupils quietly in their midst – was, off-stage among his friends, presented by Betjeman as if it was a huge joke.[28]

Publicly no-one advanced Comper's cause in the post-war years more than Betjeman, but his championship was often ambiguous. His discovery of Comper's work was a gradual process that continued long after the publication of his article on Comper in the *Architectural Review* in 1939. It was not, for instance, until 1943, that he discovered the Chapel of St Sepulchre in the crypt of St Mary Magdalene's, Paddington (1895) – a work that by then Comper had repudiated, even though he had recently restored the painted decoration.[29]

> I saw for the first time the other day your crypt at St Mary Mag, Paddington. My! It is a gleaming vision of Perp resplendence. I have already taken the following people to see it: H. de C. Hastings, Editor of the *Architectural Review*, Dr N. Pevsner, John Piper, Osbert Lancaster, T. D. Kendrick, Keeper of Brit and Medieval Antiquities at the BM and I have recommended it to Sir Kenneth Clark. All are stupefied to silence by its magnificence.[30]

Later, in 1948, he even took Christian Bérard, the stage designer and friend of Jean Cocteau, who was in London designing sets for Covent Garden: 'He was ravished. He thought you were the greatest architect living. You are. He could not understand why you were not knighted. I explained that artists aren't knighted in England. "Administrators" are.'[31] Betjeman was an unfaltering upholder and promoter of Comper's cause: 'I am continually demolishing highbrow functionalists by giving them my London course of Comper which is a visit to St MM, Paddington, and then on to St Cyprian's and then photographs of Cosham and Wellingborough.'[32]

So to what did this surfeit of praise add up? Was Betjeman sincere, satirical or merely spontaneous? Perhaps something of all three. In 1968 – prior to the full force of Betjeman's later television fame and laureateship – Summerson examined the enigmatic nature of his association with the subject of Victorian architecture, his occasional writings, the influence of his poems, but found it difficult to account for the 'enormous influence it has had'.[33] 'A better answer,' he suggested, 'may be simply the inflation of what was once a private joke, to which Betjeman's name came to be attached, into what can only be described as national humour. Back in the early Thirties, observation and classification of Victoriana was, indeed, a joke, shared here and there. It was a game of recognition, and such games tended to be wildly infectious. Then came the war and the new literacy, county guides, Pevsner, television; and the little private joke of *Architectural Review* circles of the early Thirties burst into the ocean in which, today, earnest scholarship, sheer silliness, poetic evocation, and crass nostalgia all go sailing.'[34]

Was it simply that the wind changed and Betjeman got stuck like it? Not entirely. He was, I believe, persuaded of the integrity of the work of Comper, Voysey and Baillie Scott and its inferences for the future of architecture, however startling it seemed to the readers of the *Architectural Review* when his articles first appeared, however jocose their origin. But in Comper's case Betjeman's enthusiasm backfired. By using him as a weapon to tease Pevsner, as well as to promote Comper's work, the reverse effect was achieved.

Matters came to a head in 1952 when St Cyprian's, Clarence Gate, was isolated for criticism *in London: Except the Cities of London and Westminster*, an early volume in Pevsner's *Buildings of England*. 'If there must be medieval imitation in the C20 it is here unquestionably done with joy and care. Beyond that appreciation can hardly go. There is no reason for the excesses of praise lavished on Comper's work by those who confound aesthetic with religious emotions.' This was the beginning of a process of denigration and dismissal in the rest of the series which (despite a warm description of St Mary's, Wellingborough in the Northamptonshire volume) has done more lasting damage to Comper's reputation than any other influence. For that, Betjeman is to blame.[35]

And what of Sir Giles Gilbert Scott, Sir Edward Maufe and others so enthusiastically vilified in Betjeman's letters to Comper? As early as 1938 Betjeman was writing flattering letters to Scott about his father, George Gilbert Scott Junior, while disparaging him (Sir Giles) to Comper.[36] Comper had lent him the younger Scott's *Essay on the History of English Church Architecture Prior to the Separation from the Roman Obedience* (1881). Comper thought it was the best book written about church architecture, it had great influence on his thought, and he taught Betjeman to believe that the author was the greatest of the Scott architectural dynasty. After the war, Betjeman made up to Sir Giles Gilbert Scott because he wanted to write a book about the younger Scott. Nothing came of this plan and it has been left to Gavin Stamp to bring it to completion. In 1950 Betjeman asked Scott to submit a testimonial to the Prime Minister in support of Comper's knighthood.

As for Maufe, some could not understand why Betjeman started to praise Guildford Cathedral so fulsomely in the early Seventies. In 1947 he had percipiently dismissed Maufe's work as 'genteelism'.[37] It seemed to them that he was running out of causes and pursuing into old age his desire to make mischief, tease and shock. 'He had a perverse empathy with the unfashionable …', suggests Mowl. 'If he could find out for himself a peculiar survival of the past, like Sir Edward Maufe's Guildford Cathedral, a custom or a person hovering on the edge of extinction, layered with textures, real or spiritual, of decay, then he was ardently for it.'[38]

In 1953 Betjeman met Maufe when they sat on the Royal Fine Art Commission. Candida Lycett Green believes that in time Betjeman had come to admire his work. In 1974 Maufe and his wife Prudence were given the full treatment:

> Don't bother to answer this letter for it is in the nature of a Collins to thank you for your church of St Thomas, Hanwell. I went there for the first time yesterday. … I was with my old friend Revd Harry Williams CR who was once Dean of Trinity and tutor to Prince Charles. We travelled in brilliant evening sunlight down the road to Brentford and there, on the right, was your noble brick tower of St Thomas. We pulled up, magnetised by the proportion and nobility of the exterior, braved the traffic, found the church locked but the vicar, a charming man called Sharp, was having tea in your neat vicarage and took us in. He did it most cunningly and dramatically, for we came in at the south-east corner and he switched on the lights so that we suddenly saw the whole mysterious length of the south aisle. Then he made us walk to the west and see the whole church. It is *terrific*: all done with scale: the decoration is beautifully subordinated and subtle, as is the skin of the brick-work on the outside with its bands of red and purple. The chancel is so grand that it has accommodated that huge reredos from St Thomas's, [Portman Square]. I see a lot of Guildford in the church. I loved the font, the Moira Forsyth glass and the statue of our Lady given by Prudence and safe in the niche in the Lady Chapel.
>
> As we stood on the vicarage lawn and in the fading sunlight saw the great bulk of the church and the north chapel and tall campanile, we realised we were in the presence of a masterpiece. I shall always remember it. I was proud to be able to tell the vicar that I had had a delicious luncheon with you both last autumn. It was good to know that while we are all here, that glorious, simple, noble and original church is still rising over its red suburb and lifting up the hearts of thousands.[39]

Was this written tongue in cheek as yet another private joke? Did he mean it? Was he simply being kind? Or was it, where Comper was concerned, the exasperating dislocation of one who mocks what he loves, and, once the laughter has died, finds that he has done more harm than good? But perhaps Betjeman's surprising enthusiasm for Maufe should be seen as an act of atonement. In later life he regretted his youthful arrogance. 'I was terribly arrogant as a young man,' he wrote. 'I regret very much having attacked certain people at that time, particularly people in architecture who were probably only trying to do their best. I see now that anybody who is true to his own ideas is probably all right.'[40]

Betjeman was so bound up with the exuberant splendour of Comper's work that he hardly came to terms with his ideas or theory of architecture. He was acutely perceptive and had a seeing eye, but he was not an analytical thinker and he despised those who were. At the same time, he recognised that some who pursue an academic study of the history of art and architecture have little love of the subject, still less aesthetic sensibility. Research without passion was abhorrent to him. Perhaps it is unfair to blame him for being what he was: an irresistible populariser, poet, and critic with a champagne sense of humour, who, nonetheless, wanted to be taken seriously. And it has to be said that Comper would have preferred his work, rather than his words, to be heeded, even though one cannot be understood without the other.

Betjeman was excited by the proposed publication of *Of the Atmosphere of a Church* as a pamphlet in 1946: 'I am *enchanted* to hear that the SPCK is going to print *Of the Atmosphere of a Church*. Eeles will be jealous. He is the man who is the authority on the atmosphere of churches!'[41] The paper was published on the recommendation of Professor E. C. Ratcliffe, an eminent Cambridge liturgiologist. When Betjeman reviewed it in *The Times Literary Supplement* in 1947, in company with the Incorporated Church Building Society's *Fifty Modern Churches*, and Ernest Short's patchy collection of essays, *Post-War Church Building* (a work in which Eeles was much involved),[42] Comper and F. C. Eden were isolated as the only church architects who could be compared to the Victorians. Comper's essay was described as an 'inspiration', frequently quoted and used as a means of defining tradition, dismissing jazz-modern and the poverty of modern church design with the exception of 'the sound work of such men as Harold Gibbons, Dykes Bower and Sir Charles Nicholson'.

Betjeman never properly took into consideration Comper's essential debt to European travel, erudition and reading. But Comper cannot be understood without recognizing its effects nor without following the most decisive itineraries of his annual journeys abroad. Pevsner, of course, did, and it was the Mediterranean influence that he least liked. Betjeman fell back on enthusiasm and descriptive writing rather than analysis. Compare his sparkling account of Cosham with Hammond's at the beginning of this essay:

He has left the lace-like Perpendicular of St Cyprian's, Clarence Gate (1903), and reached what he calls 'unity by inclusion'. His church of St Philip,

Cosham, (1937), is an example. It is a vaulted white parallelogram built for a golden altar under a ciborium (or baldachino) with a lady chapel east of it. The columns of the church are Classic, the vaulting which springs from them Gothic, and the windows are deliberate eighteenth-century Gothic. The font, as in most Comper churches, is the chief feature at the west end, and its gilded cover leads the eye up to the gay organ case in the west gallery. As in all Comper churches there are chairs and stalls but no pews. His work is distinguished by its remarkable sense of scale, and its colours – rose-pink predominating, white walls, golden woodwork – the whole effect of a transparency of coloured richness to which his many imitators cannot attain.[43]

Most will prefer it, as poetically it brings the church to life and makes you want to see it, but there is little recognition of St Philip's liturgical plan and significance. Unlike Hammond, Betjeman concentrated on aesthetics. Both balance each other, but all he acknowledged is that 'He builds a church from the altar outwards.' This was an understanding uninfluenced by the principles of the liturgical movement and he should not be judged by what he did not fully understand. What Mowl has described as Betjeman's 'glorious technicolored prose' has, despite its powerful contemporary influence, in the end relegated Comper to ridicule.

Maybe too much heavy weather has been made of these difficulties, but their inconvenient truth cannot be ignored. There is no pleasure in writing about Betjeman's failings, but they belong to a sketch, however slight, of his attachment to Comper. Even allowing for a change of mind, it is Betjeman's two-facedness that offends. His friendship with Comper exposed the complexity and contradictions of his character. Betjeman found Comper funny, and laughed at him (as he did at most of his friends), but he was enchanted by his company and charm, had genuine affection for him and treated him with generosity and kindness. Comper had a touching confidence in him, and was unaware of Betjeman's friendly mockery behind his back. They sometimes thought alike and had in common a similar sense of humour. Both could be great haters. Voysey died in 1941, Baillie Scott in 1945; thereafter, only Comper survived from the original triumvirate rediscovered by Betjeman in the Thirties. He lived for another fifteen years, during which time Betjeman's friendship remained constant. Betjeman shared Comper's religious convictions, recognised him as an artist, found work for him, and his sympathetic attention enabled his genius to flower. He introduced him to his friends and helped to give him an interesting and happy old age. Their friendship has resulted in much reflected glory. But perhaps it would have done Comper more good if it had been Piper, rather than Betjeman, who had championed him. Piper was never reconciled to Sir Giles, Sir Edward, or genteelism, nor was he intimidated by academic rigour. What Piper could not have given him was the emotional confidence that consoled Comper's old age. In his last letter to Betjeman, written in a frail hand when he was ninety-five,

Comper said, 'Yes, the years are passing on ever more quickly as we grow older and friendship grows deeper and amongst the chiefest among them do I value yours.'[44]

V

In 1957 Hammond gave a talk on the Third Programme, 'Contemporary Architecture and the Church', in which he took up the theme of *The Artist and the Church* and praised the post-war gains in church architecture on the Continent achieved by the liturgical movement. He favourably compared them with what he perceived to be the timidity and retrogression of contemporary English church architecture. He excepted the work of George Pace in the chapel of the University of Ibadan, Nigeria, and launched an attack on conventional Anglican taste embodied in the antiquarian legacy of Eeles which continued after his death in 1954.

> Everywhere we find the same uncritical acceptance of late-medieval tradition, the same nostalgic regard for the Middle Ages as the Christian era *par excellence* … This Gothic fixation reveals itself in the furnishing of our churches with their rood beams, their 'English' altars, their Gothic chairs and lecterns – all the stock in trade of the ecclesiastical furnisher …. It is also apparent in the persistence of a plan which … is equally at variance with the new understanding of the Mass which has found expression in so many fine contemporary churches in Europe and America.[45]

The future of church art and architecture, he believed, was heralded by the Crucifixion and Virgin and Child at Northampton, by Piper's windows for Oundle School Chapel, the work of Pace, and Maguire and Murray at St Paul's, Bow Common. There was no attention paid to Comper's insistence on the primacy of beauty. The results of Hammond's strategy lie all around us. His ideology, and what grew from it, has bedevilled the natural development of sacred art, for which Comper pointed a way forward, in the same way that Dearmer had earlier stultified evolution by applied antiquarianism and derivative aesthetics. The irony today is that Hammond's principles have become as tired and formulaic as those pursued by Eeles, as the pages of *Church Building* painfully and wearisomely demonstrate.

The problem is not, of course, confined to Anglicanism; the British dilemma is only part of a greater whole. Betjeman, in his letter to Comper of 1944, had identified in society 'the unchanging and spiritual for which your architecture stands and in which you stand head and shoulders above any other architect. The function of a church does not alter.'[46] That confident immutability was soon to change. The Anglican liturgical movement was a provincial offshoot of a more powerful Catholic force for change on the Continent. It had a Benedictine source, was deeply rooted in patristic, biblical and liturgical scholarship and in its early application was carefully considered. After the Second Vatican Council of 1962–5 the fruits of the movement were universally applied by mandate to an unsuspecting Church which was unprepared to receive them. The compasses began to point in all directions. Idealistic and soundly based in scholarship though the principles of the move-ment were, they led in Northern Europe and America to a puritan rage which, like Occam's razor brutally wielded, swept out and left bare the household of the Catholic imagination. More destruction was achieved in the name of reform on a universal scale than the entire results of the iconoclasm of the Protestant Reformation. Beauty was repudiated in the name of *aggiornamento*, bringing up to date. In a Pastoral Letter, read in Lent 1965, Cardinal Heenan compared this activity with post-war slum clearance.[47] It was only in the Mediterranean, parts of Central, Eastern and Southern Europe, in Central and South America and in rare instances elsewhere that the application of the reforms was characterised by continuous architectural development. It is only now that the Church is beginning to recover from the effects.

In the Church of England, Pace and Robert Potter, a pupil of W. H. Randoll Blacking, himself a pupil of Comper, attempted to apply the principles of *Of the Atmosphere of a Church* in their early work, distorted by perverse artistry which made them almost meaningless. The Majestas would not have been chosen as the subject of Sir Jacob Epstein's sculpture in Llandaff Cathedral nor for Sir Graham Sutherland's tapestry in Coventry Cathedral if Comper had not insisted in his papers on its iconographical application. Powerful though they are as works of modern religious art they betray their source. Few but the fading remnant of a half-remembered *avant garde*, the preservationist and the architectural historian actually like modern churches. The high hopes of the New Churches Research Group and the Birmingham Institute have resulted in a rash of mediocre churches and the ruination of many old ones which depress their congregations, starve them of transcendence in worship, and deprive them of a sense of place. 'A merciful Provid-ence,' wrote Brian Brindley, 'has ordained that high-alumina cement, blue asbestos, leaky flat roofs and general building "fatigue" – to say nothing of ugliness and unlovability – will ensure that few of them survive to celebrate their centenaries.'[48]

VI

To many modern readers *Of the Atmosphere of a Church* may seem to be an anachronism. It deplores plays, concerts, and women acting in churches, children's corners, propaganda sold in tract cases, the invasion of commercial-ism in cathedrals, over-lit churches, inorganic gilding and colour, pale wood surfaces and Modern church architecture and design. All and worse have become part of the fabric of contemporary church life. Comper's ideal was King's College Chapel, Cambridge. 'Alone perhaps of any ancient English church, King's has preserved its atmosphere; and it is because of these two things, which there are one, viz., colour and lighting …. Of King's Chapel it may be said that there is not one pane of perfectly clear transparent glass and this is what largely accounts for the atmosphere … King's Chapel is as much favoured by night as by day, for it is still lighted only by candles, the authorities having tried and rejected electric lighting.'[49] He wrote of the era of Eric Milner-White, the Dean of King's, who had used him in the chapel and went on to use him at York Minster. Would he say the same today in a building vulgarised by artificial lighting and coarse sanctuary furniture, stripped at the east end of its dark panelling, the medieval floor-levels as laid down in the will of King Henry vi destroyed, the despoliation by Sir Martyn Beckett for the intrusion of a painting of the Nativity by Rubens which has resulted in a permanent war between two works of art? I suspect not.

Comper described a world that has gone. A world which Anthony O'Hear has identified as one 'in which Latin, plainchant, the Book of Common Prayer, the King James Bible were all dignified, mysterious, resonant, powerful and historically sanctified symbols of a transcendent reality.'[50] But it would be shallow to relegate *Of the Atmosphere of a Church* to the half-light of archaic curiosities. Some will see it simply as reminiscent of a displaced period of Anglican history governed by bourgeois values. Hammond and many of the English promoters of Modernism also came from that world and turned it upside down. Others will acknowledge that behind its period interest lie constant values.

Comper's profoundly Catholic imaginative insight has lessons that go far beyond the period of history in which it was executed and the Church for which it was designed. His work and theories point to a future where the threads of continuity might re-emerge in church architecture new born, made one with the Christian centuries. Comper, more than any other English church architect of the twentieth century, endeavoured with passionate conviction to penetrate to the very core of Western civilization by studying the church art and architecture of Europe to find there spiritual values applicable to his own time. The ideological *impasse* in which modern church architecture sleeps could be broken without compromising the integrity of its liturgical principles by applying Comper's understanding of the indispensability of beauty and the legacy of Christian tradition. His theories have hardly been tested since his death in a way that he would have recognised. The only architect who came close to them was Stephen Dykes Bower, for whom beauty in architecture was imperative. All that is needed is the courage and independence of mind to follow his direction, recover beauty, and learn the lessons taught by St Philip's, Cosham. Comper's day is yet to come.

1. Peter Hammond, *Liturgy and Architecture*, London 1960, 28.

2. *ibid*, 75–6.

3. Peter Anson, 'The work of John Ninian Comper: a pioneer of the modern liturgical revival', *Pax*, 27 (1937), 177–84; John Betjeman, 'A note on J. N. Comper: heir to Butterfield and Bodley', *Architectural Review*, 85 (1939), 74–82; Anthony Symondson SJ, 'John Betjeman and the cult of J. N. Comper', *Journal of the Thirties Society*, 7 (1991), 3–13, 52.

4. Elain Harwood, 'Liturgy and architecture: the development of the centralised eucharistic space', *The Twentieth Century Church: Twentieth Century Architecture 3*, Journal of the Twentieth Century Society, 1998, 52.

5. J. N. Comper, *Of the Atmosphere of a Church*, London 1947, 9–10 (or see below in this reprint, page 234).

6. J. N. Comper, 'Further thoughts on the English altar, or practical considerations on the planning of a modern church', *Transactions of the St Paul's Ecclesiological Society*, 10, pt 2 (1933), 32.

7. J. N. Comper, *op cit*, 9.

8. Letter from Comper to Irvine, 16 October 1948. (Unless otherwise stated, this letter and others quoted in the essay are from a private collection.)

9. J. N. Comper, *ibid*.

10. Letter from JB to JNC, Vigil of St Thomas, 1939.

11. Anthony Symondson SJ, 'Unity by inclusion: Sir Ninian Comper and the planning of a modern church', *The Twentieth Century Church, op cit*, 23.

12. Symondson, *ibid*, 24–6.

13. Hammond, *op cit*, 75.

14. *The Cicestrian: The Magazine of Chichester Theological College*, X, (68), (Michaelmas 1939), 103–4.

15. Letter from KT to JNC, 16 December 1939.

16. Letter from JB to JNC, *ibid*. Donald Findlay has defended Eeles's side of the enmity with Comper in *The Protection of Our English Churches: The History of the Council for the Care of Churches 1921–1996*, London 1996, 21–5, 45–7. He was not in full possession of the facts when he wrote it nor was he aware of the extent of Betjeman's part in encouraging it. New evidence has been presented in this essay. Betjeman and John Piper later sat on the Oxford Diocesan Advisory Committee, and Betjeman published pamphlets, promoting Comper's theories, for the Central Council and eventually sat on the main committee.

17. Letter from JB to JNC, *ibid*.

18. John Piper, *The Artist and the Church*, Exhibition Catalogue, London 1944, 3.

19. *ibid*, 4.

20. *ibid*, 3.

21. Letter from JB to JNC, 1 March 1943.

22. *op cit*, 12–13.

23. Letter from JB to JNC, 15 March 1943.

24. He refers to Sir Herbert Baker and Sir Reginald Blomfield.

25. Letter from JB to JNC, 15 March 1943.

26. Timothy Mowl, *Stylistic Cold Wars: Betjeman versus Pevsner*, London 2000, passim.

27. A. L. Rowse, 'Architectural contacts', *The Betjemanian*, 2, December 1990, 46.

28. Letter from John Summerson to Anthony Symondson, 23 February 1989.

29. The present scheme of lighting and decoration, in Mediterranean blue, was a misinterpretation of his father's intentions by J. Sebastian Comper in a restoration

of 1966–7. Comper had left them in their original dark Northern European tone despite the later developments in his work.

30. Letter from JB to JNC, 17 October 1943.

31. Letter from JB to JNC, 31 May 1948.

32. Letter from JB to JNC, 23 December 1945.

33. John Summerson, *Victorian Architecture: Four Studies in Evaluation*, New York and London, 1970, 16–17.

34. Summerson, *ibid*.

35. Anthony Symondson SJ, *The Life and Work of Sir Ninian Comper (1864–1960)*, London 1988, 3–4. Mowl also came to see this incident as central to the antagonism between Betjeman and Pevsner.

36. Candida Lycett Green (ed.), *John Betjeman: Letters*, I, 1926–1951, London 1994, 220.

37. John Betjeman, 'Church building', *The Times Literary Supplement*, 6 December 1947.

38. Mowl, *op cit*, 16.

39. Candida Lycett Green (ed.), *John Betjeman: Letters*, II, 1951–1984, London 1995, 477.

40. 'The lonely Laureate', unidentified article quoted in Lycett Green (ed.), *op cit*, 511.

41. Letter from JB to JNC, 12 December 1946.

42. Betjeman, *op cit*.

43. John Betjeman, 'A century of church building', *The Times Literary Supplement: Religious Books Section*, 27 April 1951, i–ii.

44. Letter from JNC to JB, 30 June 1959.

45. Peter Hammond, 'Contemporary architecture and the church', *The Listener*, 21 November 1957, 839.

46. Letter from JB to JNC, 15 March 1943.

47. Scott M. P. Reid (ed.), *A Bitter Trial: Evelyn Waugh and John Carmel, Cardinal Heenan, on the Liturgical Changes*, Curdridge 1996, 55.

48. Brian Brindley, 'Churches for twentieth century flocks', *The Catholic Herald*, 14 August 1998, 6.

49. J. N. Comper, *op cit*, 26–8.

50. Anthony O'Hear, *After Progress: Finding the Old Way Forward*, London 1999, 166.

Of the Atmosphere of a Church

J. Ninian Comper

PREFACE

THE FOLLOWING ARTICLE was written for *The Cicestrian* by invitation of the Principal of Chichester Theological College in 1939. At his suggestion S.P.C.K. undertook to publish it, but for various reasons, did not do so at that time. Now, some eight years of continuous study have added to its writer's convictions; but, with a few corrections, it seems to him best to leave it, such as it is, to speak for itself, merely adding the illustrations.*

Its appeal is, however, greatly strengthened by the accompanying plates; and he would emphasise its condemnation of plays in churches, in view of the importance recently laid upon them as one of the means to the Conversion of England.

---

*PUBLISHER'S NOTE. The original 1947 SPCK edition had eight illustrations. It is notable that none is referred to by Comper in his text. Two of the original illustrations are reproduced below (pages 237 and 239), and another, a plan of the fourth-century church at Theveste, on page 213 above. The other five illustrations were of various Comper churches, which are dicussed elsewhere in this volume, using the same or different illustrations: the plates were of the high altar of St Andrew's Cathedral, Aberdeen (the photograph on page 178 above); St Mary's, Wellingborough (two plates originally, those on pages 193 and 203 above); St Philip's, Cosham (two plates originally; that on page 169 above and one similar to that on page 167); the organ and font cover at Lound, Suffolk (discussed above, page 122).

Note: other footnotes in this chapter are from the original edition.

The introduction of women actors into churches would be a direct contradiction of the precise enactments of St Paul so lately and persuasively restated by Pope Pius X.

If, however, men and boys only are intended it is too high a standard to attain today without such a Choir School as at All Saints, Margaret Street, and the genius of Canon H. F. B. Mackay to train it. Boldly observing the rule and Shakespeare's example who conceived his matchless women characters to be acted by boys, he produced not only the Roman scenes from *Julius Caesar*, but the whole of *Twelfth Night*; and so perfect was the acting that it drew tears from Ellen Terry and Forbes Robertson. Needless to add, the plays were not in church, but in the parish hall.

The facts, however, are that plays in churches are indirectly ruled out with other late medieval abuses by the Book of Common Prayer, and directly by Canon 88 of the English Church, which reads as follows:

> The Churchwardens or Quest-men, and their assistants, shall suffer no plays, feasts, banquets, suppers, church-ales, drinkings, temporal courts, or leets, lay-juries, musters, or any other profane usage, to be kept in the church, chapel, or church-yard, neither the bells to be rung superstitiously upon holy-days or eves abrogated by the Book of Common Prayer, nor at any other times, without good cause to be allowed by the Minister of the place, and by themselves.

★   ★   ★   ★   ★

I

THE DOYEN OF FÉCAMP ABBEY, IN NORMANDY, years ago said to me of his church that it 'prays of itself'. It was a beautiful way of expressing what we mean when we say that a church has an atmosphere.

Kipling, to whom I quoted this, wrote me one of his inspired extravagances in a private letter in which he said what should be done to architects who 'restore' Cathedrals in order that 'we should be saved scraped and cleaned bones', and added 'There are very few churches which 'pray of themselves' 'when stripped out'. Since then the work of the cleaner and scraper has advanced in strides, and added to it is the violence of startling inorganic colour, which we see after the repainting of old wall frescoes, isolated arch mouldings, gilded bosses or other carving, or where an old shield has been picked out in garish tinctures – new patches on old garments.

Then there is the use of a church for lantern shows and for the revival of medieval plays. Whatever may be said in defence of the plays in churches in the middle ages, we forget that we cannot re-create the medieval atmosphere which made them possible. I doubt if they would be attempted on the continent today, even in those places which have a background, so to say, of reverence and tradition which does make possible some things which are still a long way from being possible with us.

And, what is this sort of museum which attracts the eye of the curious visitor in some chapel or at the end of an aisle? – It is a 'children's corner'. But why should we put children in a corner in their Father's House? I do not think they do so anywhere else. In France and in Italy the children still come in to pray where they will and to lay their offerings of flowers where they will. I remember an Epiphany at Siena (in 1888) when, even during the Cathedral High Mass, children were playing below the altar steps, like the cherubs before the throne of the Madonna and Child in pictures of the Renaissance, and, much later, I recall, standing in a crowd of worshippers at High Mass in Budapest, and seeing a child's balloon with a face painted on it floating above our heads.

These were instances of freedom within the limits of what destroys the atmosphere of worship.

The atmosphere of a church should be such as to hush the thoughtless voice. It once was so amongst ourselves and still is so in France even when the building may not be of arresting beauty. I have been rebuked for talking to the organist about his music within one of the doors of Dijon Cathedral, and I remember being told by the Vicar at Hughenden the year Disraeli died that if anyone spoke to him in the church he would take him out into the porch before he answered. Surely here today with all our new materialistic organizations we have lost something of the sense of what a church is.

'My Father's house is a house of prayer, but ye have made it a den of thieves.' It is a most stern saying; and as then, so now, it is commercialism that is at the bottom of these activities ('greed and careerism' as a modern writer has put it), though it may be disguised in such fine words that the users of them may not be conscious of it. 'The tables of the money changers' – have they not literally invaded some of our Cathedrals? And even when the money changers are not there, are we not reminded of the tables in visible shape in too many churches in England, both Anglican and Roman, for the sale of tracts of (often controversial) propaganda? Seldom are the books on these tables the Holy Gospels which I have seen in beautiful form at the west end of the Cathedral at Rheims.

But party propaganda and the sale of the Gospels (and even the preaching of the Gospel) is not the purpose of a church: for what is a church? – It is a building which enshrines the altar of Him who dwelleth not in temples made with hands and who yet has made there His Covenanted Presence on earth. It is the centre of Worship in every community of men who recognise Christ as the *Pantokrator*, the Almighty, the Ruler and Creator of all things; at its altar is pleaded the daily Sacrifice in complete union with the Church Triumphant in Heaven, of which He is the one and only Head, the High Priest for ever after the order of Melchisedech.

There is then no such thing as a Protestant church. A church is of its very nature Catholic, embracing all things. There are Protestant Meeting Houses for preaching, and for praying and hymn-singing in common, and they are not to be despised; but if they are more than a plain room, they have become a meaningless imitation of that from which of set purpose they broke away.

A church built with hands, as we are reminded at every Consecration and Dedication Feast, is the outward expression here on earth of that spiritual Church built of living stones, the Bride of Christ, *Urbs beata Jerusalem*, which stretches back to the foundation of the world and onwards to all eternity. With her Lord she lays claim to the whole of His Creation and to every philosophy and creed and work of man which His Holy Spirit has inspired. And so the temple here on earth, in different lands and in different shapes, in the East and in the West, has developed or added to itself fresh forms of beauty and, though it has suffered from iconoclasts and destroyers both within and without, and perhaps nowhere more than in this land, it has never broken with the past: it has never renounced its claim to continuity.

To enter therefore a Christian church is to enter none other than the House of God and the Gate of Heaven. It is to leave all strife, all disputes of the manner of Church government and doctrine outside – 'Thou shalt keep them secretly in Thy tabernacle from the strife of tongues' – and to enter here on earth into the Unity of the Church Triumphant in Heaven. It cannot be otherwise, since He Himself, who is the Temple of it, the Lamb slain from the foundation of the world, is there also. Such a conception of a church, however faintly realised, must put to shame the quarrels of Catholic Christians, who profess the same creeds but set up Church against Church.

It must, moreover, reduce to folly those terms of 'self-expression' and 'the expression of the age', used to cover what is merely such incapacity and ugliness as every age has in turn rejected. Is an artist, the instrument of the Creator Spirit, to express *himself* in building the Temple of Christ? Is there such a supremacy of goodness, beauty and truth in the present age as to mark it as distinct from the past, and demand that we invent a new expression of it? The purpose of a church is not to express the age in which it was built or the individuality of its designer. Its purpose is to move to worship, to bring a man to his knees, to refresh his soul in a weary land. This would seem to be the Creator's purpose towards man in giving him the beauty of nature, and it should be the purpose of all art. In art man partakes in this purpose of his Maker and objectively he brings the best of all that He has given him to create of beauty (in liturgy, poetry, music, ceremonial, architecture, sculpture and painting) to be the expression of his worship. For mankind in the mass the neglect of beauty spells the hardness and narrowness either of a puritan or of a materialist; though the saint and the mystic may pass directly, without the aid of external beauty of art, and even of nature, to God Himself.

The note of a church should be, not that of novelty, but of eternity. Like the Liturgy celebrated within it, the measure of its greatness will be the measure in which it succeeds in eliminating time and producing the atmosphere of the heavenly worship. This is the characteristic of the earliest art of the Church, in liturgy in architecture and in plastic decoration, and it is the tradition of all subsequent ages. The Church took over what is eternal in the Jewish and Greek temples, adapting and perfecting it to her use, developing and adding to it in unbroken sequence, and evolving new forms, some which came to stay and some which needed correction. For the religion of Christ knows no moment of perfection here on earth although it retains all perfections to which man has attained and rejects all imperfections of barbaric or evil days. It should have no use for the incapacities and crudities of primitive society in the invitation of which some take refuge today, this is rather a time to look to the rock whence we are hewn, *respondere natalibus*. While we cling to every loveliest form that man's work has produced just as we cling to every loveliest flower of nature, we must again make the architecture of our churches in complete harmony with the liturgy, as Rome has done so notably of late for its music. And yet again, just as no moment is perfect, so no reform is perfect, for it will always go a little too far. The admission of later music and a stringed orchestra for the ordinary of the mass at Barcelona on Easter Day, 1935, in addition to the unaccompanied plainsong and contrapuntal music, was no contradiction of the new ruling. For is there not room in the Kingdom of Eternity here for all manner of music that it has entered into the heart of man to conceive as existing there?

And so it should be with architecture, the other handmaid of liturgy. No beautiful style should be excluded. But the plan, the 'layout', of the church must first he in accord with the requirements of the liturgy and the particular needs of those who worship within it, and the imagery must express the balanced measure of the Faith; and for guidance in both we must look to tradition. There is no need to apologise for doing so in architecture, any more than in music, unless we need apologise for the guidance of tradition in the interpretation of the New Testament and the creeds of the Church. There are those who do so apologise, and for them tradition in the arts has naturally no appeal. They are consistent; since modernism in art is the natural expression of modernism in doctrine, and it is quite true they are both the expression of the age, but of one side of it only. Rome has condemned modernist doctrine but has not yet condemned its expression in art. The attraction of the modernistic* is still too strong. It is flattering to think that, like the ages of Faith, this age can produce a new style of architecture. But the real strength of

---

*It may he useful to define the difference between what is modernistic and what is truly modern, and I cannot do it better than by quoting Mr John Betjeman: 'A modernistic Church,' he writes, 'is often a brick building which apes with its outline and proportions a steel construction. It is sham engineering. King's College Chapel, Cambridge, was genuine engineering in stone and glass, an aeroplane is genuine engineering – both products are genuinely modern in their respective times. But a new church in what is called the "modern style" is often no different in its plan and

the appeal of the modernistic lies not, I think, in any claim which it may sometimes make to beauty but rather in a supposed antagonism between the arts of beauty and, as a correspondent expresses it, 'the masterful and pervading influence of science. What is out of place in pure and applied science' (and beauty is assumed to be out of place in it), 'seems an intrusion on all serious work whatever today. What is wrong is the breach with tradition which no one would have ventured upon but for the overwhelming appearance, awesome power, and obvious superiority of science to all else, applied as it is now to every side of human life. Science was a very big thing in the nineteenth century, but tradition could still hold its own. Today everything is puny compared with science, and science is everywhere.'

Really there is no antagonism. The trouble is simply that art, which in its great days was scientific, has today ceased to be so, and one of the requirements for its recovery is that it should become scientific again and thereby be in harmony with the best spirit of the age. The man who sets to work to design an aeroplane or a motor cat has no self-conscious strivings to express himself or his age, like the pathetic architects and artists of today. His one business is to make it go and, if possible, to go one better, and he would not be so mad as to think he could do this without knowing the tradition of all that went before. Moreover, if he fails, there is no question of his failure; he cannot hide it by fine words and theories. Let us apply this to architecture and have an end of humbug. After all, deep in the human heart is the sense of beauty and when a man sees it he will respond unless his eye is hypnotised by words. And so, first of all, the mists and fogs of theory and fashion must be cleared away. Science is not the enemy: rather it is to science we must go.

And do we want originality? I quote Dr Inge: 'What we call originality is generally the power to see old things in a new light – it is the reading of some open secret, as we know it to be in the natural Sciences.' And the

---

construction from the dullest Victorian Gothic church in brick; the effect is "unusual" but not truly modern, and is obtained by mouldings and shapes and colours which are the result of indigestion after a visit to Stockholm Town Hall, and the *neue Baukunst* of Germany. This is "modernistic." Some young man has thought that he would invent new mouldings, new window shapes, new pews, new light-fittings and in his anxiety to avoid the admittedly bad "churchiness" of ecclesiastical fittings, he has gone to the other extreme and produced an arrogant decoration of his own – because he is not an artist, really, but a professional man taught in a school. Only a consummate artist can produce mouldings, shapes, and details, which are more suitable than those used for centuries in Europe from Greece and Sicily to East Anglia. The sun still shines at the same angle on us and at the same intervals. You cannot suddenly run up a new style in an office with the aid of a prize-medallist from the Architectural Association.

'The trouble is that a "modernistical" as opposed to a "modern" architect, mistakes unusual detail for the truly modern. The thing that matters is the function of the church. It is the adaptation of the plan of a church to contemporary needs which should be the first consideration of a modern architect. "Style" is a side issue.'

'The Pilgrim Entering the Church'.
A restoration of the Church of
St Felix of Nola by Rohault de
Fleury in 'La Messe', reproducing a
ciborium upon a bronze medal of the
fourth or fifth century in the Vatican.

(One of the illustrations in the
original edition of this essay.)

correspondent whom I have quoted before sums up: 'What passes for originality today is at its best no more difficult to accomplish and is less *original* than what a man does who not only has studied the past, but bears the past within him when he is at work on some quite modern need.'

II

Knowledge of Tradition is the first requisite for the creation of an atmosphere in a church and I should like in illustration of what is said above to touch upon some of its main details.

In the fourth century we find fully established, so as to postulate an earlier origin, the 'layout' of the plan of a church which is suited to the needs of today in a way in which the medieval plan, to which we in England still adhere amidst all vagaries of styles, is not suited, developed as it was for monastic use. The main feature of the early plan is the position of the altar, one might say, in the midst of the worshippers, and not separated from them by any choir but only by a very open screen, or merely by low *cancelli*. This may be seen in the unaltered plan of the ruins of the North African churches, and, most worthy of note, a return to it in principle may be seen in Spain from the end of the fifteenth century onwards. For there, while keeping the medieval arrangement of the altar against a great solid screen, they put the choir westwards leaving space for the body of the worshippers between it and the altar.

And inseparable from the primitive plan of the open altar is the *Ciborium* over it. It has survived in Italy, Dalmatia and in other Mediterranean countries unto this day. It survived also the advent of Gothic architecture, until the high reredos was introduced and the altar was set against a wall or solid screen, when the *Ciborium* was, so to speak, taken to pieces. Its canopy, was always kept in one form or another, and sometimes also, its isolated columns with the curtains between them; sometimes the curtains were hung on projecting wands without the columns. There is, however, no need to be historically shocked by the restoration of a *Ciborium* in its original form to a gothic church. A metal *Ciborium* of the thirteenth century may still be seen over the high altar at Gerona in Spain, and later examples exist over side altars elsewhere. The *Ciborium* above the high altar, with the tabernacle hanging against it, is assumed in the *Magdalen Pontifical* (ascribed to Canterbury and the second half of the twelfth century), and it was restored by Henry VII to Westminster in his new Lady Chapel. A late classical form of *Ciborium* was designed by Wren for St Paul's, and in the early eighteenth century another was set up in the chapel of Trinity College, Cambridge. An early form was revived by Pearson in Victorian times at Peterborough and Perth Cathedrals, and there are better modern revivals by J. D. Sedding in two parish churches in London. At the present moment I am engaged on a richer version of the Cosham *Ciborium* for the Cathedral choir I am adding to the eighteenth-century gothic St Andrew's, Aberdeen; and another, more classical in form, is part of the accepted plans which I have made for the Cathedral enlargement of the Georgian All Saints, Derby. It is worth mention that in strict ecclesiastical language a *Ciborium* and a *Baldacchino* are not the same thing. This is noted by Dr Rinaldo Pilkington, a Chaplain of the Cathedral of Florence, in *La Chiesa e il suo arredemanto* (Turin, 1936). The canopy is called a *Baldacchino* when made only of woven stuff (because the richest stuffs came from Baghdad, which is *Baldaccho* in Italian), and is either suspended or, as sometimes, combined with a dossal. It is in fact this which was condemned by the St Barnabas, Pimlico Judgement, and not the *Ciborium*. It is the permanence of the *Ciborium* through the ever changing forms of architecture that I would indicate. Indeed the origin of the *Ciborium* is pre-Christian. It is possible that it stood over the great image of Diana at Ephesus as it is shown in a recent model of 1932; and quite certainly it is covered by the 'Ornaments' of the English Church in 1548.

Against the ceiling of the *Ciborium* was the suspended tabernacle. We have documentary evidence of it in the sixth century, if we have not yet found inescapable proof of its being earlier. Thus the altar and the abiding covenanted Presence were the centre of the church; and the centre of its imagery was, not the Rood, but the great figure of the *Majestas*, i.e., of our Lord enthroned, above the altar. This we can still see in perfection in mosaics of Sicily of the twelfth century.

The distinctively medieval conception of the altar and the Rood loft is indeed beautiful if adequately treated, in the setting of an exquisite Gothic

A restoration by Rohault de Fleury of St John the Evangelist's. (Ravenna, fifth century.) Showing the ciborium above the confessio *and behind an open screen, somewhat similar in plan to Raphael's drawing of Old St Peter's, Rome.*

(One of the illustrations in the original edition of this essay.)

building and its wealth of painted glass. None would grudge an individual preference for it and freedom to attain it for who so can. But the old way of concentration upon the altar itself by the *Ciborium* would seem the better way. Nothing has ever so combined magnificence with simplicity – nothing so separates the altar from everything else in the building and gives it such prominence that we see at once that it was to contain this that the church was built. And if we realise this, may it not be that we have something new to do today, as Spain had in the early sixteenth century, but in a manner of our own? Why not adapt the great tradition of our glorious east windows to the service of the figure of our Lord enthroned in larger scale than life and dominating the church and still, it may be, appearing above the Rood over a screen, but with the altar beneath a *Ciborium* and the east window, perhaps at the length of a Lady Chapel, behind it, and the worshippers brought all round it? Why not combine once again, as has been done before, but in a new way, the Greek and the Gothic? Such in fact has been my own development from St Cyprian's, Marylebone, through St Mary's, Wellingborough, and the (unfinished) All Saints Sisters' Chapel, near St Albans, to the simpler church of St Philip, Cosham, at Portsmouth.

It has been allowed to none, I believe, to record the exact appearance of the Parthenon when Iktinos and Phidias had finished their work but we know it was built for and dominated by the great image of the virgin Athene within it, which cost more than the whole building. We know too that when the Parthenon, still in its pristine beauty and robbed only of its great image, became indeed the temple of the Virgin – 'Our Lady of Athens' – the place of the image was taken by a *Ciborium* over the Christian Altar. And so the highest achievement man had ever reached in architecture was predestined and ready for its perfect use. Christianity made it her own and saved it from death. She brought the life of revealed religion into that which was the ultimate human perfection and which without that life could have gone no further. Rome added her material engineering to it, but could create nothing higher. It was left for Christianity to absorb the best of Greece and Rome, and, again borrowing the pointed arch from the East (as Greece before her had done), to soar with it into heights unknown before, though not without some losses. But henceforth architecture could never be final, never at rest, though in every finest achievement giving rest to the human soul and so partaking of the Divine.

III

Now with regard to rules. I would ask, is the prescript of the Ornaments Rubric – or the prescript of the Sacred Congregation of Rites in Rome – ever intended to be followed literally everywhere and in every particular? Are they both not rather meant as a guide and as an authority by which a serious, or a too careless, disregard of them can be checked? And, seeing that we have neither so much learning nor such a long tradition as Rome, would it not be well if at least we followed her example in the liberty which she gives? The rigid requirement of Faculties, based on the contradictory and sometimes unconvincing opinions of Advisory Committees and Chancellors, are no more than a source of irritation because they carry no intrinsic weight, and where they try to prescribe in matters of taste they go beyond Rome herself. I incline to the idea that the Advisory Committees should do what they were formed to do, viz., what the State control of our churches would do, and that the activities which have been added were better dropped, as indeed I hope they will be in proportion as the Committees gather experience.

Many have felt that an authoritative rule based on the antiquarian findings of 1548, did neither convince nor satisfy, and from such individual interpretations some have turned to equally individual acceptance of the clear-cut handbooks of the Roman Archdiocese of Westminster. But in truth, if we follow what lies behind both, no ecclesiastical authority will quarrel with us, and no Catholic authority will wish to make us all of one pattern. That is reserved for ecclesiastical fashion which has created church furnishers and architects who will set up what they call 'English altars' alike in every ancient cathedral and parish church and in the most modernist of new buildings, quite independently of suitability of position and surroundings. Our need is to break away from fashions, whether the modernist fashion of the moment or the persistent medievalism which survives them all; and, if it be possible, without the tragic consequence of creating another fashion.

Take the detail of altar lights. There is the idea that six candles on the altar are Roman and two are English. But note what Edmund Bishop tells us, viz., that two were the universal use of Christendom until the lack of space in the strait days of the Avignon Captivity which caused the seven candlesticks of the Roman Orders to he placed upon the altar instead of in front of it. The English Church requiring two and two only upon the altar is merely continuing the universal custom which Rome then broke and we followed suit for some three centuries only till we turned in this to Catholic practice at the Reformation. It is a sad irony that we should break from it in breaking our rule today, and breaking at the same time, by keeping six candles always on the altar, what is the strict Roman rule. Then look at Spain. There as elsewhere today the use at a Low Mass is two candles. But at Huesca in 1935, as in other Spanish Cathedrals, there were six for a High Mass on a festival and four on the previous day, and out of service-time none. And this is, I believe, not at variance with the Roman rule but rather a more strict interpretation of the ceremonial, as well as being in agreement with late medieval use. It is the practice of leaving six candles on the altar always, whether used or not, and adding two or more when required for lesser occasions that seems to be irregular, as indeed it is scarcely reasonable.* And different uses may still be found, such as the six candles on the steps, three at each end of the altar and none upon it, at Chartres and, as I observed quite recently, at Dreux also; the only detail which differs from medieval use is that the candles at that time seem to have been of an odd number generally and not only the seven for the Bishop still prescribed. The arrangement at Seville was, I noted, four on the north side and three on the south.

Another instance of a supposed conflict between English and Roman use is the method of Reservation. The 'hanging pyx' of English inventories is spoken of as if it were different from the 'tabernacle' as now prescribed by Rome, the essential of which is the veil all round it, *'tabernaculum* – a tent,' as Cardinal Bourne once insisted to me, agreeing that it is the suspended tabernacle let down upon the altar and fixed there. The only difference is its position permanently upon the altar and not above it. What is out of order is the cupboard form of tabernacle, whether on the altar or apart from it. The suspended tabernacle is not out of order in the Roman Church, but special permission must be obtained for it where it has not been continually in use, as it has been in certain places in France. I have been told of a definite case in which it is hoped to obtain leave to introduce it in the Roman Communion in England. The monks of Solesme resumed its use when they returned to France. Unfortunately, their whole high altar is of ugly modernistic design, but the use is admirable. They told me that they reserved only for the sick; and, in the beautiful old transept chapels at mass, we noticed that communion

---

*Cf. Dr Rinaldo Pilkington, of Florence Cathedral, in his recent work *La Chiesa e il suo arredamento*, p. 50.

was given from the paten and that, as afterwards explained to us, the serving monk collected the wafers at the offertory from intending communicants in a small silver pyx. I cannot refrain from mentioning the beautiful cut of their full chasubles like those of the finest old effigies. The tabernacle at the high altar was used also for 'Benediction' and we saw it descend and ascend by an electrical arrangement such as I had made at All Saints, Margaret Street. The practical and important point about the 'suspension' is that it enables the tabernacle, while it is in the central position of honour and separated from the actual table of the altar at which the Holy Sacrifice is offered, to be reached without the need of climbing up to it. This must have been unavoidable in the case of the beautiful renaissance examples of aumbries high up in the altar screens of Portugal and Italy. An example may he seen in the Victoria and Albert Museum in the reconstructed chapel from the church of Santa Chiara, Florence. Nor was it always an aumbry in the reredos, or wall. The tabernacle of St Mary Major in Rome lifted high above the Papal altar by great bronze angels is a case in point. The position of the tabernacle high up above the altar, and more particularly if it is suspended, does moreover suggest its immaterial nature, let down as it were from heaven, as St John describes the Holy City, the new Jerusalem.

IV

No observance of rules even in these most important details on which I have touched can in itself produce an atmosphere. Colour plays a large part in that, and lighting still more. It is in Spain that this can best be learnt, and our nearest approach to it is King's Chapel in Cambridge. Alone perhaps of any ancient English church, King's has preserved its atmosphere; and it is because of these two things, which there are one, viz., colour and lighting. To give a point to my meaning, perhaps the telling of my own experience is pardonable and unavoidable. I have worked all day in a church decorating in gold and colour and felt a deep despair, when suddenly, with the evening light, what before had seemed so hopeless became beautiful. This happened so often that I began to think: and then my later visits to Spain brought it home to me, completing my understanding of Milton's lines: 'storied windows richly dight, shedding a dim religious light' – not the darkness of a St Barnabas, Pimlico, before the whole church was ruthlessly 'improved' – from which it was almost pardonable to revolt, nor the darkness of some of the altered and 'restored' Spanish churches like León, nor yet of Chartres – but literally 'a dim religious light', like the light of early morning or of the evening when the Lord God walks in the garden. It may have its shafts from the rising or setting sun breaking through the trees, but not the even all-over glare of midday. Apply this lesson from nature to a church, and it will be seen why decoration cannot look well in a strong and evenly distributed light. When the painted glass of our churches was smashed and the gold and colour of their altars and screens destroyed, the substituted clear glass and the plain oak and marble monuments, with slight touches of heraldic colour, had an effect of simple beauty not inharmonious with the Book of Common Prayer in its severest interpretation. The church indeed had an atmosphere, but it was largely that of the outside and still beautiful world of trees and buildings seen through its windows; and moreover curtains shaded the too full blaze of the sun. But directly the return is made to richly decorated altars and screens, all is out of gear, and it becomes of first importance that the light should be qualified. Of King's Chapel it may be said that there is not one pane of perfectly clear transparent glass and this is what largely accounts for its atmosphere. No frosted or artificially made glass will do, nor a dead even stippling but, failing painted glass, some uneven stippling is required to give the effect of the qualified light of painted glass as nearly as possible, or curtains of canvas-colour should be drawn across the windows. At Toledo curtains are sometimes drawn across the painted windows. Occasionally in the South, as at Siena and Valencia, windows have transparent alabaster slabs which transmit the softest light; and sometimes in Italy a window here and there will let in a shaft of light with telling effect. How great is the effect of the management of light in creating an atmosphere, I have seen most vividly illustrated in St Peter's, Rome, at a Canonization, before electric light was substituted for candles. All the windows were veiled except one or two which let in a shaft of sunlight across the thousands of burning tapers. Also the exaggeratedly huge details of the architecture were veiled by crimson hangings, and the result was that the whole church looked its vast scale, which under ordinary conditions it fails to do.

King's Chapel is as much favoured by night as by day, for it is still lighted only by candles, the authorities having tried and rejected electric lighting. Indeed electric lighting is one of the greatest of problems. The appeal which I have made to nature will probably rule out every proposal which the electrician will make, who is too often called in without instructed guidance. His great aim is to create precisely those conditions of lighting which are not suitable to a church and which have the power of destroying the whole atmosphere of even the most beautiful buildings, as may too often be seen. Flood lighting, I think, of any kind may at once be dismissed. Rarely, and with all the care and skill of the best stage-lighting, a concealed lamp may be used to throw a light on one side only, just as a shaft of sunlight can come from only one point. For the power of electric light is comparable with sunlight and not with candle light; though in the only beautiful use of it that I have seen, which was in Barcelona Cathedral in 1935, the lamps at the ends of tall tapers in the chandeliers were of such low power that in the subdued light of the church they were indistinguishable from the wax tapers. Clearly the secret is to have many lights of as low power as possible and not to hide them. But at present for the purposes of reading it seems impossible to get lamps of sufficiently low power to avoid some skilful and unnoticeable shading to prevent dazzling.

Frosted lamps or shades should never be allowed, because of their conspicuousness in the day time, but an efficient and quite narrow shade can be devised for the ordinary low power lamps, and pendants are still the best method of artificial lighting.

And as to colour itself, it is essential that it should subserve and enhance the proportion and main lines of a church. That is just what the restoration of early medieval paintings on the walls of our English churches does not do. They were lime-washed over even in later medieval times, and the present fashion of bringing them again into prominence is the greatest mistake. They are easily, it is true, lime-washed over once more, but their real interest, which is antiquarian, is destroyed by the repainting which more or less accompanies their disclosure. Some are not without beauty of drawing, and for that reason also it destroys their value to retouch them. This was an axiom until these recent times which seem incapable of holding fast that which has been proved. Still more fatal in their effect are the violent patches of strong colour and gilding which destroy the rhythm of the architecture. How colour can be rightly used on the vaults and walls of the building itself can now be seen best in unrestored churches in Italy and Spain, but particularly in Spain where, as formerly in England, colour is mostly in the glass, corresponding to the mosaics of the South, and in the altars and screens, and often hardly at all in the fabric of the building. This is characteristic of those churches which are most conspicuous for the richness and beauty of their colouring. The fabric is generally left a uniform tone of French grey so that the lines of architecture have their full value, undistracted, as now so often in England, by the jointing of differently coloured stones and plaster, or by one part of the building being scraped or newly lime-washed, while the rest remains, admittedly not as it originally was, but as time has weathered it. And what can more destroy the architectural atmosphere than such patchwork

V

Finally, it has to be remembered that an atmosphere cannot be produced by a number of people working either independently of each other or in committee. It must be the product of one mind so steeped in tradition as a second nature that, as we have seen above, he can receive the inspiration to apply it to the needs which he has to meet, bringing forth from his treasures, like the householder in the parable, 'things new and old'. Let not people be beguiled by the pleasant doctrine which has been preached to them in recent times, that there are certain things which the priest himself or a committee can undertake independently of the one controlling mind: things such as frontals and vestments, or the most difficult and important questions of heating, lighting and cleaning, on which the whole atmosphere of the church may depend. Very rarely the controlling mind might be the priest himself or some other layman, but practically it is impossible for even the most gifted amateur to control all that is included in the architecture of a church, and probably the more he knows the more insistent he will be to seek out and be guided by one individual whom he has found not by reputation but by seeing the works which he has already produced. In the *Memorabilia* (11, vi, 6) Xenophon makes Socrates say: 'What test do we apply to a sculptor? We don't judge by what he says, but we look at his statues, and if we see that the works he has already produced are beautiful, we feel confident that his future works will be as good.' Today the priest and the architect ate so pressed by 'forms to fill up' and by every kind of activity external to their own proper work, that it is almost impossible for them to find the time essential for doing it. Looking back on the days in which this was not the case, it seems to me that they produced better fruit in both priest and architect. Certainly the work of the architect (and it cannot be less for the priest) demands all his time for study and for the exercise of his skill with undivided attention. He should be one who is called by name as Bezaleel was called, not from among the priests but out of the tribe of Judah, 'to devise cunning works, to work in gold, and in silver, and in brass, and in cutting of stones to set them, and in carving of timber, to work in all manner of workmanship.' If such are rare, it should be the first care of the Church to create the demand for them and not, as now, to suppress it.*

But the first care now is to make money and avoid sacrifice with the forlorn hope that in this way the people can be won. Old churches are pulled down that the money got for their sites may build new ones, and the objectives of the

*A recent book on the *History of Spanish Architecture*, by Bernard Bevan, although one may not agree with all its judgements any more than with Street's, gives some very important facts which are significantly at variance with prevailing opinions. The author brings out the individuality of the architects and the blending of styles in the later work. He says (p. 135): 'Every prominent architect was an individualist, but very often he was also the master of several styles. "Riano" (sixteenth century), the great Sevillian architect, built at one and the same time in Gothic, Renaissance, Plateresque, and the most severe Graeco-Roman.' Also he points out (p. 148) that 'prominent architects' designed the great 'rejas', or metal screens, and not the craftsmen who carried them out. And most important of all (p. 169) in view of what has been taking place in England during the last twenty-five years – 'The real significance of the Bourbons in Spanish architecture lies not in the buildings they erected, but in the foundation of academies of art modelled on the Academy in Paris. In 1744 a national school for architects was founded. A royal decree prohibited the erection of any public building the plans for which had not been approved by the Academy. In addition, no one was allowed to assume the title of architect or master of works or be entrusted with the construction of any building before he had passed the Academy's examination. The authorities of St Ferdinand's Academy thus became a sort of artistic police force. All freedom of design was lost, and with it those most precious of gifts, originality and vitality.

'Spain, governed, or rather paralysed, by the Royal Academy, produced few great architects in the latter half of the eighteenth century, for the official classical style, sober, frigid, and cosmopolitan, gave little scope for imagination.'

new ones are cheapness and pretentiousness. It is the pretentiousness of these modernistic churches which is unforgivable. Their architecture expresses the self-satisfaction which has produced them. They display the names of the architects who designed them and the bishops who blessed them. There is no shame that in an age so wealthy the house of God should he so poor. Granted the crying need, created by the development of housing estates, for four walls within which to worship and the lack of self-sacrifice to provide a worthy building, a lesson might be taken from the simplest of our medieval churches whose fabrics were little more than a barn – hardly so fine a barn as barns then were – but which became glorious by beautiful workmanship within. To so low and plain a fabric a worthy altar has only to be added and the white-washed barn will have an atmosphere of prayer and love instead of being reminiscent of the cinema and its impersonal efficiency.

Part 2: Gazetteer

Stephen Arthur Bucknall

To my father AB and brother JSB, whose lives were spent assisting JNC in the creation of beauty

Foreword to the Gazetteer

Stephen Arthur Bucknall

IT HAD LONG BEEN MY DESIRE TO PRODUCE A GAZETTEER of the work of Sir J. Ninian Comper, one of the last of the great Gothic Revival architects, given the increasing number of those who realise his importance. A first edition, published privately in 1986, had an enthusiastic response. I realised this should be the basis for further research for a second edition, here being published by the Ecclesiological Society in association with Spire Books.

I am particularly pleased that in two ways the publication has expanded far beyond the original conception. First, it now includes a substantial introduction to Comper and his work, written by Fr Anthony Symondson, in the form of an extended commentary on historic illustrations. Secondly, the volume now contains a reprint of *Of the Atmosphere of a Church*, Comper's best-known essay. It is now nearly seventy years since he wrote it, and it has long been out of print. To place it in context, and make it understandable to the modern reader, Anthony Symondson has written a helpful introduction.

I hope that the introduction, the reprint of Comper's own thoughts, and the gazetteer, will encourage a new generation to discover the work of this great ecclesiastical architect.

★ ★ ★ ★ ★

My interest in Ninian Comper, my great-uncle, stems from the atmosphere of the home in which I was brought up in South London.

In the early years of the practice, Comper was in partnership with William Bucknall (1851–1944), his brother-in-law. The partnership lasted from 1888 until dissolved by Comper in 1904. William was largely responsible for the structure of their early buildings. My father, Arthur Bucknall (1876–1952),

William Bucknall's nephew, was apprenticed to Comper at the age of sixteen. The 'Study', as Comper insisted on calling his drawing office, was close by our family home so I lived in a world of architecture, looking at churches and cathedrals and what they contained. After the Study was bombed in 1944 it was moved to 'The Priory', Comper's large early nineteenth-century house which was close by. The double drawing room became the drawing office and the large kitchen became the area where the glass was painted, fired and leaded. During working hours the only sounds came from the noise of the furnace. After staying at The Priory, John Betjeman observed how 'silently the saintly office assembled'. This was a perceptive remark: no one ever spoke above a hushed whisper. Under these conditions was beauty created. When writing to Comper, Betjeman would often extravagantly refer to him as the greatest living architect in England.

Arthur Bucknall became Comper's 'other pair of eyes' and ran the business side of the practice. All lettering whether on stone, wood or glass was designed by him, while the tabernacle work in stained glass was also usually his. He accompanied Comper on all his travels both at home and abroad. Sadly he died eight years before Comper. Arthur's second son, John Samuel (1917–89), my brother, was also apprenticed at the age of sixteen. Comper would not appoint artists with qualifications from schools or colleges of art just as he would not have letters after his own name. He only accepted his knighthood in 1950 at the age of eighty-four after much persuasion from friends and relations.

John continued the painted glass practice for several years after Comper's death; he added a bee to the wild strawberry plant plus date which Comper had used as his insignia since about 1908. The architectural practice was inherited and continued by J. Sebastian Comper, Comper's pupil and eldest son.

When the painted glass practice finally came to an end in 1968 most of the thousands of drawings and his official correspondence were deposited by Sebastian Comper with the Drawings Collection of the Royal Institute of British Architects. They have not yet all been catalogued and many are at present not even stored in London.

Just as Comper disliked schools of art, so he disliked Diocesan Advisory Committees. They had no right to dictate to architects. The Central Council for the Care of Churches had the power to recommend that a parish should not have Comper as its architect. It considered that it might not be able to cope with his idiosyncrasies. It was also tragic that Sir Nikolaus Pevsner was so derogatory about Comper's work although he admitted that St Mary's, Wellingborough, 'glistens and reveals and conceals to one's heart's delight'. There is no knowing how much beautiful work was lost because of these factors.

Comper died in 1960. His ashes were interred in the north aisle of the nave of Westminster Abbey beneath his glass of abbots and kings. A few years later The Priory with its beautiful terraced garden, woodland and lake had been sold and submerged under the rising tide of suburbia. There is nowhere today where a blue plaque could be placed to commemorate that Sir J. Ninian Comper lived there.

★ ★ ★ ★ ★

There are in the gazetteer some six hundred place names arranged by county, with a further list of places abroad. I have often given the name of the architect of buildings of recent date; Comper took great care in making his designs harmonise with their architectural style. Dates of work are usually given, though the resources at my disposal mean that there will undoubtedly be some inaccuracies, and the lapse of time between commissioning, installation and dedication can also cause difficulties. A great many of the entries have been checked on site, but some rely on documentary sources: in both cases there is room for misunderstanding, error, and the changes that time brings.

County names are always a problem with historical gazetteers. An index of places in the Gazetteer is included on page 321 to allow the reader to check the county in cases of doubt. I have been pragmatic. For England, the list generally uses the traditional county names, preserving the historic counties of Middlesex, Huntingdonshire and Rutland, and joining the Isle of Wight with Hampshire. However the old Cumberland and Westmorland are merged into Cumbria, and I have used the new four-part division of Yorkshire. I have taken account of the latest boundaries, so some places will appear in a different county from that shown in older guide books. English cities are listed under their historic counties (Bristol is under Gloucestershire, York under North Yorkshire), except for London which is treated separately, and thus subsumes some of its neighbouring counties.

In Scotland and Wales the reorganisation of counties has been more drastic, and this sort of compromise arrangement is not really feasible. So in Wales I have used the 'preserved' post-1974 counties (in their anglicised form). Despite administrative reorganisation in the 1990s, these counties still have formal existence, each, for example, having a Lord-Lieutenant. In Scotland I have used the modern administrative areas, which to some extent respect the ancient counties; for convenience I have placed Dundee in Angus and Edinburgh in Midlothian.

I have allocated stars (explained on page 254) to indicate the relative importance of the work. Any system is, of course, subjective and personal, but it is hoped that some indication is better than none. If an entry has no star it does not mean that it is not worthwhile, just that I am not encouraging someone to travel many miles out of his or her way.

St Mary's, Wellingborough is Comper's greatest work. Other masterpieces are St Margaret's, Braemar; St Cyprian's, Clarence Gate, Marylebone; the conventual church of All Saints at London Colney; St Michael's, Newquay;

and St Philip's, Cosham. His restorations are also very important as can be seen at St Wilfrid's, Cantley, South Yorkshire; St Mary's, Egmanton, Notting-hamshire; St John the Baptist, Lound, Suffolk; and St Petroc's, Little Petherick, Cornwall. Then there is his important work in Westminster Abbey and the rebuilding of St Giles, Wimborne St Giles, Dorset. The Welsh National War Memorial at Cardiff is his main non-ecclesiastical work.

★ ★ ★ ★ ★

In the production of the list, I am indebted to several hundreds of people from cathedral closes to remote villages, both here and abroad, for their help over the years from 1983 to the present day, but particularly to my brother John before he died in 1989, my nephew John F. Bucknall (architect), and the Revd Anthony Symondson SJ for thoroughly reviewing the list after completion. A work of this sort will never be completely accurate so I apologise for inaccuracies. As explained in the preface from the Ecclesiological Society on page ix, amendments can be notified to me c/o the Society, and will be posted on the website of the Society.

STEPHEN A. BUCKNALL

Contents of the Gazetteer

Abbreviations used in the Gazetteer

AB	Arthur Bucknall (1876–1952), JNC's nephew-in-law. He became JNC's 'other pair of eyes' and managed 'The Study' from 1904 to 1952.
Bucknall	William Bucknall, JNC's brother-in-law. He was in partnership with JNC from 1888 to 1904.
Butchart	William Butchart, painter and gilder
BVM	Blessed Virgin Mary
HABS	H. A. Bernard Smith, painter, decorator and gilder
JB	John Betjeman
JBSC	Sebastian Comper (1891–1979), JNC's eldest son. He became an architect in his own right.
JNC	Sir John Ninian Comper (1864–1960), architect, the subject of this book
JSB	John Samuel Bucknall (1917–1989). Son of Arthur Bucknall, who took over after JNC died in 1960
LB	Lucy Bucknall (1859–1937), JNC's sister-in-law. She was trained by the Sisters of Bethany and produced work for JNC.
SSB	Society of the Sisters of Bethany. This community in Clerkenwell, London, under JNC's direction produced the finest church embroidery both for him and other designers.
SSJE	Society of St John the Evangelist, Oxford
V&A	Victoria & Albert Museum, London
WFK	Frank Knight, base metal worker, blacksmith and silversmith
WWI	World War I (and WWII for World War II)

Stars (for background to the star system, see page 251)

★★★	Very important buildings designed by JNC. Outstanding 'restorations'. Buildings containing very good work.
★★	Less important buildings. Good 'restorations'. Good contents.
★	Worth a detour!
(★)	Brackets mean that the work no longer exists in its original state or has been demolished, or was never built.

Proposed works
Where a work is described as 'proposed' it will almost always be the case that it was not eventually executed. No attempt has been made to provide a complete list of unexecuted work.

Gazetteer

Stephen Arthur Bucknall

ENGLAND

Bedfordshire

ASPLEY GUISE, St Botolph (Architect: JBSC)
   Glass: 1956
DUNSTABLE, St Peter
   1894   Painting on east wall
   1901–7   Screens
WYMINGTON, St Lawrence
   1934   Oak kneeling desks
   1938   Reredos figures

Berkshire

ASCOT, Priory
   Glass: 1908; 1918, Fr Suckling memorial
   1923–30 Electric light pendants and standards, holy water stoup
             Proposed decoration of west part of ceiling
             Embroidery
CAVERSHAM, St Andrew
   Glass: 1918 nave; 1919–21 window in north aisle (Haslam memorial);
               1920–21 proposed Mott memorial window; 1946 window
   1916–25 Lengthened chancel
CLEWER
—ST ANDREW
   Glass: 1932
—ST STEPHEN
   1932–6   Window in Brocas Chapel
EARLEY, St Peter
   1912   Oak kneeling desk (south chapel)

HURST, St Nicholas
   1940–41 Wimberley memorial brass

MAIDENHEAD, Boyne Hill, All Saints (Architect: G. E. Street)
   Glass: 1958 east window of Lady Chapel

NEWBURY, St Nicholas
   1905   Reredos, carved figures

READING, St Bartholomew
   Glass: 1907 north aisle; 1945 east window
   1913–21 Lectern, banner, Lady Chapel
   1919–21 New porch to south door, proposed choir gallery and hanging pyx
   1939   Design for tomb for Lord Reading
   1939   Carved figure
   1943   Medallion of the Risen Christ
   1945   Decoration & cutting down of altar pillars

★★★ STOCKCROSS, St John the Divine (*see page 118*)
          Patron Sir Richard Sutton
   Glass: 1905 east window; 1920–22 east window of WWI war memorial chapel;
            1952 north window of north transept
   1905–7 and 1920–35: Restoration
          Wrought-iron chancel screen, font, kneeling desks, English altar with
            angels, alabaster reredos, screen, panelling & seats in chapel, priest's
            desk, candlesticks, 2 altar frontals (red & green), chalice & paten.
          JNC proposed designs for a larger church which would incorporate the furniture
            executed for St John's

SULHAMSTEAD ABBOTS, St Mary
   Glass: 1937–40 east window (Beatrice Gilbey memorial)
          Altar & reredos, panelling, altar rails, oak priest's chair, gilded and
            decorated altar frontal, Harris memorial tablet

SUNNINGDALE, Holy Trinity
   Glass: 1934–5 east window (Cunliffe-Owen memorial)
   1934   Scheme for decoration of chancel

WINDSOR

—WINDSOR CASTLE

——PRIVATE CHAPEL
          1901–2 Frontal (made by the Royal Irish School of
            Art Needlework) (*lost*)

——ST GEORGE'S CHAPEL
          1954 Silver crucifix and candlesticks

—WINDSOR GREAT PARK
   Glass: 1918; 1928
   1920   Kneeling desks, hangings, credence table
   1924   Lectern
          Oak altar, altar cross & 2 standard candlesticks

WOODLEY, St John
   Glass: 1935–6 window on south side of chancel

Buckinghamshire

★ BEACONSFIELD, St Mary

Glass:	1896–7 five windows (restoration for Dr Mann, Christ Church, Oxford)
1898	Memorial to Edward Burke (south wall); altar; altar in Jesus chapel, veil, stole (*these not extant 1986*); candle stands on choir stalls, restoration of medieval wooden screen (south side of choir stalls), roof decoration. (*The rood screen was later removed to St Paul, Wooburn Green, Buckinghamshire, 1899.*)

★ BLETCHLEY, St Mary

Glass:	1958, 1959 (porch)
1947	Altar frontal, reredos, riddel angels, panelling, frontlet (SSB), banner, paving of nave, roof, chandeliers
1947	Flags (hung in nave)
1948–51	Candlesticks & cross (using old designs)
	Processional cross, plaster figure of Virgin & Child
1958	Credence table, kneeling desk
1961	Mothers' Union banner

(★★★) BURNHAM

—HOUSE OF PRAYER

	Sold 1985. Now (1990) called 'Grenville Court'. Converted into offices. Grilles remain in the chapel, but all other furnishings removed.
Glass:	1956 small panel (*now at the shrine of our Lady of Walsingham, Little Walsingham, Norfolk*)
1932–5	Building of chapel and a new cloister. Fittings and furnishings, including: altar, ciborium, wrought-iron screens and grilles, including old ironwork. Altar cross and candlesticks, sedilia, vestments, canopy over Bishop's throne, faldstool, carpets, electric light fittings
1942	Stalls
	(*Six candlesticks and monstrance now at Mirfield, Community of the Resurrection, West Yorkshire; crucifix and vestments now at Quainton Hall School, HARROW-ON-THE-HILL, Middlesex*)

—NASHDOM ABBEY (Anglican Benedictines)

	Now at Elmore Abbey, Newbury, Berkshire
1945	Cross & six candlesticks (in memory of Brother Thomas More Bishop) (*now at Elmore Abbey*)

CALVERTON, All Saints

1893	Churchyard cross
1904	Gravestones

CHICHELEY, St Lawrence

1907	Rood

CLIFTON REYNES, St Mary the Virgin

1905–21	Fittings
1919–21	War memorial cross. Proposed Doughty memorial tablet and steps outside tower

ELLESBOROUGH, St Peter & St Paul
Glass: 1901; 1907; 1912 Astley memorial window
1900–1901
Furnishings; altar & reredos

FARNHAM COMMON, St John
Glass: 1939–40 east window & south window (St Nicholas)

GREAT LINFORD, St Andrew
Church now (1989) ecumenical and all furnishings removed
1921–2 Uthwatt memorial tablet

HEDSOR, St Nicholas
1943 Memorial tablet

HOGGESTON, Holy Cross
Glass: 1949 east window

ICKFORD, St Nicholas
Glass: 1919; 1934–5 east window of south aisle (in memory of Revd Vernon Staley)

LAVENDON, St Michael
Glass: 1933–5 south window of Lady Chapel (Hulse memorial)
Limewashing of the walls; removal of the organ from the Lady Chapel to the west end; proposed altar and candlesticks and restoration of the Lady Chapel

★★ LITTLE KIMBLE, St Nicholas
Glass: 1901 south chapel, 2 windows
1900–1904
Complete restoration
1903 Tester & reredos with small window behind; screen for south chapel; altar frontal, south chapel

NASHDOM ABBEY
See BURNHAM

NEWPORT PAGNELL, St Luke
Hanging pyx (from St Mary's, Wellingborough, Northamptonshire)

STOKE POGES, St Giles
1915 Hasting's chapel

STOKENCHURCH, St Peter & St Paul
Chandeliers (undated)

STONY STRATFORD, St Giles (Architect: F. Hiorn)
1922–35 Furnishing of sanctuary, altar & reredos, oak pulpit, hanging candelabra
1930–35 Altar frontals

TAPLOW, St Nicholas
1936 Lectern

WENDOVER, St Mary
1952 Lectern

WEST WYCOMBE, St Lawrence
Churchwardens' staves

WING, All Saints
Glass: 1910 south window

WOOBURN GREEN, St Paul
1899 Screen (originally for Beaconsfield); two angels (Bucknall & Comper; decorator HABS) (*removed from screen some years ago; exhibited V&A 1971–97; now lost*)

Cambridgeshire

BARRINGTON, All Saints
1915–23   Repairs to church tower. Decoration and furnishing of Bendyshe
          chapel, including reredos and screen

★ BOURN, St Helen & St Mary
Glass: 1934–6 east window; 1949 east window of north transept
1936   Altar & reredos, electric light standards & pendants, 2 small carved
            figures of vested priests in chair

CAMBRIDGE
—CAVENDISH HOUSE ORATORY OF THE GOOD SHEPHERD (*not extant 1985*)
1920–27   Interior decoration of chapel, altar hangings & furniture

★ —LITTLE ST MARY
Glass: 1912 east window lower panels (upper panels Kempe); 1963 north aisle
            window (JSB)
1912   High altar, riddel posts & hangings
1913   Altar cross & candlesticks

—ST GILES
Glass: 1938 memorial window to Bishop Gore
1925–6   Oak panelling, cove and cresting at west end; red altar frontal and
            furnishings; processional cross

—UNIVERSITY
——CHRIST'S COLLEGE
1935–9   Decoration of the hall, including three heraldic achievements on the
            gallery end wall, painting of the walls, electric light fittings
1961   Design for coat of arms of Henry VI
1963–4   Carving in low relief on end wall in hall to JNC's design

——KING'S COLLEGE
1937–9   Altar frontal (Strawberry cloth of gold with blue orphreys, SSB)

——MAGDALENE COLLEGE
1924   Chapel restoration

——TRINITY COLLEGE
Glass: 1913 in hall (presented by Lord Harding)
1925   Panels

ELY
★ —CATHEDRAL OF THE HOLY TRINITY, Bishop West's Chapel
Glass: 1936 east window tracery lights and central figure (1946 window
            completed)
1934–5   Bishop White Thompson memorial altar frontal and carpet
1936–40   Restoration, paving, altar, wrought-iron riddel posts, reredos & frontal
            (SSB), banner of painted linen (Church of England Men's Society)
1945   Wrought-iron riddel posts

★ —ST PETER (*see page 29*)
1889   Screen & rood (JNC's first)

GREAT STAUGHTON, St Andrew
Glass: 1916
            Churchyard memorial cross & gravestone

KINGSTON, All Saints and St Andrew
1894   Restoration of church and addition to vicarage

LITTLEPORT, St George
- 1960 — Altar furnishings (Lady Chapel in south aisle)
  Two chandeliers

PETERBOROUGH, Cathedral of St Peter, St Paul & St Andrew
- 1911 — Bishop's mitre, embroidered with pearls
  Altar cross of silver and lapis lazuli for private chapel

STRETHAM, St James
- *Glass:* — 1933–4 east window

WALSOKEN
See under Norfolk, in which county lies the church of All Saints

Cheshire

BIRKENHEAD, Benedictine Priory of St James
- *Glass:* — 1920–22 east window of chapter house
- 1921 — Fittings

CHESTER, St Mary-on-the-Hill, St Mary
- 1891 — Altar frontal (SSB)
  (V&A exhibition 1971 – drawing only)

Cornwall

BLISLAND, St Protus & St Hyacinth
- *Glass:* — 1899 east and south windows of Jesus chapel; 1911 east window

GUNWALLOE, St Winwalloe
- 1906 — Altar (granite), riddels, hangings, frontals
- 1910 — Screens

★★★ LITTLE PETHERICK, St Petroc Minor
Patron Athelstan Riley, patronage transferred to Keble College, Oxford 1948
- *Glass:* — 1908 east window
- 1908 — Restoration; rood screen & loft across aisle & nave
  High altar & chancel panelling
- *c.*1916 — Bronze monument to Hon. Mrs Riley
- 1920 — Riley chantry chapel (south of high altar)
- 1947 — High altar reredos
  Organ gallery at west end
  Lady Chapel altar & reredos

★★★ NEWQUAY, St Michael
Seriously damaged by fire 1993. Reopened 1996 with new narthex and vestry.
Nearly all furnishings have been restored except high altar riddel posts,
hangings, panelling in aisles, pulpit, lectern and litany desk.
- *Glass:* — 1925–30 east window; 1945 east window of south aisle
- 1911–16 — Church built, furnishings
- 1921 — Proposed steps and gates for north side of the church
- 1930–37 — Screen and rood, figure of St Michael with dragon for the front of the loft, panelling at west end
- 1945 — Font cover (*damaged, in storage*)
- 1949 — High altar frontal painted and gilt
- 1961 — Tower (JBSC)

PADSTOW, St Petroc
- 1902 — Brass chandelier

★ PENRYN, St Gluvias
    1954   Organ gallery (south aisle west end), case for memorial book, brass cross & 2 candlesticks, 2 standard wood candlesticks, simple wood altar rail, rose-red damask altar frontal, 25 chandeliers. Whole church limewashed including piers. (*JNC did drawings, parish did the work.*)

PENZANCE, St Mary
    1902   Brass chandelier

PERRANARWORTHAL, St Piran
    1941–2   Gravestone (M H N C Atchley)

ST ERTH, St Erth
    1916–17 War memorial cross

TRURO

—CATHEDRAL OF THE BLESSED VIRGIN MARY
    1910   Hanging pyx in St Mary's aisle, placed here in 1997 (made for Caldey Abbey, Pembrokeshire; donated by Athelstan Riley)

—CONVENT OF THE EPIPHANY, Tregolls Road
    Became Alverton Manor Hotel in 1993. Nuns took 20 stalls to Copeland Court, Kenwyn, Truro.
    1897–1900 Clock tower, main entrance (*extant*); altar carving in chapel, frontal, stalls (*not extant*)

Cumbria

CARLISLE, Cathedral of the Holy Trinity
    1947   Banner (SSB)

CASTERTON, Holy Trinity
    1919–20 Churchyard war memorial cross

THRELKELD, St Mary
    1947   Fittings

WARCOP, St Columba
    Glass: 1898

★★ WORKINGTON, St John
    Glass: 1932 east window
    1915   Proposal to restore church
    1915   Altar frontal
    1930–33 Complete restoration and refurnishing of the church. Altar & ciborium with figure of the Risen Christ with rays; pulpit; font cover; decorative plaster ceiling

Derbyshire

BAKEWELL, Holy Cross
    1918–20 Furnishing of the Holy Cross chapel: altar, frontal, side hangings in rose-red damask, reredos and attached small tester (war memorial)

BUXTON, St James the Less.
    1903   Fittings

CHESTERFIELD, St Mary & All Saints
    Glass: 1941 east window of Holy Cross chapel; 1943 south window of St Peter's chapel (St Helena and St Thomas; Dilworth Harrison memorial window)

DERBY

★★ —CATHEDRAL OF ALL SAINTS (Architect: James Gibbs)

    Glass: 1955

    1927–30 *In 1927 All Saints church was raised from the status of a chief parish church to that of a cathedral. JNC was first consulted in 1922 and in 1927–30 made plans for the conversion. His work included:*

        Alteration of the altar, pews, steps and screen; altar hangings and cushions; altar pillars; altar cross and candlesticks; communion rails; reredos. Carpet. Faldstool. Sedilia bench and hanging. Archdeacons' stalls and canons' stalls, and alteration of the Bishop's throne. Electric light pendants and brackets. Heating system. Cleaning and painting of the interior. Altar for the north aisle, with a cross and candlesticks. Tester. Alterations to the pulpit. Floor paving. Mace cupboard. Repositioning of the Bakewell screen.

        Proposed, not executed: angels for the high altar; processional cross; purchase of a Renaissance pulpit from St Gregory's, Small Heath, Birmingham

    1935   Figure of Virgin & Child (from Convent of the Holy Name, Malvern Link, Worcestershire, after closure in 1980s)

    1939–45 Oak sedilia. Name tablets for the canons' stalls. Pulpit soundboard. The 'Forty-five' memorial tablet (commemorating the visit to Derby of Prince Charles Edward in 1745).

    1939–60 In 1939 JNC proposed an extension eastwards to form a new sanctuary with high altar beneath a ciborium. This was prevented by the war, but was completed to a modified design by JBSC in 1967–72. The original reredos was incorporated as the soffit of the ciborium. JBSC also designed the organ case in the west gallery and a monument was erected to his memory in 1978.

—ROLLS ROYCE LTD

        Painting by D. Eyre (1963) of the Sir Frederick Royce memorial window in Westminster Abbey (the last of the series of eight: see WESTMINSTER, London)

EDALE, Holy and Undivided Trinity

    Glass: 1896; 1906; 1932

ELVASTON, St Bartholomew

    Glass: 1934–5 nave & clerestory (Prodgers memorial on north side with tablet)

LITTLEOVER, St Peter

    Glass: 1961 (JSB)

LONG EATON, St John

    1920–22 War memorial cross

SHIREBROOK, Holy Trinity

    Glass: 1968 (JSB)

WIRKSWORTH, St Mary

    1919–22 War memorial tablet

             Proposed oak screen

Devon

AXMINSTER, St Mary
    1924   JNC's advice sought on proposed alterations
BOVEY TRACEY, St John
    1909   Banner
CHERITON BISHOP, St Mary
    Glass: 1966 (JSB)
                Cross & candlesticks
CLOVELLY, All Saints
    Glass: 1905
DARTMOUTH, R.N. College chapel
    1925   Altar candlesticks & cross
DENBURY, St Mary
    1919–20 War memorial tablet on village conduit wall
EXETER
—CATHEDRAL OF ST PETER
    Glass: 1947 east window of north transept (memorial to the fallen of
                HMS Exeter)
—ST MICHAEL
                Banner
FENITON, St Andrew
    Glass: 1946
HAM (Plymouth), St James the Less
    Glass: 1958 east window
HOLBETON, All Saints
    Glass: 1911
LITTLEHAM, St Margaret
    1926–7   Churchyard gravestone to Revd Dr Salisbury Price
PAIGNTON, St John the Baptist
    1947–8   Altar & reredos, oak kneeling stool, candlesticks, chandeliers, credence
                table, book desk, hangings, carpet
PLYMOUTH, St John
    Glass: 1916; 1919 west porch
    1913–19 Aumbry
    1919   Figure of Joan of Arc
THROWLEIGH, Okehampton, St Mary the Virgin
    Glass: 1911 east window; 1912 south window

Dorset

ATHELHAMPTON, St John
    Glass: 1917–18 north wall of nave (de la Fontaine memorial)
BOURNEMOUTH
—ST MARY (Architect: C. A. Nicholson)
    Glass: 1930–32 east window; 1944–6 Lady Chapel; 1949 north aisle
                Church closed 1997, now Youth Centre; glass well cared for.
—ST PETER (Architect: G. E. Street)
    Glass: 1914; 1936–7 east window of south aisle

1913–37	Fittings
1919	War memorial
1921	Silver-gilt chalice
1925–7	Building and furnishing of the chapel of the Resurrection
1930s	Low relief plaque of Risen Saviour (south wall)
	War memorial
	Vestments
1930	Altar cross in copper mercurial gilt
	Proposed organ case (drawing at St Peter's)
	Seats and flooring in the nave

—ST SWITHUN (Architect: Norman Shaw) (*Church closed 1988*)

| 1919–25 | Decoration and furnishing of chapel (*destroyed*) |

BROADSTONE, St John

| *Glass:* | 1934–5 south window |

COLEHILL, St Michael (Architect: W. D. Caröe)

| *Glass:* | 1957 |

GILLINGHAM, St Mary

| *Glass:* | 1929 |

LYTCHETT MINSTER, Parish church (dedication not known) (Architect: J. Tulloch)

| 1919 | War memorial |
| 1933–7 | Hargreaves memorial tablet |

MILTON ABBAS, Abbey Church

| 1896 | Proposed restoration of altar screen |

★ PUDDLETOWN, St Mary

| *Glass:* | 1906 south chapel |
| | Early restoration |

SHILLINGSTONE, Holy Rood

| *Glass:* | 1914 |
| 1914 | Furnishings in Lady Chapel |

WEYMOUTH, Portway Hospital chapel

| *Glass:* | 1941 (roundel for the Countess of Shaftesbury) |

WIMBORNE MINSTER, St Cuthberga

| 1920–22 | War memorial cross in churchyard, war memorial tablet in church |

WIMBORNE ST GILES

—ST GILES' HOUSE (Lord Shaftesbury)

Glass:	1906–7 seven lights at east end
1905–7	Private chapel
	Reredos has detached open screen as at Moreton Corbet, Shropshire
1942	Calvary in garden

★★★ —ST GILES (*see page 112*)

Glass:	1910 east window of north aisle; 1921–6 west window; 1934 proposed silver-wedding windows for the Earl and Countess of Shaftesbury; new panels for Coronation windows; 1936 panel of Virgin & Child; 1949 one panel
1910	Church rebuilt by JNC after 1908 fire (only walls & tower were left)
	Mortuary chapel altar & tester
	Screen & rood
1920	War memorial (*fallen down*)
1921	Cross
1926	Seven rood lights for screen

1940	Font cover
1957	Paschal candlestick
	Organ case
1958	Memorial tablet on wall
	Two banners
	Three frontals:
	1. Gold silk damask & cloth of gold riddels
	2. Rose-red silk with matching riddels
	3. Lenten of calico with reredos veil to match
	Chasuble, stole & veil

WITCHAMPTON, St Mary & St Cuthberga
Glass: 1935–9 east window

Co. Durham

BARNARD CASTLE, Bowes Museum
1919–21   War memorial cross for 4th Battalion Durham Light Infantry in grounds of Bowes Museum

BRANCEPETH, St Brandon
1920   Proposed war memorial cross

DURHAM, Cathedral of Christ & St Mary
1923   Proposed altar hangings
1950   Tester and four standard candlesticks for shrine of St Cuthbert

EASINGTON COLLIERY, Church of the Ascension
*c.*1950   Altar and screen (JBSC)

STOCKTON-ON-TEES
—EGGLESCLIFFE, St John the Baptist
Glass: 1904
Fittings (undated)

—ELTON, St John
1907   Rood screen & figures, hangings
1936–7   Tombstone in churchyard (Revd H. S. Milner)

Essex

BOCKING, St Mary the Virgin
1950   Figure in low relief of the Majestas, gilt & painted hangings on west wall
1950–55   Rood, north & south screens

CHIGWELL, Chigwell School war memorial chapel
1923   Proposed window and reredos

GREAT BADDOW, St Mary the Virgin
1929–31   Lych-gate

HATFIELD BROAD OAK, St Mary
Gravestone to Geoffrey Bright

ILFORD, St Mary's Hospital chapel
1920–23   Altar & reredos in Lady Chapel

★ LITTLE ILFORD, St Barnabas
Glass: 1954
1901–9   Church and vicarage (largely Bucknall)
1901   Font

ORSETT, St Giles & All Saints
    1911   Chancel, rood screen

PRITTLEWELL, Annunciation of the Blessed Virgin Mary
    1907   New vestry

RIVENHALL, St Mary & All Saints
    Glass: 1919 Willmott memorial window

SOUTHCHURCH, Holy Trinity
    Glass: 1918–21 west window of north aisle (Philpott memorial)
    1906   New church, fittings, including old Norman church as an aisle.
                Completed by F. C. Eden.

Gloucestershire

ALMONDSBURY, St Mary
    1914   Pulpit, made from oak grown in Cirencester Park

BERKELEY, St Mary
    1917–18 Pulpit (stone)
    1942–50 Monument to the last Earl of Berkeley in Berkeley memorial chapel: a
                heraldic achievement with figures of St George and St Francis in full
                relief

BRISTOL
—FISHPONDS Diocesan Training College chapel
    1912   Brass standard candlesticks
    1921–5   Chapel furniture, altar frontals, vestments and alms bags

—ST MARY-ON-THE-QUAY (Roman Catholic)
    1920–22 Decoration of nave and chancel, alteration to the high altar and steps,
                tester, altar frontals, two painted reredos panels for Lady Chapel,
                sanctuary lamp-bracket, carpets (proposed war memorial)

★ —ST MARY REDCLIFFE
    Glass: 1911–14 south window in south transept (Cabot memorial)
    1916   Proposed high altar

★★ —STOKE BISHOP, St Mary Magdalene
    Glass: 1924 south chapel, 2 small lancets
    1922–3   Lady Chapel furnishings: altar, frontal (LB), dossal (LB), reredos
                (alabaster), riddel posts with angels, panelling, screens, pews,
                2 chandeliers
    1922   Cross & candlesticks
    1928   Altar vessels
    1951   Additional pews & panelling

CHELTENHAM, Warden Hill, St Christopher
    Glass: 1961 east window (JSB)

CIRENCESTER
—CIRENCESTER PARK
    1921   Figure of St George in garden

—ST JOHN THE BAPTIST
    1908   Altar frontal (Lady Chapel) (SSB) (*Altered by S. E. Dykes Bower 1950s*)
                Altar hangings, riddel posts (Lady Chapel) (*Altered by S. E. Dykes Bower
                  at a later date*)
    1911   Litany desk (*extant*), chasuble (*no trace, 1986*)
    1917   Proposed market cross

1917–23	War memorial (west of south porch) – a Calvary, modelled on one at Fécamp
1930s	Two black standard candlesticks
	Communion rails & pavement
1938	Recumbent stone in cemetery (Munn)

COLD ASHTON, Holy Trinity

1942–3	Oak kneeling desks
1947	Two five light pendants

DUMBLETON, St Peter

1920–21	War memorial cross

EASTINGTON (near Stonehouse), St Michael

Glass:　1908 east window; 1909 south window of south aisle

FAIRFORD, St Mary

1915–30	Alterations of the chancel, including: new altar with riddel posts, hangings, cloth of gold frontal (LB), chancel paving, altar cross (WFK)
1949	Angels & decoration of riddels added

HARESCOMBE, St John the Baptist

*c.*1910　Altar, riddels, dorsal & frontal (almost certainly by JNC)

HENBURY, St Mary

1922	JNC's advice sought over scheme by C. F. W. Denning to reform the Lady Chapel

IRON ACTON, St James the Less

Glass:　1901, south aisle

NORTHLEACH, St Peter & St Paul

Altar frontal (made & restored SSB)

★ RANGEWORTHY, Holy Trinity

Glass:　1919 east window – St Michael, Risen Christ, St George

1926–38 south window of nave (Hull memorial)

1926–38 west window, Annunciation

1949 window on south side of chancel (in memory of Revd P. Sullivan, Vicar)

1952 north window, Christ in Majesty

STANTON

★★★ —ST MICHAEL

Patron Sir Philip Stott, Bart

Glass:　1915; 1920 east window, war memorial including resetting of fifteenth-century glass from Hailes Abbey; 1926 east windows of north and south transepts

1915	Alabaster reredos (sculptured by W. Gough)
1918	West gallery dormer windows & organ loft
1919–21	Churchyard war memorial cross
	South transept altar & communion rails by JBSC
1919–36	Organ-case and gallery
*c.*1923	Rood screen & rood, credence table & kneeling desk

—WAR MEMORIAL

1919	War memorial converted from village pump in wall of Dumbleton Court at Broadway turning

STANWAY, St Peter
- 1897   English altar & candlesticks (metal riddel posts with angels) (*1988, front two posts not in original position*)

TEWKESBURY, Abbey Church of St Mary the Virgin
- 1914   Restoration of Beauchamp chapel
- 1950   Proposed design for English altar & baldachino & Lady Chapel altar; cross & candlesticks

WHADDON, St Margaret
- *Glass:*   1920 east window

WITHINGTON, St Michael
- *Glass:*   1948 east window of south chapel

Hampshire and the Isle of Wight

ALDERSHOT, Parish church (dedication not known)
- Altar frontal

BIGHTON, All Saints
- *Glass:*   1904 south window; 1924
- 1899   Rood screen
- Other fittings

CATHERINGTON, Catherington House
- 1924–5   Proposed calvary for the garden of the Retreat House

★★★ COSHAM (Portsmouth), St Philip & St James (*see page 165*)
- *Glass:*   1937
- 1935–9   New church with internal decoration and all fittings and furnishings, including east window, ciborium and font
- (Vicarage & parish hall by JBSC)

EAST MEON

★ —ALL SAINTS
- *Glass:*   1906; 1907 east window of Lady Chapel; 1912 east window; 1920; 1924–8 north aisle (Essington memorial); 1946 north window
- 1890   Restoration of steeple (the start of a long association with the church)
- 1905   Altar frontal
- 1907   Restoration
- 1920–22 War memorial cross, memorial tablet
- 1924–8   Oak kneeling desk
- 1939   Funeral pall
- 1941   Gravestone (Masters)
- 1948–9   Painted decoration of lectern
- Oak frontal case

—ALMS HOUSES
- Alms houses by JNC in their external design, and by Bucknall in their planning

EMPSHOTT, Holy Rood
- 1911   Altar & frontal

EMSWORTH, St James
- 1920–21 Proposed baptistery

GOSPORT
- *Glass:*   1904 two windows (*original location and current whereabouts unknown; possibly destroyed WWII*)

MILFORD-ON-SEA, All Saints

Glass: 1943–8 south window (Power memorial)

MILLBROOK (Southampton)

—HOLY TRINITY

1919–37   Altar, reredos, sanctuary lamps & west-end screen, all in war memorial
            chapel; processional cross, figures of SS Michael & George

1923–6   Tester for high altar, vestments, electric light fittings

1933–4   Interior fittings, chancel, ciborium
           (*1980s church stripped and robbed except for chalice and paten*)

—ST CLEMENT

1937   Plans for proposed new church

PORTSMOUTH

—CATHEDRAL OF ST THOMAS OF CANTERBURY

1923–8   Crozier for Bishop of Portsmouth, Ernest Norille Lovett

1934   High altar cross, Lady altar and cross, copes (SSB)

1938   Linen for 3 altars (SSB)

—EASTNEY, St Andrew (Garrison Church)

1934–43   Proposed: additions to the altar, wall hangings, credence table, kneeling
            desks, carpet, lime-washing of walls

—MILTON, St James

Glass: 1933 east window

1937–9   Hangings, carved figure of Risen Christ, 3 brasses, banner of St James
           (painted on canvas)

SHEET, St Mary

1923–8   Screens & lectern, pulpit, credence table, choir-stalls and desks

SOUTHAMPTON

—MISSION TO SEAMEN

Glass: 1959

—ST LUKE

1923–4   Vestments; proposed new porch and glass for the east window and
           north wall of the sanctuary

—SOUTHAMPTON CEMETERY ANGLICAN CHAPEL

1924–30   Aumbry, ciborium, lamp & proposed furniture

—SOUTHAMPTON WORKHOUSE CHAPEL

1924–30   Proposed scheme of decoration

UPPER WIELD

           See WIELD

VENTNOR (Isle of Wight), St Alban

Glass: 1931 Lady Chapel

WEYHILL, St Michael and All Angels

Glass: 1947

WHERWELL, St Peter and Holy Cross

Glass: 1927–30 west window, partly completed (memorial to Ernest Lascelles
           Iremonger)

WIELD, St James

           Side altar

WINCHESTER

—CATHEDRAL OF THE HOLY TRINITY

1921–5   Figure of St Joan of Arc

Three chasubles, given by Sisters of Bethany when they moved house
in the 1970s

Mothers' Union banner

1928–32   Redecoration and furnishing of the east end of Bishop Waynflete's
chantry chapel and effigy

1932   Pastoral staff for Bishop of Winchester, memorial to Herbert Edward
Ryle

Proposal for memorial brass to William of Wykeham for Wykeham
chantry

Decoration of altar screen and three alabaster figures for niches

—HOLY TRINITY

1948   Altar, reredos & fittings in Lady Chapel

Herefordshire

BRAMPTON BRYAN, St Barnabas

1896   Altar frontal *(not extant 1995)*

★★ BRINSOP, St George

Glass: 1917; 1920 west window, war memorial; 1920–24 east window,
restoration (some new glass); 1925 south window; 1928, Bishop
Wordsworth; 1931 east window of Lady Chapel

1914   Heraldic panel in Brinsop Court

1920–24   Alabaster reredos & altar; rood figures & ceilure, pulpit, panelling, stalls.
The reredos is a version of the reredos at Stockcross, Berkshire.

Hertfordshire

ALDENHAM, St John the Baptist

1901   Memorial tablet

BALDOCK, St Mary

1923–4   Processional cross (bronze, gilt)

BAYFORD, St Mary

Glass: 1898

1898   Gravestone (Thornton memorial)

1919–20   War memorial cross on Bayford Church Green

ELSTREE, St Nicholas

Glass: 1950

1927–8   Gravestone (Martha Ray)

1948   Tablet

HERTFORD, St Andrew

1919–20   War memorial cross

HITCHIN, Langley End Cemetery

1925–7   Gravestone (designed by AB)

LONDON COLNEY

See ST ALBANS

LONG MARSTON, All Saints

1943   Altar cross, 6 candlesticks, kneeling stools

NORTHAW, St Thomas of Canterbury

1917   Village cross

1948   New cross & shaft

RICKMANSWORTH, St Mary

Glass: 1921–2 Removal of stained glass to the V&A and installation of new glass by JNC

ST ALBANS

★ —CATHEDRAL OF ST ALBAN

Glass: 1920–26 west window (the St Albans Diocesan War Memorial)

1920–26   Gallery front of iron under west window, brass inscription

1940   Stalls & desks in Lady Chapel

★★★ —LONDON COLNEY, Conventual church of All Saints (now All Saints Pastoral Centre) (*see page 151*)

Glass: 1930 east window (Jesse window, dominated by a figure of the Majestas); 1957 outer lights of the window completed

1921–4   Planning of the new church

1924–8   Building of the chapel, cloister, sacristy and priest's room

Choir stalls with panelling

High altar

Lady altar with hanging pyx

Altar cross and candlesticks (WFK)

Altar frontal (given to St John's Home, Oxford)

Sedilia

Heating system

Tester

1926–30   Building of St Anne's Home

1930–38   Eleven iron grave-crosses

Altar book-desk

Two extra front desks for the choir and Lady Chapel

Figure of St Anne and the child Mary for St Anne's Home

1945–7   Tabernacle, canopy and ciborium

1960–64   Completion of final bays of west end to a modified design by JBSC

SOUTH MIMMS, St Giles

Glass: 1938–9 east window of Lady Chapel; 1939 north window of Lady Chapel additions

1939   Font cover

★ WATFORD, St John

1902   Brass standard candlesticks

1907   Screens on north and south side of chancel

1915   Choir stalls

1919–21   Lady Chapel screen. Figures of SS Michael & George, & BVM. War memorial tablet.

1926–7   Figure of the Virgin & Child, with pedestal and steeple

South aisle screen

Panelling of east end of the south aisle; organ screen

WESTMILL, St Mary

1958   Chancel additions, reredos, 4 riddel posts with angels

Huntingdonshire

★ BRAMPTON, St Mary

1918–21   Alterations to chancel

Screen with shields for the war memorial chapel, floor of chapel and altar

1925–8   Interior fittings & south aisle Lady Chapel

1928   Mothers' Union banner

1940   Altar rails & priest's desk for Lady Chapel

1941   Proposed extra seating; proposed new paving in the cross aisle

1948   Silver altar cross & candlesticks & standard candlesticks

HAMERTON, All Saints

1919–24   Proposed scheme for decoration of the chancel

HUNTINGDON, St Mary

1920–21   Altar, riddels, frontal (LB), hangings, communion rails, seats & desks

★★★ ST IVES, All Saints (*see page 39*)

Glass: 1894–6 south aisle; 1910; 1925–9 north aisle (Watts memorial window)

1894–9   Restoration, organ case, screen & rood, figures on nave pillars, brass lectern, vestry

1920–23   Oak roof and other restoration work
           Proposed rebuilding of spire and introduction of bells to tower

1931–3   Proposals for improvement of the church

1935–6   Floor, carpet, mats; proposed ringers' gallery, new chancel floor, Osborne memorial

YAXLEY, St Peter

Glass: 1949 east window

1936   Grave cross in churchyard

1946   Altar & reredos

Kent

BARMING, St Margaret

Glass: 1900

1898–1900

Restoration

Pulpit etc.

New paving of chancel

Two kneeling desks

BROMPTON, St Luke

1937   Altar rails, altar book desk of English walnut, 2 silver bowls

CANTERBURY

—CHRIST CHURCH CATHEDRAL

Glass: 1954 Coronation window

1929–31   Proposed shrine to St Thomas of Canterbury

1953   Two tablets (nave & cloister)

1954   Proposed reredos for Martyrdom chapel

—ST MARTIN

1905   Choir stalls (*removed*)

—ST PETER

Glass: 1905 east window of south aisle

CHATHAM, St Mary

1895   Altar frontal

DENTON, St Mary Magdalene

1917–20   Proposed Kitchener memorial cross

DOVER, St Bartholomew
    1921–2   Altar cross

EAST BARMING
        See BARMING

EAST MALLING, St James
    1919   War memorial
    1931   Candlesticks
    1947   Memorial tablet (Blunden)

EASTCHURCH, Royal Naval Air Service Church
        Not extant
    1917   Altar hangings & figures (*not extant*)

ELMERS END (near Bromley), Cemetery
    1903   Gravestone (Revd W. A. Bolton)

FOLKESTONE, St Mary & St Eanswythe
    1912   White chasuble

FRITTENDEN, St Mary
    Glass: 1892
    1920–21   War memorial cross in churchyard
    1924–5   Gravestone (Revd Charles Henry Moore)

GILLINGHAM, St Luke
    Glass: 1891 west window; 1900 east window of south chancel; 1916
    1936–8   Lady Chapel furnishings – frontal, hangings (SSB), tester, blue carpet,
              cross & candlesticks

GOUDHURST, St Mary
    Glass: 1914 (Strathconna memorial window)

HEADCORN, St Peter & St Paul
    Glass: 1895 east window
    1895   Restoration and high altar

★★ KEMSING, St Mary (*see page 81*)
    Glass: 1901 two windows; 1907 west window; 1910 west window in
              north aisle
    1900–1909
              Restoration, high altar, rood figures, hangings, decoration of
              chancel walls
    1909   Brass (Skarratt memorial)
    1914   Lectern
    1933–4   Restoration of central panel of the reredos

LOOSE, All Saints
    1920   Proposed war memorial lych-gate

LYMINGE, St Mary & St Ethelburga
    1913–15   Reredos & candlesticks

NEWENDEN, St Peter
    1927–8   Proposed scheme for decoration and furnishing of chancel

OSPRINGE, St Peter & St Paul
    Glass: 1898–9

ROCHESTER, Cathedral of Christ and the Blessed Virgin Mary
    Glass: 1911 part of tomb of Walter de Merton

SIDCUP, St John
    Glass: 1946 Lady Chapel; 1951 east window; 1958 Baptistery window

TUNBRIDGE WELLS, St Barnabas
 1890s Banner of Our Lady
 1899 Altar & hangings
 1951 Plaster figure of St Barnabas with canopy & pedestal
WEST MALLING, St Mary
 1922–6 Proposed scheme for chancel
WESTERHAM, St Mary the Virgin
 1920 War memorial churchyard cross
 1946 Additional names
WROTHAM, St George
 1907 Reredos in Lady Chapel (*see page 84; similar design to St Paul, Bow Common, London; now in St Wilfrid, CANTLEY, South Yorkshire*)
 1908 Altar frontal

Lancashire

ASPULL, St Elizabeth
 1925 Altar cross
BLACKPOOL, St Cuthbert, South Shore (RC)
 1928–31 Furnishing of chapel of Sacred Heart: altar, embroidered panels of reredos, altar frontal, candlesticks, tabernacle, rood, figures of St Augustine and St Teresa, floor paving and carpet
BURY, St Mary
 1924–5 Roll of Honour of the Lancashire Fusiliers (chained book on a stone desk)
LIVERPOOL
—CATHEDRAL CHURCH OF CHRIST
 1921 Elizabeth Hoare Collection: sampler depicting St Agnes for chasuble (SSB)
—TUE BROOK, St John the Baptist (Architect: G. F. Bodley)
 1952 Figure of St John the Baptist
MANCHESTER
—THE BISHOP'S COURT
 1923–4 Alterations for the Bishop of Manchester (William Temple)
  Altar frontal and curtains, cross and candlesticks
—GRAMMAR SCHOOL HALL
 1964 Heraldic plaque in carved wood, painted & gilt (JSB), celebrating 400th anniversary of school
★★★ ROCHDALE (Wardleworth), St Mary (*see page 127*)
  1980s threat of redundancy. Offer of Grant Aid from Historic Buildings & Monuments Commission 1985. Structural repairs by S. E. Dykes Bower 1989
 Glass: 1910 east window; 1923 west window (war memorial); 1926 small window under gallery (Healey memorial)
 1908–12 New church by JNC, incorporating the nave of the old eighteenth-century church as the north aisle; screen, rood and complete furnishing
 1919–26 Chancel screen, rood beam and images
STONYHURST COLLEGE, Clitheroe
 1924–7 Proposed decoration of dining hall, long room, galleries and sacristies

Leicestershire

HUNGARTON, St John the Baptist
  1897–8   Restoration
  1926–7   Furnishing of the Quenby chapel
LEICESTER
—CATHEDRAL OF ST MARTIN
            Altar frontal
—ALL SAINTS (*in care of Churches Conservation Trust*)
  Glass: 1916 east window of north aisle

Lincolnshire

ALFORD, St Wilfrid
  Glass: 1947 east window of north aisle
(★) BURGH-LE-MARSH, St Paul's Missionary College
            1967 chapel demolished, no trace of glass, but stalls now in Holy Spirit Chapel,
                Sheffield Cathedral
  Glass: 1898; 1914; 1919 29 east and west windows
  1894–5   Chapel built and furnished by Bucknall & Comper
CAISTOR, St Peter & St Paul
  1919–22 War memorial cross
★ GOSBERTON CLOUGH, Mission chapel, now Parish Church, St Gilbert & St Hugh by
            Bucknall & Comper
            Church recently repaired
  Glass: 1920–21 east window
  1902–4   Half timbered nave, stone chancel & fittings (a very small church)
            Stone tablet, font, oak lectern, brass altar cross and candlesticks
  1941   Chair & desk
GRIMSBY, St Augustine (Architect: Sir Charles Nicholson)
  Glass: 1959 two north windows
  1959–61 Candlestick for Paschal candle
  1959   Four candlesticks
KELSTERN, St Faith
  Glass: 1952; 1954; 1957 south window in nave
LINCOLN
★★ —ALL SAINTS
  Glass: 1923 window on south side of chancel; 1926 east window of chapel;
                1928–39 five windows on south, four on north; 1945, St Thomas
  1920–25 Vestments; nave arcade shields; rood beam
  1920–39 St Hugh's chapel, including altar, hangings, reredos, crucifix
  1953   Memorial stone (Canon Harding)
  1955   Tablet in chapel
            Vestments, including red chasuble
—ST ANNE'S BEDEHOUSES, Sewell Road (Architect: William Butterfield)
  Glass: 1955 east window
—ST FAITH
  1948   Figure of Virgin & Child
—ST MARY LE WIGFORD
  1936   Aumbry

★★ NORTH SCARLE, All Saints
    Glass: 1898; 1899
    1898–1901 Major restoration
SAUSTHORPE, St Andrew
    1919–20 Proposed war memorial cross
SAXILBY, St Botolph
    Glass: 1934 north aisle
★ SKEGNESS, St Matthew (Architect: James Fowler)
    Glass: 1950
    1949–56 Font cover, priest's chair, processional cross, reredos (1953), frontal and
        super-frontal (1953), banner (St Mary)
★ SLEAFORD, St Denys
    Glass: 1923 proposed window for Canon Langdon
    1919–42 Rood loft & figures, chancel screen gates
    1923–9 Carved figures of the remaining six apostles for the rood loft; new brass
        and rearrangement of existing brasses
    1938–42 Proposed high altar and ciborium
SPILSBY, St James
    Screen (north aisle east end)
    1919–21 War memorial chapel
STAMFORD, St Mary
    1940–42 Hangings for east wall and altar (SSB)
STOW, St Mary
    1945–6 Pendant for candles & electric light; proposed Waterhouse memorial
        window in Lady Chapel
THORGANBY (near Louth), All Saints
    Glass: 1946 south window in chancel; 1948 north window; 1956 north
        window
WAINFLEET, Magdalen College School
    1924–6 Silver and enamel Challenge shield, with the Magdalen College arms
        School transferred to Skegness Grammar School, 1933. Current whereabouts of
        shield unknown.
WEST KEAL, St Helen
    1919–21 War memorial cross in churchyard

London (including Greater London)

ACTON, St Peter, St Alban's Avenue
    1927   Banner
BAYSWATER, Priory of the Resurrection, Westbourne Terrace
    Not extant
    1926–8 Room furnished as chapel
    Four candlesticks and crucifix (*now at Mirfield, West Yorkshire*)
BETHNAL GREEN, St John (Architect: Sir John Soane)
    1911–12 Altar & alterations to Bodley reredos
    Light fittings
BOW COMMON, St Paul, Burdett Road
    Destroyed in WWII
    1904   Screen, reredos & fittings (*reredos now in St Wilfrid,* CANTLEY, *South*
        Yorkshire)

BROMPTON, Holy Trinity, Brompton Road

    1936–7   Altar rails, with two silver-plated flower-bowls; altar book-desk; proposed altar cross

CAMBERWELL, St Giles, Camberwell Church Street (Architect: Sir George Gilbert Scott)

    Glass: 1954; 1955 (south transept)

    1940s   Decoration & fittings

CAMDEN TOWN, St Michael, Camden Road (Architects: Bodley & Garner)

    1924   Banners

CHILD'S HILL, All Saints

    Destroyed in WWII

    1922–6   Decoration of east end

CITY OF LONDON

—BISHOPSGATE, St Ethelburga

    Church partly destroyed by bomb April 1993. Now the St Ethelburga Centre for Reconciliation and Peace. None of Comper's surviving furniture has been incorporated.

    1911   Restoration, screens & fittings (*not extant*)

    1919–22   War memorial chapel, roll of honour, seat in south aisle, panelling, Rectors board

    1944   Two candlesticks stained black (*not extant*)

—EASTCHEAP, St Clement (Architect: Sir Christopher Wren)

    1932–4   Wren reredos gilded & coloured & side panels; whitening of walls & ceiling; rose-red frontal (SSB)

—EMBANKMENT, EC4

    1919–22   War memorial table for the Metropolitan Asylum Board

—FOSTER LANE, St Vedast

    1916   Altar cross and candlesticks

—HOLBORN VIADUCT, St Sepulchre

    1920–22   War memorial board

    1922–3   Memorial tablet to Revd A. Cunningham-Craig

CLAPHAM

—HOLY TRINITY, Clapham Common Northside

    Proposed scheme for decoration and furnishing of chancel

—ST MARY (Roman Catholic), Clapham Park Road

    1947   Advice on decoration of domestic oratory

CLERKENWELL

—ST JOHN OF JERUSALEM (*destroyed in WWII*) (*see page 184*)

    1907   Cope (*extant 1985*)

(★)   1943   Proposal for rebuilding the church, with detailed perspective drawing of interior of church to replace the original – never built

—ST PHILIP, Granville Square

    Demolished 1930s

    1896   Screens, stonework, banners (SSB now in Our Holy Redeemer, Clerkenwell)

CRICKLEWOOD, St Barnabas Home

    1907   Reredos, riddels & frontals

CROUCH END, Christ Church, Crouch End Hill

    1940   Banner

DARTMOUTH PARK, St Mary Brookfield, Dartmouth Park Hill (Architect: William Butterfield)

1911	Rood beam
1919–21	Organ case; new vestry; war memorial panelling; St George's altar with hangings, reredos and tabernacle
1928	Oak panelling round St George's altar

EALING

—ST BENEDICT ABBEY (Roman Catholic), Charlbury Grove

   Glass: 1964 south transept (JSB)

(★) —ST HELENA'S HOME, Wantage Sisters

        Sold 1979; little of JNC's work remains

   Glass: 1913 east window

| 1913 | Chapel built (one of the first examples of unity by inclusion) |
| 1930–36 | Blue frontal with 4 orphreys (*no trace 1990s*) |

—ST SAVIOUR, The Grove, off Ealing Green (*Church destroyed in WWII*)

| 1920–22 | Banner of St Catharine of Siena |

EAST DULWICH

—LORDSHIP LANE

| 1913 | Proposed design for St Thomas More's Roman Catholic church |

—ST JOHN, East Dulwich Road

   Glass: 1958; 1963, St Cecilia

        Church restored JBSC

EDGWARE, St Lawrence Whitchurch, St Lawrence Close

| 1931 | Interior restoration |

FINSBURY, House of Bethany, the Convent of the Sisters of Bethany, Lloyd Square

        Not extant

| 1903 | Rood and statue of BVM for chapel (*see page 107*) |
| 1923 | Chalice, paten & frontals |

FITZROVIA, St Luke's Hospital chapel, Fitzroy Square

| 1909–10 | Altar reredos & fittings |

FOREST GATE, St James, Forest Lane (*demolished 1964*)

   Glass: 1919–21 east window of war memorial chapel

| 1919–21 | Furniture in war memorial chapel |

FOREST HILL, Christ Church, Church Rise (*declared redundant 2003, due for conversion into residential accommodation with place of worship retained in the chancel*) (Architect: E. Christian)

   Glass: 1934–9 three lights (Paddon memorial window)

FULHAM, Fulham Palace, Bishop's Avenue, domestic chapel

   Glass: 1953 east window (Wand memorial)

        Wall paintings

HACKNEY, St Peter, de Beauvoir Square

| 1931–2 | Proposed high altar and furnishings |

HACKNEY WICK, St Mary of Eton, Eastway (Architect: G. F. Bodley)

   Glass: 1893; 1898 east window (*destroyed in WWII*)

HAMPSTEAD

—ST JOHN, Church Row

| 1928 | Gravestone (John Wallis-Jones) in churchyard |

—ST PAUL, Avenue Road

   Glass: 1896 (*destroyed in WWII*)

HIGHGATE, St Anne, Highgate West Hill
      Medallion of Risen Christ & tablet

HOLBORN

(★★★) —ST ALBAN, Brooke Street (Architect: William Butterfield) (*see page 135*)
   Glass: 1914; 1924–9 three windows in Stanton chantry (*destroyed 1941*); 1945
               Stanton chantry replacements
   1891   Chasuble (SSB)
   1892–4   Vestments (white – high mass set) (SSB) (*extant*)
   1909   Font cover based on Ufford, Suffolk (*destroyed 1941*)
            Statue of St Alban (*extant*)
   1914–29   Stations of the cross and memorial tablets (*mostly destroyed 1941*)
   1917   Stanton chantry built (*destroyed 1941*); tomb-chest (*extant*)
   1936   Canopy for figure of Virgin & Child (figure seventeenth century)
               (*canopy destroyed 1941*)
   1946–8   Plans for restoration
—ST JOHN, Red Lion Square (Architect: J. L Pearson)
            Destroyed WWII
   1922–4   Oak figure of St John with canopy and spire (Cowan memorial)
   1922–3   Vestments, candelabra (*destroyed WWII*; see TWICKENHAM, Middlesex)
—ST MONICA'S ORATORY, Brooke Street
            Not extant
   Glass: 1892
KENNINGTON, St John the Divine, Vassall Road
   1944–50   Proposed restoration of the church
KENSAL GREEN
   1917   Gravestone
KENSINGTON
—41 EGERTON CRESCENT, SW3
   1927–8   Garden room for Seymour Obermer, with wrought-iron gates
—2 KENSINGTON COURT, Private Oratory belonging to Athelstan Riley
            Not extant
   1895   Altar & alabaster reredos (*went to 14 Davis Street in 1905 & then to
               CAVENDISH, Suffolk*)
—ST CUTHBERT, Philbeach Gardens (Architect: W. D. Gough)
   1933–5   Banner of Blessed Sacrament, pall, chasuble and purple velvet High
               Mass vestments
—ST HELEN, St Quintin Avenue (Architect: JBSC)
   Glass: 1958 east window; east window of chapel; west end rose window
—ST MARY ABBOT'S, High Street
   1903–9   Altar frontal (*not extant, cut up 1985*)
—VICTORIA & ALBERT MUSEUM
   *c.*1890   Embroidered altar frontal: St Barnabas, Beckenham (Circ.715:1960)
   *c.*1890   Cope (T671:1974) (SSB)
   1897   Pyx from St Mary, Egmanton, Nottinghamshire (*see page 69*)
   1900   Hood to cope, morse & stole by Pugin 1840 (T284:1993) (SSB)
   1908   Cope of red silk damask (T333:1970) (SSB)
KENTISH TOWN, St Benet & All Saints, Lupton Street (Architect: Cecil Hare)
            JNC proposals only, not executed
   Glass: Proposed: 1893, 1896, 1900
   1897   Proposed chancel and altar fittings

KILBURN

—PADDINGTON CEMETERY, Willesden Lane

    1920   Gravestone (Revd Francis Cobb; no. 12301, section 1A)

—ST PETER'S HOME (*destroyed WWII*)

               Brass (Revd W. Cleaver)

LAMBETH

—ST ANNE, South Lambeth Road

   Glass: 1904 (Morris window)

   1904   Memorial tablet

(★★★) —ST JOHN, Waterloo Road (Architect: Francis Bedford)

               Church extant, but all JNC's work destroyed WWII. Restored 1951 by Thomas Ford & Partners.

               St John's was the most advanced application of JNC's mature church-planning theories after his experiments at the Grosvenor Chapel in 1912. The high altar was brought into the body of the nave, enclosed in communion rails, and protected by a ciborium. The former sanctuary was made into a chapel. It was the first experiment in a parish church of JNC's discovery of Constantinian church-planning at Theveste in North Africa and anticipated a similar solution at St John's, Workington, Cumbria, in 1930–33, and the building of St Philip's, Cosham, Hampshire, in 1935–9.

   1924–5   Replanning, decoration and furnishing, including: altar, tester, altar hangings, altar cross and candlesticks; repaving of the chancel, carpet, electric light fittings

   1926–30 Pulpit hanging; two chairs and two desks, with cushions; communicants' rails; seats; aumbry; removal of the choir seats and iron screens; cushion for the Bishop's Chair; memorial brass

   1931–3   Altar cross and six candlesticks; proposed children's chapel

   1940–41 Salvage and demolition work, after the destruction of the church by enemy action

LEWISHAM, St Stephen, Lewisham High Street

   1893   Vestments & banner

LEYTONSTONE, Holy Trinity, Birkbeck Road

               Demolished 1970s

   Glass: 1910 window on south side of chancel; 1930 windows in chapel of All Saints; 1938 west window of chapel (in memory of Ernest William Saunders)

   1908   New chapel

               Proposed carved wood figures of SS Mary & John

MARYLEBONE

★★★ —ALL SAINTS, Margaret Street (Architect: William Butterfield)

   1909   Restoration of the altar screen by William Dyce on the east wall. Dyce's panels had almost entirely perished and JNC replaced the series, painted on mahogany boards with zinc backings, in order to protect what was left of Dyce's originals. The main figures were lengthened in order to improve the proportions. In 1916 new figures were added to the blind tracery on the north and south sides of the sanctuary. (*Cleaned by Peter Larkworthy in 1980*)

1911	Chancel vault decorated and sets of silk-damask hangings provided for the lower east and south walls; high altar lengthened; wrought-iron brackets for the sanctuary lamps. White chasuble.
	(JNC's work on the east wall, vault, and the addition of later furniture effectively changed the character of All Saints by drawing the sting from Butterfield's constructional polychromy. His proposals for lime-washing the interior were not accepted.)
	Lady Chapel, altar, carved altar screen and tester (*cleaned by Peter Larkworthy in 1980*)
1912	Green altar frontal for high altar
1918	Proposed war memorial chapel of the Holy Angels
1925	Hearse, platform and heraldic achievement for Queen Alexandra's requiem
1927–8	Hanging tabernacle of silver in the form of a *turris*, presented by the Duke of Newcastle as a war memorial to the men of the choir, with an electric hoist, dedication brass and marble slab
1928	Proposed *reja* of black iron for chancel screen
1928–34	Silver ciborium
	Advice on the restoration of the chancel gates
1937–40	Memorial brass to Prebendary H. F. B. Mackay

—ALL SOULS, Langham Place

1921–2	Proposed altar hangings
	Altar frontals

—ALL SOULS CHURCH OF ENGLAND SCHOOL, Foley Street

1922	Interior cleaning with repairs

★★★ —ST CYPRIAN, Clarence Gate (located north end of Glentworth Street) (by Bucknall & Comper) (*see page 87*)

Glass:	1903 east window one light
	1918 east window lower lights
	1927 east window of Lady Chapel
	1946 east window completion
1902–3	Built & furnished
1920–22	Completion of central screen
1922–7	Completion of main screen; altar cross and candlesticks; credence table. Completion of structure of the front screen north aisle. Completion of the screen between the north aisle and the north chancel. Standard candlesticks. Decoration of the Lady Chapel screen. Lady Chapel altar hangings. Figure of the Virgin & Child. Holy water stoup. Decoration of the rood loft. War memorial panel for the boys of Arnold House School. Proposed cope.
1933	Carved seraphim for rood
1944	Figure of the Assumption of the BVM
1946	Tester over high altar with Majestas

★★ MAYFAIR, Grosvenor Chapel, South Audley Street, (Chapel-of-Ease to St George's, Hanover Square) (Architect: Benjamin Timbrell)

Glass:	1927–8 south-east window in nave (Longman memorial window); 1929–32 easternmost window of north aisle; 1942 north aisle (Nepean memorial window); south aisle (Orme memorial window)
1911–12	Remodelling and planning of the chapel. The Grosvenor Chapel was the first English church of the twentieth century to have the high

altar brought forward to be in visual relationship with the congregation. A consistory court case, which questioned the legality of a baldachino, or ciborium, above the high altar prevented the scheme from being completed. Two giant Ionic columns were erected at the east end, which were intended to be the first of a series extending west.

Executed work includes: altar screen and rood; ciborium over the high altar (only partly erected); altar hangings; decoration in white and gold

1919–22 Pyx, with pyx-cloth and canopy, suspended from an angel with a crook above the reredos in the Lady Chapel.

1922–8 Vestments – four Low Mass sets; alteration and decoration of the rood beam and images; electric lighting in the chancel; altar book-desk. Proposed completion of the ciborium

1932 Proposed floor brass in memory of Bishop Gore

1938–9 Two oak chairs; two chair cushions from Watts & Co. Embroidered altar linen

1946 Canopy in the form of a triple crown above the pyx gilded in burnished gold

1949 Electric chandeliers in nave

MUSWELL HILL, St Andrew, Alexandra Park Road *(badly damaged WWII, reopened 1957)*

1937–9 Figure of Risen Christ, hangings and altar frontal (SSB) *(destroyed WWII)*
Bronze memorial tablet to Revd M. C. Blakelock *(extant)*

NEWHAM, Church of the Ascension, Baxter Road, Victoria Docks
Glass: 1918–23 east window, St Joan of Arc (repaired 1949)

NORTH FINCHLEY, St Elizabeth's Home
1947 Redecoration of figure of BVM

★ NOTTING HILL, All Saints, Clydesdale Road
Glass: 1955 east window of Lady Chapel; 1957 south window of Lady Chapel
1912 Vestments
1952 Lady altar & fittings, triptych
1958 Pulpit sounding board
1955 St Columba altar (hangings, frontal, reredos)

★★★ PADDINGTON, St Mary Magdalene, Clarendon Crescent (Architect: G. E. Street) *(see page 60)*
Glass: *c.*1895 (drawing in V&A exhibition 1971)
1895 St Sepulchre's crypt chapel; red high mass vestments and altar frontal (made by St Mary Magdalene's Guild of Embroidery; V&A exhibition 1971); mitre
Painted ceiling, screen, organ case, reredos
Sanctuary lamp (V&A exhibition 1971)
1897 Gate to staircase, altar frontal
Monumental brasses to Revd Richard Temple West (d. 1893) and Revd W. Bleadon (1915)
1937 Four candlesticks

★★ PIMLICO, St Barnabas, St Barnabas Street (Architect: T. Cundy) *(see page 75)*
Glass: 1901 Lady Chapel *(damaged WWII, restored 1945)*; 1953 east window *(replacement for one destroyed in WWII)*
1889–90 Iron screens, rood beam and lamp in crypt

1890–1901
   Lady Chapel, painted screens & altar; sacrament house in sanctuary,
    statue of Our Lady on chancel south wall, decoration of lower
    chancel walls

1931–2 Oak memorial tablet to the Revd and Hon. Alfred Hanbury-Tracy

POPLAR, St Saviour, Northumbria Street (*closed 1985*)
 Glass: 1893 (*destroyed in WWII*)

PORT OF LONDON, Mission to Seamen
 Glass: 1948 Sankey memorial

PRIMROSE HILL, St Mary, King Henry's Road
 Glass: West window of south aisle (early)

REGENT'S PARK
★★ —ST MARK, Prince Albert Road
 Glass: 1957 east and south windows of Lady Chapel;
    1959 Lady Chapel round window;
    1960 north aisle, St Thomas & St Mary Magdalene windows;
    1961 north aisle, Journey to Emmaus

1936–8 Painted Triptych (high altar) (*destroyed in WWII, restored 1955 from original
    drawings with improvements*)

1955 Restoration

1957 Cross & candlesticks (high altar & Lady Chapel)
    Frontal (Lady Chapel)

1958 Altar pillars with angels, 2 standard candlesticks, painted predella and
    triptych (Lady Chapel)

—ST MARY MAGDALENE, Munster Square (Architect: R. C. Carpenter)
    Proposed rood, and Lady Chapel screen
    Vestments

ST PANCRAS, Church of the Holy Cross, Cromer Street (Architect: Joseph Peacock)
 1914 Banner of St Pancras

SHADWELL, St Paul, The Highway (Architect: John Walters)
    Altar frontal (*decayed 1980*)
    Churchwardens' staves

★★ SOUTH NORWOOD, St Alban the Martyr, junction of Grange Road and
    Whitehorse Lane
    (Architects: Bucknall & Comper; more Bucknall's work than Comper)
    1889–98; from 1905 Bucknall took responsibility for completing
    the church.

 Glass: 1905 Lady Chapel
 1895 Lady Chapel
 1922 Proposal by Bucknall to alter steps of high altar
 1951 Hanging rood, & pulpit with sounding board (AB)

SOUTHWARK
★★ —CATHEDRAL OF ST SAVIOUR (*see page 144*)
 Glass: 1923 proposed window in Lady Chapel;
    1929 north side of choir ambulatory, middle light of window; proposed
    window in south side of Lady Chapel
    1945–7 east window (Majestas)

1899 Altar frontal for Lady Chapel and burses and veils
1921–3 War memorial tablet, with St George in a wreath, in retro-choir.
    Advice on the treatment of the Gower tomb.

1923–6   Works in the Lady Chapel, including: altar, altar pillars and four gilt
                angels, altar frontal and upper frontal. Paving. Two communicants
                kneeling desks. Carpet.
            Pulpit cushion
            Deaconess Gilmore memorial tablet, incorporating a portrait relief by
                Arthur George Walker (south transept west wall)
            Harvard chapel: altar frontals and oak altar top
            Cope and set of high mass vestments of *lama d'oro*
            Vestment chest
            Altar frontal chest
            Proposed furnishing of the Chapel of the Social Worker's Guild (the
                Good Samaritan chapel), including the altar, altar hangings,
                panelling, credence table, communion rails with flower bowls,
                screens to the top of the cornice, decoration of the ceiling bays, and a
                carpet
            Proposed chairs and stools for the Lady Chapel
1927–9   Furnishing of St Christopher's chapel, including: altar, altar hangings,
                reredos, communion rails
1928–31   Decoration of the high altar, including pillars with angels and hangings.
                High altar reredos. Decoration of the high altar screen, between the
                altar pillars.
            Mothers' Union banner
            Embroidered pulpit hanging
            Restoration of the decoration on Bishop Lancelot Andrewes's tomb
            Alteration to the Bishop's throne; embroidered hanging provided
                behind it
            Lady Chapel screens
            Limewashing of the Lady Chapel and choir aisles
            Lowering of the floor of the retro-choir, and provision of new heating
                system, under the delegated supervision of W. A. Forsyth, Architect
                to the Cathedral
            Works in the Missionary chapel, including: oak altar, reredos, altar
                hangings and candlesticks
            Candlesticks for St Christopher altar
            Proposed tapestries of rose-red Van de Weyden silk damask for the
                chancel and the two western piers of the nave crossing
            Proposed decoration of the Gower tomb
1935   Banner for the Girls' Friendly Society
1936–7   Mitre of *lama d'oro*, low mass vestments, altar frontals for the high altar,
                including one of Strawberry cloth of gold
1938–9   Bishop Preston memorial footstool
            Memorial stone to Provost J. B. Haldane
1945   Proposal for ciborium for the crossing
1949   Oak altar in retro-choir
1954   Six kneeling desks; priest's chair and desk
—GUY'S HOSPITAL
1922   Proposed alteration to chapel
1937   Blue chasuble & altar frontal (SSB)

—ST ALPHEGE, Lancaster Street (*redundant, closed 1985*)

1936   Reredos

1985   Statue of St Alphege

—ST PETER, Sumner Street (*church destroyed WWII*)

1922–32   Furnishing of sanctuary

1925–6   Banner (*worn out 1985*)

1929–30   Limewashing of the walls

Tile floor in the chancel

Enlargement of the Lady altar

Altar hangings

Chalice

Proposed wrought-iron lectern

1933   Festival frontal (Strawberry cloth of gold) (SSB)

1935   White chasuble

STEPNEY, St Augustine, Settles Street (*church destroyed WWII*)

Banner

STREATHAM

—NORWOOD GROVE, SW16

1927–8   Stanton Covington testimonial bird bath (following acquisition of Norwood Grove as a public open space)

—ST ANSELM (*demolished*)

Glass: 1956 east window around apse, 14 lancets

1899   Altar frontal

—ST PETER, Leigham Court Road

1909   Sacrament house & safe in vestry

1953–5   Altar & reredos in chapel

Small font cover

STROUD GREEN, Holy Trinity, Granville Road

1893   Brass lectern

1920   War memorial tablet (*not extant*)

UPPER NORWOOD

—ALL SAINTS, Beulah Hill

1919–29   War memorial and decoration in chancel

—ST JOHN, Sylvan Road (Architect: J. L. Pearson)

Glass: 1894 east window of south transept; 1893 rose window in north transept (repaired 1954, with a Majestas in centre)

1891   Vestments

Seven sanctuary lamps, thurible, incense boat, censer

*c.*1898   Cope

Banners

*c.*1898   Chalice veil & burse

—ST JOHN'S COTTAGE HOSPITAL

1890–94   Chapel & interior fittings

Sanctuary lamps

—ST MARGARET (*church declared redundant 2003*)

1943   Two standard candlesticks of oak

VAUXHALL, St Peter, Kennington Park Road (Architect: J. L. Pearson)

Banner

VICTORIA & ALBERT MUSEUM
        See KENSINGTON, London

WALWORTH

—ST JOHN, Larcom Street (*damaged WWII*)

1927	Six candlesticks & cross & 4 chandeliers
1936–9	Rood & beam, with rood figures and pelican
1943	Proposed carving of Virgin & Child, with design for stone corbel

—ST PETER, Liverpool Grove (Architect: Sir John Soane)
        Interior fittings

WANDSWORTH, St Anne, St Ann's [*sic*] Hill (Architect: Sir Robert Smirke)

1911	Proposed figure of Risen Christ
	Church lime-washed
	Hangings (*decayed 1986*)

WEST DRAYTON, St Martin, Church Road

Glass: 1896; 1899 west window; 1906 two windows; 1908

WEST DULWICH, All Saints, Rosendale Road
        Church and glass destroyed by fire 2000, church restored 2006

Glass: 1952 east window of Lady Chapel

1930–33	Oak cresting and coving behind high altar
	New heating system

WESTMINSTER

★★★ —WESTMINSTER ABBEY (*see page 159*)

Glass: north aisle (series of eight):

        1908–9 Edward III & Archbishop Simon Langham, Sir B. Baker

        1913 Henry V & Abbot William of Colchester, Lord Kelvin

        1919 Richard II & Abbot Littlington, Baron Strathearn

        1919–22 Edward I & Abbot Wenlock, J. W. Barry

        1923–7 Henry VI & Abbot Harweden, the Gerard window, British
            P.O.W. Germany 1914–18

        1923–7 Edward the Confessor & Abbot Edwin, Royal Army Medical
            Corps

        1950 Henry III & Abbot Richard de Vere, G. A. Parsons

        1962 King Edgar & St Dunstan including arms of JNC, Sir Frederick
            Royce

Other glass:

        1910–11 north transept, Bunyan memorial window

        1951 east window of triforium

Banners: 1923 (Girls Friendly Society); 1923–7 Mothers' Union; 1938 Church
            of England Men's Society (SSB)

1923–7	Cope (*cut up*)
1924	Cross (for Lady Margaret Beaufort chapel) in association with Detmar Blow
1925–32	The Warriors' chapel (chapel of St George, originally the Holy Cross), wrought-iron screens & other fittings
1932	Candlesticks
	Altar frontal (for Coronation of George VI)
1960	Stone tablet (floor of north aisle, marking position of interment of JNC's ashes) (JBSC)

—CHAPEL OF THE COWLEY FATHERS, 22, Great College Street

        Not extant

1906   Simple rearrangement of chapel, red altar frontal (*not extant*)

—MISSION OF THE GOOD SHEPHERD, 12 St Matthew Street, SW1 (*church destroyed WWII*)

1922–3   Enlargement of the altar, hangings, limewashing of walls, electric lighting

1925–7   Incorporation of statue of Our Lady of Peace, by Martin Travers; carved cross, corbel and canopy of *lama d'oro*. Paving stones round altar, carpet.

—ROYAL MILITARY HOSPITAL CHAPEL, Millbank (*demolished*)

1910   Altar cross

(★★) —ST MATTHEW, Great St Peter Street

    Glass: 1893 east window of Lady Chapel

1892   Vestry, built with Lady Chapel above

            Decoration & furnishing of Lady Chapel

            First 'English Altar' since Reformation with suspended tabernacle (see also CANTLEY, South Yorkshire)

1901   Hearse & funeral trappings (for requiem of Queen Victoria)

            4 candlesticks (*stolen 1977*)

1914   Decoration of east wall of Lady Chapel

1977   *Church destroyed by fire; subsequently restored*

1980   Chasuble (*small portion survives as part of reworked chasuble*)

1984   Lady Chapel completely restored (with modifications and elaboration by Donald Buttress)

★ —WESTMINSTER HALL, Palace of Westminster

    Glass: 1952 Parliamentary war memorial

            Case for book of names (Designed by AB made by Albert Webb)

WIMBLEDON PARK, St Paul, Augustus Road

1915   Proposed altar cross

Middlesex

BEDFONT (near Feltham), Chapel

1907   Chapel of Community of St Mary the Virgin, Wantage. Rebuilt at THORPE, Surrey, 1931.

HARROW-ON-THE-HILL

—QUAINTON HALL SCHOOL

            Crucifix, vestments (from the House of Prayer, Burnham, Buckinghamshire)

—ST MARY

    Glass: 1906 east window

1928–9   Conversion of north chancel aisle into a side chapel, with fittings

NORTHWOOD, Holy Trinity

    Glass: 1928–30 baptistery

PINNER, St John the Baptist

    Glass: 1906; 1912

1906   Gravestone

TWICKENHAM

—ALL HALLOWS

1922–3   Candelabra (the larger of two from St John, Red Lion Square,
HOLBORN, London)

—CEMETERY

1925–6   Gravestone (Major-General Willoughby Garnons Gwatkin)

Norfolk

EAST WINCH, All Saints

1913   Font cover

★ GREAT RYBURGH, St Andrew

1912   Reredos; plaster vaulting with angels in the chancel
Kneeling desks

1912–17 Other fittings

1919–20 Proposed choir stalls and rood screen

HOLT, Gresham School Chapel

1917   Altar and hangings

HOVETON, St John

Glass: 1912–14 north window

HUNSTANTON, St Edmund (Architect: F. Preedy)

Glass: 1911 south window

★ LITTLE WALSINGHAM, Church of St Mary and Shrine of Our Lady
of Walsingham

Glass: 1931; 1952; 1956 small panel from House of Prayer, Burnham,
Buckinghamshire

1933   Red vestments, given by the Guild of the Servants of the Sanctuary

1959   Altar frontal, gilt & painted; reredos & tester; candlesticks & crucifix;
carved shells & rays either side of niche (figure of BVM not by JNC);
brass chandeliers (JSB, executed by Butchart)

1961   Figures from rood in House of Bethany, Lloyd Square, Clerkenwell,
unrecognisably incorporated by Lawrence King in hanging rood in St
Mary's church

★★ MUNDFORD, St Leonard

Glass: 1911 east window

1911   Restoration; chancel decoration; screen, reredos, riddels & frontals
(SSB), pulpit, organ case

1946   Electric light chandeliers & brackets

NARBOROUGH, All Saints

1912   Font cover

NORWICH

—CATHEDRAL OF THE HOLY AND UNDIVIDED TRINITY (*see page 102*)

1900   Bishop's cope of Russian cloth-of-gold, worn at coronation of
Edward VII (SSB). Morse, crocketted mitre and jewelled gloves of red
silk. Morse of silver-gilt for the Dean's cope. Both morses made by
Barkentin & Krall

—ST PETER MANCROFT

1895–1902

Restoration of tower and sanctuary levels

1929–33   Reredos (by J. P. Seddon, 1885) remodelled & enlarged, with figures of the Risen Christ, St Augustine, St Columba, St Alban, St Felix and the Virgin & Child; altar frontal, hangings and cushions

STRATTON STRAWLESS, St Margaret

Glass: 1900 south aisle (*destroyed WWII*)

1898–1902

Alterations and additions by Bucknall & Comper, including new floor, seats and screens, font, new altar and altar hangings (*not extant 1980s*)

WALSINGHAM

See LITTLE WALSINGHAM

WALSOKEN, All Saints

1920–21   Proposed window over south door

WATLINGTON, St Peter & St Paul

1915   Reredos, altar cross, altar frontal (*no trace 1980s*)

1955   Reredos & tester (*extant 1980s*)

WOODBASTWICK, St Fabian & St Sebastian

1906   Churchyard Cross

Gravestone (Cator)

★★★ WYMONDHAM, Abbey Church of St Mary & St Thomas of Canterbury (*see page 131*)

1913–34   Restoration

1919–34   Altar screen (cleaned and conserved 1993); altar; tester; rood

1926   War memorial tablet

1933   Lady Chapel

1938   Paschal & standard candlesticks

1946   Memorial tablet (Daniel)

1947   Virgin & Child figure

Cross & 6 candlesticks

1948   War memorial tablet

YARMOUTH, St Nicholas

Destroyed WWII; restored S. E. Dykes Bower

Glass: 1903 (*destroyed WWII*)

Northamptonshire

★ BENEFIELD, St Mary (Architect: J. M. Derick)

Glass: 1896

1894–8   Rood, English altar and reredos, ringers' loft

1918–20   War memorial cross in churchyard

BRACKLEY, Magdalen College School

Glass: 1897 east window, five lights

CASTLE ASHBY, St Mary Magdalene

Fittings

CROUGHTON, All Saints

Glass: 1924–7 two south aisle windows: east and Lady Chapel window

1924–7   Altar frontal and upper frontal

★ GEDDINGTON, St Mary Magdalene

Glass: 1903 east window; 1934 Lady Chapel

1890   Restoration; early reredos (JNC's first restoration, including features such as the black and white marble floor which he later repudiated)

1912   Stalls

HIGHAM FERRERS, St Mary
    1911–19   Fittings
    1918–22   Rood loft, carved woodwork
               Memorial tablet to William Havers Pope
KETTERING, St Peter & St Paul
    Glass: 1937 east window of north aisle
NORTHAMPTON, St Peter
             Redundant 1990s, in care of Churches Conservation Trust
    1942–4   Moving of the font; electric lamp
             Proposed scheme for the chancel, including new high altar, hangings, chancel screen, rood beam with Christ in Majesty in vesica, ciborium, decoration of the existing reredos (by John Oldred Scott), and whitening of the walls and roof
OUNDLE
—ST PETER
    Glass: 1896; 1916 south window
    1896–8   Oak kneelers & other fittings
(★) —WORKHOUSE CHAPEL
    1889–91   Chapel built (JNC's first work in England). *Now converted to a house.*
ROCKINGHAM, St Leonard
    1921   Lych-gate
THORPE MALSOR, St Leonard
    1920–35   Proposed alterations to high altar
    1934   Gravestone
★★★ WELLINGBOROUGH, St Mary (*see page 190*)
             Complete church, fittings & furnishing. 1904–31; work begun in 1907 and built gradually over the following decades. JNC's most important work.
    Glass: 1920–22 east window; 1922 St John's chapel; 1935 east window of Jesus Chancel, in memory of Grace Comper (JNC's wife); 1950 windows of St John's chapel completed; 1958; 1965 sacristy (JSB)
    1907–15   Building of chancel and north and south chapels
    1920–22   Tester, high altar hangings, screens with decorative iron work and bronze angels, iron balusters for chancel; iron candlesticks, hanging pyx (*now at NEWPORT PAGNELL, Buckinghamshire*)
    1923–6   Decoration of the tester; altar cross and candlesticks; rood loft and figures
    1940   High altar decorated
    1945–6   Majestas
    1946–7   Font cover proposed; superseded in 1966 by a design by JBSC

Nottinghamshire

CLUMBER PARK (National Trust), St Mary the Virgin (Architect: G. F. Bodley)
    Glass: Four small windows
    1897   Statues of Virgin Mary, St George, St Barnabas
             Altar frontal; vestments
CODDINGTON, All Saints
    1901   Altar hangings
DAYBROOK, St Paul
    1919–22   War memorial tablet

EAST MARKHAM, St John the Baptist (*see page 70*)

    Glass: 1897 east window

1896–9   Restoration (incomplete)

               High altar; vestments

★★★ EGMANTON, St Mary (*see page 69*)

               Church recently restored

    Glass: 1896 east window

1897   Restoration (for Duke of Newcastle)

               Rood screen, organ case, font cover

               Open pulpit (V&A exhibition 1971)

               Hanging pyx (now (2006) in V&A)

★ NEWARK-ON-TRENT, St Mary Magdalene

1930–32   Chapel of the Holy Spirit

1935–7   Triptych & high altar, alterations to the sanctuary floor, credence table, altar hangings

NOTTINGHAM

—ST PETER

    Glass: 1963–4 four 3-light windows (JSB)

—TRENT COLLEGE

    Glass: 1963 (JSB)

RETFORD, East, *(original location and current whereabouts unknown)*

1928   Gravestone (Canon A. J. Mason)

SHIREOAKS, St Luke

1899   Proposed chapel over end of south aisle

TUXFORD, St Nicholas

1906   Furnishings

Oxfordshire

BURFORD, St John the Baptist

1909   Minor restoration

CUDDESDON, Theological College (*see page 174*)

1934   Proposed plans for a new chapel

DRAYTON ST LEONARD, St Leonard

    Glass: 1897 east window of chancel; 1898 east window of south aisle

1898   Painted and carved pulpit

★ EWELME, St Mary

1903–4   English altar, painted frontal, reredos in Jesus chapel

HENLEY-ON-THAMES, St Mary

1895   Painting of chancel; altar frontal

IFFLEY, St Mary

1907   Pulpit (*now in St John the Evangelist, New Hinksey; see under* OXFORD)

OXFORD (and surrounds)

—CHRIST CHURCH CATHEDRAL

               Tablet (on north nave pillar)

1918   Scott Holland memorial

               Chandeliers (*not extant 1984*)

1919–21 War memorial book with silver and enamel work

1924–6	Fittings, including: Chapter House brackets; stalls and altar frontals for Latin and Trinity chapels; communion kneeling desks; priests' kneeling desks; kneeling stools; electric light fittings

—COWLEY

★ ——MISSION HOUSE OF SSJE, Marston Street (Architect: G. F. Bodley)

1937–9	Transeptal altar & end of chapel of the Holy Name; ciborium (first proposed in 1913); Benson memorial

——ST BARTHOLOMEW'S CHAPEL

1908–37	Simple restoration
1924–35	Inner roof of oak, with cornice
1936	Electric light pendants & brackets, limewashing, oak cupboards, almsbox

★★★ ——ST JOHN'S HOME (The Society of All Saints), Leopold Street, by Bucknall & Comper (*see page 97*)

Glass:	1907 east window tracery & centre light (completed later); 1910 east window of south aisle; 1946 west window
1902–33	Chapel (completed 1907), extension to dining-room wing
	Rood screen (stone)
	Stalls
	Figure of Virgin & Child on plinth – gilt & coloured
	High altar with riddel posts
	Silver-gilt ciborium (*sold*)
	Two large free-standing silver candlesticks on stone plinths
1932–3	Altar frontals, funeral pall
	Altar frontal from London Colney (*under repair 1985*) (see ST ALBANS, Hertfordshire)
	Following alterations of 1980:
	Removal of 2 brass chandeliers (to Magdalen College, Oxford); removal of gates (wooden) in stone screen; nave altar to replace screen altar

——ST MARY & ST JOHN, Cowley Road

Glass:	1893; 1907; 1913; 1922
1889–90	Altar furnishings
1916–17	Benson memorial Calvary
	Bucknall & Comper: parish room (1892–3), parish schools (1894), Vicarage (1902)

—HEADINGTON QUARRY, Holy Trinity (Architect: G. G. Scott)

Glass:	1952 east window

★★★ —NEW HINKSEY, St John the Evangelist by Bucknall & Comper (*see page 84*)

1898–1900	
	Nave only built
	Aumbry
1937	Roof painting
1942	Lobby to south door
1950	Frontal & frontlet (Watts & Co.)
	Church also contains JNC's pulpit from St Mary, IFFLEY

★★★ —PUSEY HOUSE, Chapel of the Resurrection (Architect: Temple Lushington Moore) (*see page 170*)

Glass:	1935 east window
1935–9	Decoration of east window splays

Ciborium

Gilded metal frontal, with foliage scrolls and the Annunciation

Alteration of the rood, and fixing of the altar in the rood loft

Alteration of the altar pace; marble altar top; memorial stone with
  bronze lozenge showing the arms of Lady Powell, from whose legacy
  the chapel was furnished

Altar pillars

Altar cross and six candlesticks

Four candlesticks for altar in the rood loft

Tabernacle

Embroidered frontlet, sedilia hanging, cushion, fair linen cloths, altar
  frontals, aumbry veil and cere cloth

Oak bookcase

Oak credence table, with wrought-iron furniture

Iron lamps for stalls

Brass chandeliers

Carpets

Vestments

Staining of the organ console

—ST PETER'S IN THE EAST

1932   Decoration and furnishing of crypt chapel

—UNIVERSITY

——ALL SOULS

1949   Memorial stone (Archbishop Lang)
          White altar frontal

——KEBLE COLLEGE

1919–21   Proposed war memorial cross

——MERTON COLLEGE

1910–11   Altar and panelling

1920–31   War memorial tablets in the choir and archway to Fellows' Quad;
          refurnishing of sanctuary

——ORIEL COLLEGE

Glass: 1909; 1913 bay window; 1915; 1924–30 Annunciation; heraldic
            windows (*all glass in the hall*)

1909–11   Screen, panelling and restoration of the hall
          Light fittings

1924–30   Altar frontals, burses and veils for chapel

RADLEY, College Chapel

1905   Altar hangings

SANDFORD-ON-THAMES, St Andrew

          Lamp

★ SOULDERN, St Mary

Glass: 1898 east window of south aisle

1894–6   New chancel and transepts by Bucknall & Comper
          Stalls

SOUTH LEIGH, St James

1934   Electric pendants, additions to pulpit, heating

1938   White chasuble (SSB)

STANTON HARCOURT, St Michael

Glass: 1914 (*not extant 1989*)

UFFINGTON, St Michael & All Angels
    1945   Chalice & paten (donated by John Betjeman)

WALLINGFORD, St Leonard
    Glass: 1934

(★) WANTAGE, St Mary's Convent
    Glass: 1924 east window
    1899   Funeral pall (*not extant*)
    1922–35 Alterations to east end of the chapel and altar; dossal, frontal, banner
                  (*none extant, except dossal to Norwich Ecclesiological Museum*)

WESTON-ON-THE-GREEN, St Mary
    1921–2   Altar canopy and hangings

WHITCHURCH (near Reading), St Mary
    1937   Processional cross & oak standards

WOOTTON, Boar's Hill, St Peter
    1937–40 Reredos and oak panelling

Rutland

ASHWELL, St Mary
    Glass: 1903

★ KETTON, St Mary
    Glass: 1906; 1916
    1920–21 War memorial cross in churchyard
    1923–5   Works in chancel, including complete refurnishing
    1925   Burroughes memorial stone
    1926–7   Altar frontal (LB)
    1945   Gravestone (General Gorton)

LANGHAM, St Peter & St Paul
    Glass: 1905 east window (Frederick Hamlyn memorial); 1909 south transept
               (Sir Henry Clarke Jervoise memorial); 1937 additional inscription
               for Hamlyn window; 1949 new head of St Michael for Jervoise
               memorial

OAKHAM
—ALL SAINTS
    Glass: 1911 (Presentation of Christ in the Temple)
    1913–45 Restoration
    1913   Altar frontal
    1914–15 Gravestones
    1919–22 Town war memorial cross, processional candlesticks
    1922–30 Vestments; crucifix in south porch; Henry Nicholson brass memorial
               tablet; bishop's chair; banner; pair of cruets and lavabo bowl
    1945   Lady altar frontal, curtains (SSB), oak altar cross & candlesticks,
               credence table, kneeling rails
               Chair
—RUTLAND CEMETERY
    1945   Gravestone (Canon Charles)
—RUTLAND HOSPITAL
               Plaque

UPPINGHAM, St Peter & St Paul
    Glass: 1909 window on south side of chancel

1919–20 War memorial cross in churchyard

1920–24 Cracks in cross repaired

Shropshire

LUDLOW, St Lawrence

      Tracery, chancel windows

1923–4 Banner (Royal School of Needlework) (*repaired 1993, now in display case*)

★★ MORETON CORBET, St Bartholomew

  Glass: 1904 chancel east & south windows (east window serves as reredos)

  1905 Restoration of chancel including: reredos, altar & ornaments, frontal & frontlet, including 2 free-standing alabaster figures; gilt tester with shields

  1917–21 Corbet memorial tablet

      Churchyard cross

  1936 Proposed vestry; proposed cleaning and repair of tester and gilded window splays

STANTON-UPON-HINE-HEATH, St Andrew

  Glass: 1913–15 east window

  1915 Altar hangings (LB)

WEST FELTON, St Michael

  Glass: 1926–7 Congreve memorial window

Somerset

BAGBOROUGH

      See WEST BAGBOROUGH

BATHAMPTON, St Nicholas

  Glass: 1914 west window in south aisle, 3 lights (centre, St George & dragon)

BATHWICK

—ST JOHN THE BAPTIST

  1920–23 Rood figures, in memory of James Dunn, Vicar

  1939–46 Figures on screen: St John the Baptist & Virgin & Child, in memory of Charles Etheridge Harris 1919–36, Vicar

  1946 Screen cornice

—ST JOHN'S PRIORY

  1924 Proposed embroidered processional canopy for the Blessed Sacrament

★★ BISHOPS LYDEARD, St Mary

  Glass: 1924; 1938 east window of south chapel

  1919–38 Alteration and redecoration of high chancel, furnishings and vestments, 2 altars, tester over main altar, chandeliers in chancel (*four stolen 1986*)

  1945 Rood loft & figures

  1947 Altar cross and candlesticks (Lady Chapel)

CLEVEDON

      See EAST CLEVEDON

COTHELSTONE, St Thomas of Canterbury

  Glass: 1919 east window

CROSCOMBE, St Mary

  Glass: 1921–6 east window (Allott memorial)

★★★ DOWNSIDE ABBEY, Stratton-on-the Fosse, St Gregory the Great (*see page 46*)

Glass: 1896 heraldic window in new lower east cloister; 1896–8 east window of Lady Chapel; 1899–1927 Lady Chapel, 9 further windows; 1912 window in entrance to crypt; 1914 three windows in Chapel of the Sacred Heart; 1934–6 east window of choir

1896–1900
    Lady Chapel stone altar screen and Gothic altar with four iron riddel posts, presented by Mgr Arthur Stapylton Barnes (*now in Chapel of the Blessed Richard Whiting*)

1905   White altar frontal of cloth of gold (SSB) for Lady Chapel; pair of cloth of gold dalmatics; green and red low mass vestments

1913   Reredos of alabaster in the form of a Jesse Tree framing scenes from the infancy of Christ for the Lady Chapel, with four feretories of gilded wood (V&A exhibition 1971) and a crucifix with figures of St Mary and St John. The reredos was based on surviving examples of fifteenth-century Nottingham alabasters

1915   Statue of Virgin & Child at entrance to the Lady Chapel

1917–31   Chapel of St Sebastian, including: the Van Cutsem tomb; altar, altar frontal and hangings of rose-red silk damask, altar cross and four candlesticks; altar screen with a figure of St Sebastian in alabaster and angels; two parclose screens of stone; tapestry curtain; (1937–9 proposed completion of the two side screens)

1919   Statue of St Benedict

1919–26   Proposed panelling and seats in the Lady Chapel
    Proposed stalls for the Choir
    Proposed scheme of decoration for the Choir and high altar, including a ciborium
    Proposed altars and screens in the upper chapels

1926–31   Lady Chapel gates in iron
    Hangings and carpets for the upper chapels
    Carvings of the four evangelists on the desk ends of the choir stalls

EAST CLEVEDON

★★★ —ALL SAINTS

Glass: 1916 north and south windows of sanctuary
    1917 sedilia window
    1918 two 3-light windows in baptistery; north aisle window
    1920 windows in sanctuary; west rose window
    1922 small windows with heraldic devices in south porch
    1923 west windows in south & north aisles
    1924 two small windows in south transept (figures with no colour); Jesse tree in Jesse chapel in north transept; small windows with heraldic devices in west porch

1920–34   Furnishing scheme
1920–22   Screen & rood loft
1920–25   Reredos (oak & mahogany except central figure of alabaster; made by W. D. Gough, decorated by HABS); crucifix & 6 candlesticks
1933–4   Tabernacle
1948   Statue of Virgin & Child, Lady Chapel (painted & gilt)

—IN VILLAGE

    1920–25   Stone figures of St Mary and St John for the village war memorial; central figure in concrete by Michael Fraund, 1948 (see YEOVIL)

EXFORD, St Mary Magdalene

    1923–5   Oak screen between the nave and the tower, with carved shields and badges

HINTON CHARTERHOUSE, Charterhouse of Locus Dei

    1919–21   Proposed alterations and limewashing

ILMINSTER, St Mary

    1941   Memorial tablet (Boughton)

KINGSTON, St Mary

    Glass: 1922 south window in nave

MAIDEN HEAD

    Glass: 1900 (*original location and current whereabouts unknown*)

MILBORNE PORT, St John Evangelist

    1919–22   War memorial tablet in church; village war memorial cross in churchyard

NAILSEA, Nailsea Court

    Glass: 1929 enamelled crest on pane of glass

OLD CLEEVE, St Andrew

    Glass: 1953 east window

PENSELWOOD, St Michael

    Glass: 1921–4 north wall (Leaver memorial window)

SALTFORD, St Mary

    Glass: 1918

    Private memorial tablet

SELWORTHY, All Saints

    Glass: 1923–5 north aisle (Acland memorial window)

TAUNTON, St Mary Magdalene

    1923   Processional cross

TINTINHULL, St Margaret

    1919–21   Churchyard cross (war memorial)

TRULL, All Saints

    Glass: 1964 (by JSB)

    1896   High altar

WELLS, Cathedral of St Andrew

    1929–30   Mothers' Union banner

    1934–5   Furnishings and decoration of St Stephen's chapel for the Mothers' Union: altar with wrought-iron posts and screen

    1937   Altar frontal, high mass vestments, cope & stole, embroidered mitre & hood, crozier (all by SSB)

    1943   Nativity panel in St Stephen's chapel parclose screen

    1945   Faldstool with 2 shields

    1959   Two kneeling desks

    1964   Flower stand for Mothers' Union chapel (JSB)

★★★ WEST BAGBOROUGH, St Pancras

    Glass: 1916 north window; 1922 east window; 1929 by porch; 1931 south window; 1931 north window; 1934; 1936 north window; 1922 small window in south chancel

1913–41   Restoration, rood beam with rood, figures and dragons
1922–6   Oak screen for organ gallery
          Decoration of rood figures; font cover; altar dorsal and curtains; figure of Risen Christ with canopy
1926–34   Decoration of the roof; tabernacle; figure of St Pancras with canopy; four silver bowls and two candle-brackets
1940   Memorial brass & gravestone to Canon J. F. Briscoe
1941   Gilt chalice & ciborium

WITHAM FRIARY, St Mary, St John the Baptist & All Saints
Glass: 1923 south windows

YEOVIL, St Mary & St John
1902   Furnishings
1918   Central figure in oak from village war memorial at East Clevedon, removed to Yeovil in 1957

Staffordshire

BURTON-ON-TRENT, Holy Trinity
          Demolished 1990s
Glass: 1914

★ CHECKLEY, St Mary & All Saints
Glass: 1919 east window of south aisle & St George window; parish war memorial and Moreton Philips window in north wall
1916   High altar with wrought-iron posts
1916–22   Restoration of south chapel
          English altar, hangings, screens
1921–2   Credence table

DENSTONE, Denstone College
1931   Reredos (altered 1960s), 6 candlesticks

KINGSWINFORD, St Mary
Glass: 1934–5 south window in nave
1955   Aumbry, sanctuary lamp, font cover, tablet

LONGSDON, St Chad
Glass: 1913–17 five lights

LONGTON, St Mary & St Chad
Glass: 1949
          Church demolished 1980s due to subsidence, glass reused in nave of new, smaller building 1989

LOWER GORNAL (Dudley), St James the Great
Glass: 1903 three lights
1903–4   Furnishings

Suffolk

★ BURY ST EDMUNDS, St Mary (*see page 163*)
Glass: 1935 east window of Suffolk chapel; 1951; 1955; 1958; 1961
1935   Decoration and furnishing of the chapel of the Suffolk Regiment; frontal (SSB)
          Proposed designs for an organ case and gallery
1936   Bronze case for regimental Roll of Honour
1958   Roses for ceiling below organ loft

CAVENDISH, St Mary

> Reredos (central panel 16th-century Flemish mounted in a semicircular frame, the whole mounted on a simple predella. Given by Athelstan Riley's daughter 1950. See 2 Kensington Court, KENSINGTON, London)

DENNINGTON, St Mary

1910   Fittings

★★ EYE, St Peter & St Paul

Glass: 1929 window in north aisle, opposite porch; east window; clear glazing of clerestory

1919–27   Restoration of rood screen and loft with figures. Completed in stages: 1919–22, 1922–5 and 1925–7. In 1932–7, proposed to continue screen across south aisle

> Proposed monument to Sir Thomas Tacon

> Grave cross for Harriet Bertha, daughter of Sir Thomas Henry and Kate, Lady Tacon, buried in Worcester Cemetery. Additional base added 1927

1922–5   Chancel paving

> Chancel carpet

> Altar hangings

> Two kneeling stools

> Limewashing of the walls

> Proposed memorial to Revd A. Oakley

1925–7   War memorial tablet

> *Consistory court case over the obliteration of a fresco by the limewashing of the walls; its reinstatement was refused*

1929–32   Font cover

> Memorial book, listing the donors to the memorial to Revd Oakley

> Enlargement of the high altar

> Altar pillars with angels

> Altar hangings

> Altar cross with figures and candlesticks

> Six rose bowls, a censer, incense boat, holy water bucket, asperser and standard candlesticks

> Altar rails

> Rearrangement of choir stalls

> Two memorial stone floor-slabs

> Chancel carpet

> Gravestone in Eye cemetery (Albert Barber)

IPSWICH, St Mary Elms

Glass: 1906 north aisle

KETTLEBASTON, St Mary

1946   Wrought-iron gate to rood loft stairs

★★★ LOUND, St John the Baptist (*see page 122*)

Glass: 1914 east window

1909–14   Major restoration; rood loft, altar of Our Lady, organ case, font cover; north wall painting of St Christopher (designed by JNC, painted by Butchart; De Havilland 'Comet' inserted during restoration 1964)

1920   Proposed war memorial crucifix on outside wall

★ LOWESTOFT, St Margaret
    1905–42 Restoration
    1919–32 War memorial chapel, north-west screen
    1923   High altar and memorial screen
    1923–4   Lych-gate, altar frontals (*no trace of latter 1980s*)
    1932   Lady Chapel screen, panelling and carving
    1939–42 Font cover
    1940   Kneeling desks
    1941   Silver ciborium
    1942   Two processional candlesticks
SOUTHWOLD, St Edmund
  Glass: 1954 east window
★ UFFORD, The Assumption of Our Lady
  Glass: 1901; 1919 east window of south aisle
    1919   South aisle screen
    1919–21 Reredos (war memorial chapel)
    1925   Advice on ventilation and other proposed alterations, including the repositioning of the font in its original position at the west end of the nave, the high altar, reredos and east window
    1934   Paving of south aisle
WINGFIELD, St Andrew
    1924–5   Furniture for Lady Chapel and chancel; kneeling desk (*not extant*)
           Altar hangings, cross and candlesticks (*not extant*)
WOOLPIT, St Mary
    1904   Font
WOOLVERSTONE, St Michael
    1892   Altar hangings

Surrey

BENHILTON, All Saints
    1931   Gravestone
BLETCHINGLEY, St Mary
  Glass: 1894–6 east window (designed by JNC, not executed by him); 1900 two south windows
    1898   Altar hangings etc., embroidery, tapestry
BROOKWOOD, Cemetery
           St Alban's, Holborn, burial plot
★   *c.*1900 Standing calvary
    1913   Gravestone to Revd A. H. Stanton
    1919   Gravestone to Canon and Mrs Edmund McClure
    1932–3   Gravestone to Frederick Edward Sidney (grave no. 197073)
           There are other stones by JNC in the plot
BURGH HEATH, St Mary the Virgin
  Glass: 1929
    1927–9   Decoration and complete furnishing of St Monica's chapel
★★★ CARSHALTON, All Saints (*see page 180*)
  Glass: 1934 west window of north aisle; window in baptistery

Reredos & altar

1920–22 Aumbry in north wall of sanctuary

1935 Decoration in burnished gold of high altar triptych, designed by
G. F. Bodley

Gilding and decoration of the Georgian reredos in the Lady Chapel

Iron screens in the chancel and Lady Chapel

1940 Raising and decoration of Bodley's screen and the rood figures placed
on a new loft

1941–3 Organ case and west gallery

1946 Sounding board and stairs to pulpit

Font cover

1947–8 Majestas above the rood

1948 Portland stone steps to chancel

1958 Chandeliers; ledger memorial

Coped gravestone in churchyard to Revd W. R. Corbauld

CATERHAM-ON-THE-HILL, St Mary

1917–18 Fittings

1930s Triptych (in 'new' church opposite old church)

CHEAM, St Dunstan

1907 Litany desk

COMPTON, St Nicholas

Glass: 1950

COULSDON

—ST ANDREW

Glass: 1958 east window; 1959 east window of Lady Chapel and three
windows on north side of the chapel

—ST JOHN

Glass: 1960 centre light of south window

CROYDON

—ST ANDREW (Architect: B. Ferrey)

Glass: 1941 east window of Lady Chapel (put in 1948 with redesigned tracery
stonework); 1953 two west windows of 2 lights each

Hanging rood

—ST MICHAEL (Architect: J. L. Pearson)

1898 Altar frontal in Lady Chapel, tester

1928–30 Furnishing of Lady Chapel

1952 Cross & candlesticks

ESHER, Christ Church

Glass: 1908 east window with new tracery and mullions; 1911 south window

1909 Altar

EWELL, St Francis

1959 Wall aumbry with door of bronze in relief

GUILDFORD

—CATHEDRAL OF THE HOLY SPIRIT

Glass: 1921 roundel displayed in 'light box' in library (wedding present to
JNC's daughter, Mary Surtees, given to Cathedral in 1988 by
Richard Surtees, his grandson)

1930 JNC submitted a portfolio of plans and photographs of the Seabury
Memorial Cathedral, Aberdeen (unexecuted); All Saints Conventual
Church, St Albans, Herts; and St Mary's, Wellingborough,

Northants: any of these, he suggested, could be adapted and used for the intended cathedral at Guildford

1930s   Figures (from THORPE) *(in storage; but claim has been made (1999) that they should be in Thorpe parish church)*

—ST NICHOLAS

1901   White altar frontal

Monumental brass

—ST NICHOLAS CEMETERY

1923–5   Grave cross for the Peake family

HAM COMMON, Richmond, St Andrew

Glass: 1901 east window (given by Mrs Scott, grandmother of Queen Elizabeth, the Queen Mother; the chancel of the church had been added by G. F. Bodley 1900)

HASLEMERE, St Christopher

1920–21   Gravestone (Henry William Mozley)

KEW, St Anne

1906   Decoration

1923–5   Proposed scheme for redecoration of the church

1954   Redecoration

KINGSTON-UPON-THAMES, All Saints

1912   Banner for Society of Mary *(kept at St Luke's)*

1951   High altar

PEPER HAROW, St Nicholas

Glass: 1902–4; 1907

1945   Memorial tablet

SELHURST, Holy Trinity

Demolished 1982

Glass: 1956 *(removed by Goddard & Gibbs Studios Ltd., London, E2; in store)*

SHOTTERMILL, St Stephen

Glass: 1906

SUTTON, St Nicholas

1926–35   Proposed extension of the chancel and vestry, with furnishings

(★) THORPE, Convent of Spelthorne St Mary

Convent sold 1974

Glass: 1922; 1934 two windows; 1957 three windows *(no trace of these windows after 1976)*

1907   Half-timbered chapel for Community of St Mary the Virgin, Wantage

1920–24   Hanging pyx, panelling, stalls, holy water stoup, window of Our Lady in sanctuary

(Chapel built at Bedfont, near Feltham, Middlesex; rebuilt at Thorpe 1931; now used as reception offices by an American School. Figures in Guildford Cathedral; tester being (1998) restored for use in Thorpe parish church.)

WEST CLANDON, St Peter & St Paul

*c.*1905   Riddels & frontals

Sussex

ARDINGLY, College Chapel

Glass: 1889–90 (in illuminated case: see HAYWARDS HEATH) JNC's first windows

BRIGHTON,

—ALL SOULS, Kem Town

   1903   Cope of cloth of gold, now in St Mary's, Rock Gardens

—ST NICHOLAS

   Glass: 1904

   1956   Statue of St Nicholas

★★★ CHAILEY, The Heritage Crafts School, Chapel of St Martin (*see page 125*)

   Glass: 1912 Ewing window

           1920–22 new chapel extension, north side: four-light window and two-light window beside it; the west (Rose) window; St Martin window; Richard Ford window; War window; Creation window; St Cecilia window; Pilgrim's Progress window

           1936–7 east window

   1913–22 Chapel and Song School by JNC

   1922–30 Chapel tower, with water tank

           Song School

           Gymnasium and workshop, with an ambulatory and figure of St George

           Chapel extension

           Girls' Heritage Chapel, plus furniture

           Chapel fittings and furnishings, including: electric light fitting; completion of the screen and rood; figure of St Martin and the beggar (over west door); hatchment; Shiffner tablet; Sir John Chailey tablet; Bridgeman tablet; carpet; decorative painting of the ceiling in blue and gold

           Proposed: west gallery; banners; cloister; new hospital wing and boys' hostel; war memorial cross

   1930–32 (JBSC)

           St George's residential block – dormitories

           Seymour Obermer block (gymnasium, workshops)

           Three Pines Shelter

   1932–3 Pulpit for the chapel

           Six almsbags – embroidered in gold

   1937   Reredos; altar frontal (SSB)

CHICHESTER, Cathedral of the Holy Trinity

   1923–7 Restoration of St Katherine's chapel

   1927   Litany desk

   1952   Banner (Mothers' Union)

   1957   Statue of St Richard

CROWBOROUGH

   1942   Statue of Virgin & Child (Driberg memorial)

           (*original location and current whereabouts unknown*)

DANEHILL, All Saints (Architect: G. F. Bodley)

   1934   Predella & triptych with carvings, altar frontal (SSB), carpet

EAST GRINSTEAD, St Mary

   1913   New chancel

   1952   In Lady Chapel: altar, ciborium, riddels, hangings, frontal and super frontal

           Figure of Majestas over screen

EAST PRESTON, St Mary

   Glass: 1949 window on north side of chancel (small)

EASTBOURNE
—ALL SAINTS HOSPITAL CHAPEL
   1920–21 Proposed aumbry
   1923–6   Altar, altar cross and candlesticks, frontal and curtains, tabernacle, oak
               screens and limewashing
            Chapel dismantled 1980s
—ST ANNE, Upperton (*destroyed WWII*) (*see page 67*)
   1896–7   Altar & reredos (*the retable survives in St Mary Magdalene, Coldean,
             Brighton*)
FOREST ROW, Holy Trinity
  Glass: 1920
HARTFIELD, St Mary
   1949   Altar cross, figure, 2 candlesticks (WFK) frontal and hangings
             (Watts & Co.)
HASTINGS, St Clement (Priory Road, Halton)
  Glass: 1939 east window
   1940   Hangings & altar frontal (SSB)
   1949   Frontal & frontlet for high altar (Watts & Co.)
HAYWARDS HEATH
—CONVENT OF THE HOLY CROSS
          (Architect: Thomas Garner. Garner gave the following commission to
            help Bucknall & Comper start their practice.)
          Convent now closed
  Glass: 1889 Glass in the south wall of the original chapel: Virgin & Child, St
            Andrew, St Cornelius. These were JNC's first windows, executed by
            Burleson & Grylls. (*Removed 1985, now exhibited in frames in* ARDINGLY
            College Chapel)
  1889–90 JNC furnished and decorated the original chapel in the style of his
            master, Bodley. Bucknall & Comper added a small residential wing
            and a new entrance.
          (A larger chapel was added 1902–6 by Walter Tower, for which JNC
            designed a white embroidered altar frontal.)
—WEST SUSSEX COUNTY HOSPITAL CHAPEL
  Glass: 1930 east window
  1928–32 Building of a new chapel with fittings and furnishings
HOVE, St Andrew
   1949   Tablet
LANCING, College Chapel
  Glass: 1941
   1910   Proposed altar screen for high altar
LEWES, St Michael
  1919–20 Proposed war memorial window
LINDFIELD, All Saints
  1920–22 War memorial cross in the churchyard wall
PETWORTH, St Mary
  Glass: 1905–6
PULBOROUGH, St Mary
  Glass: 1928–30 west window (Burnett memorial window) and south aisle
            westernmost window (Children's window); 1958; 1968 (JSB)
   1929   Tower screen

1937–8   Headstone & kneeling stone (Charles Reginald Haines); stone
            commemorating JNC's ancestors

ROGATE, St Bartholomew

1920   War memorial cross in churchyard

1948   New dates & names added

RUSTINGTON, St Peter & St Paul

1908   Panelling, riddels, Lent hangings, upper & nether frontals

WILLINGDON, St Mary the Virgin

Glass: 1948 south window

1954   Rood & figures

WORTHING, Ramsey Hall Chapel

1904–7   Altar & reredos (*no trace 1980s*)

Warwickshire

(★) BILTON

—CHAPEL OF THE NUNC DIMITTIS

Glass: 1893 three windows

1894   Memorial chapel (built by Bucknall and Comper). In memory of
            C. E. W. Assheton; tower added 1904 probably designed by
            R. O. Assheton (1863–1909)
            Plain alabaster reredos (*dismantled*)
            1975 chapel redundant; 1980–81 converted to dwelling (glass extant)

—ST MARK

            Iron lectern
            Cross & 2 candlesticks (wood)
            One free-standing candelabrum
            Four 12 inch high apostles & crucifix (alabaster)
            (*All of these from Chapel of the Nunc Dimittis*)

CLIFFORD CHAMBERS

1919–21 War memorial cross

COMPTON WYNYATES, The House

Glass: 1931 ten lights

COVENTRY

—CATHEDRAL OF ST MICHAEL

1919   Proposed scheme for the restoration of the choir, side chapels and
            western screen

—HOLY TRINITY

Glass: 1955 east window

1949–52 Fittings for south transept chapel, including: gilt figure for altar cross,
            kneeling rail

—See also WESTWOOD HEATH

CURDWORTH, St Nicholas & St Peter-ad-Vincula

Glass: 1907

1905–7   English altar (hangings decaying & only 2 riddels with angels, 1990s),
            brass cross, candlesticks & candelabras, communion benches

ERDINGTON ABBEY, Birmingham (*see page 57*)

            No longer extant

Glass: 1896 (*whereabouts unknown*)

1896   Feretory for one of the heads of St Ursula's Virgin companions (made for Dom Bede Camm, OSB) (*destroyed*)

FILLONGLEY, St Mary and All Saints

1961   Majestas (on nave wall, intended to hang from chancel arch)

LEEK WOOTTON, All Saints

1934–5   Pulpit

LITTLE PACKINGTON, St Bartholomew (*redundant 1991, now privately owned*)

Glass: 1911 (*vandalised 1980s*)

RUGBY

—HOLY TRINITY (Architect: Gilbert Scott)

           Demolished 1983

1919–22 Lych-gate with rood and war memorial cross

—ST ANDREW

           War memorial

STRATFORD-ON-AVON, St James

           Demolished

1905   Choir stalls and additions to chancel

WARWICK, All Saints

           Demolished 1960s, whereabouts of furnishings unknown

1939   Altar (north aisle), upper frontal, hangings, Mothers' Union banner

1946   Figure of St Gregory & Child

1952   Reredos (Lady Chapel)

1955   Memorial tablet

           Loft and rood added to screen

WESTWOOD HEATH (west Coventry), St John the Baptist

1919–20 War memorial tablet

Wiltshire

BRADFORD-ON-AVON, St Lawrence

1911   Red altar frontal (LB)

CORSHAM, St Bartholomew

Glass: 1905

CRUDWELL, All Saints

Glass: 1901 north window, restoration only

           Altar

DEVIZES

1919   War memorial

EAST KNOYLE, St Mary

Glass: 1934 east window (George Wyndham memorial: died 1913, window dedicated 1934)

EDINGTON, Westbury, Priory Church

           Altar frontal (made for Colombo Cathedral, Sri Lanka; recently repaired)

FROXFIELD, St Peter

1905–13 Fittings

GREAT SOMERFORD, St Peter & St Paul
   1901   Chancel roof (barrel & painted)

MARLBOROUGH College Chapel
   1950–52 Reredos & altar, including 2 standard candlesticks, copper & silver plated, with central candle surrounded by 16 smaller candles (*restored 1985*)

MIDDLE WOODFORD
        See WOODFORD

SALISBURY

—CATHEDRAL OF THE BLESSED VIRGIN MARY
   1923–4 Set of High Mass vestments

—ST GILES THEOLOGICAL COLLEGE CHAPEL
   1905–6 Interior fittings

SAVERNAKE FOREST, St Katherine
   1915   Figure of St Margaret of Antioch (on altar frontal?)

SHREWTON, St Mary
   Glass: 1925–6 south wall

WOODFORD, All Saints
   Glass: 1924–8: Grenville memorial window; Olding memorial window; east window with new tracery
   1926   Altar

Worcestershire

BREDON, St Giles
   Glass: 1913 north chancel
   1912–14 Fittings
   1913   Gravestone
   1919   Weather vane

MALVERN

—COLLEGE CHAPEL
   Glass: 1934–5 (Foster memorial window)

—ST MARY & ST MICHAEL
   1910   Banner (V&A exhibition 1971) (*in glass case 1988*) (Made by St Mary's Convent Embroidery School, Wantage)
   1915   Proposed reredos for St Anne's chapel

(★★★) MALVERN LINK, Convent of the Holy Name (*see page 41*)
   Nuns moved to Derby in late 1980s. In 1994 sold to 'Day of Salvation' Ministries; convent chapel adapted as the chapel of the 'Christian Conference Centre'. When unoccupied, much vandalism took place.
   Glass: 1898 ante-chapel window; 1901 Lady Chapel (*stolen*); 1925 south window; 1923–6 east window (*almost undamaged*); 1923–6 north window (*badly damaged, remains were removed*); 1950 cloisters (*nothing remains*)
   1893–1926 Church built, dedicated 1893 (Bucknall & Comper); enlarging of sacristy & rebuilding of cloisters; all fittings (*not many remain*); reredos (*damaged*)
   1924   Hanging pyx (made by W. F. Knight) (*taken to Derby*) Jewelled cross

              Vestments

              Sanctuary lamp and bracket

              Electric light fittings

1935   Figure of Virgin & Child (*now in Derby Cathedral*)

1940   Panelling over stalls (*only a little remains*)

SHELSLEY WALSH, St Andrew

              Pulpit (undated)

WICK, St Bartholomew

Glass: 1947 west window

1939   Gravestone (Revd Charles Hudson)

1948   Font cover

WORCESTER, St Paul

Glass: 1931–3 memorial window to John Polycarp Oakey

Yorkshire, East

KIRBY UNDER DALE, All Saints

Glass: 1919 south window

Yorkshire, North

ACKLAM (Middlesbrough), St Mary

1911–12 Church Congress banners

1920   White altar frontal

1957   Banner

DRINGHOUSES, St Edward the Confessor

Glass: 1935–6 memorial to Lady Green

EASINGTON (near Guisborough), All Saints

1923–6   Redecoration and repairs, new high altar, banner

EASINGWOLD, St John & All Saints

Glass: 1936

HARDRAW, St Mary & St John

Glass: 1914

★ HARROGATE, Christ Church

Glass: 1938 south chancel

1938–40 Reredos (upper part in form of a triptych), hangings, frontal, figures

LOTHERSDALE, Christ Church

Glass: 1917

MYTON-ON-SWALE, St Mary

Glass: 1908

★ RIPON, Cathedral of St Peter & St Wilfrid

Glass: 1924: north aisle (Bishop Boyd Carpenter memorial window); south aisle (Florence Bickersteth memorial window)

1919–26 High altar, reredos, screen

              Brass (on chancel step); Barnbrough memorial tablet (in south aisle of choir); Reginald Mansfield Owen memorial plaque

WHITBY, St Ninian

1909   Vestments

YORK, Minster of St Peter

1912	Banner of St Hilda (for Middlesborough Church Congress 1912; made by Wantage Sisters)
1942	Frontal & frontlet (SSB)
1942–5	Font cover in crypt
1948	Nave pulpit in memory of Archbishop Cosmo Gordon Lang and Archbishop William Temple

Yorkshire, South

CANTLEY

—CANTLEY LODGE

1893	Alterations and additions

(★★★) —ST WILFRID (*see page 32*)

Glass:	1894 east window; 1894 west window of north aisle; 1909 north-west window of north aisle; 1915 'Angels' window
1893–4	Restoration of arcade and aisle and reinstatement of rood screen, chapels, parclose screens and medieval floor levels; altar (JNC's second 'English altar'), frontals (red, green & gold), vestments (purple & red chasubles, purple & white copes), rood loft, hanging pyx
1922–6	Proposed seats for south aisle
1929–36	Electric lighting, choir seating, heating apparatus, cruets
1944	Paschal candlestick
	In 1986 the church was enlarged and Comper's interior arrangements altered

DONCASTER, Christ Church

1899	Furnishings

★★ FRICKLEY (Clayton), All Saints

	Closed 1990 due to mining subsidence; completely restored to its former beauty and rededicated 1994
Glass:	1909 east window
1929–34	Restoration, warm air heating, altar, reredos, seating, pulpit, panelling, organ case at west end
1942–5	Further alterations in the chancel

HICKLETON, St Wilfrid

Glass:	1910–11 two windows in north chancel
1909	Screen west end
	Halifax tombs

★★ HIGH MELTON, St James

Glass:	1907 west window
1904–8	Rood screen, altar, stalls, door furniture, purple frontal, blue, purple & red frontlets
1925	Gravestone (Ethel Mary Crawford)

HOOTON PAGNALL, All Saints

Glass:	1929–30 window in side chapel

MEXBOROUGH, St George

	Demolished 1980
1899–1900	
	Fragment of major church built. Nave unfinished
	Organ case

SKELBROOKE, St Michael
- 1942   Kneeling desks, priest's desk & oak chair

★ SPROTBROUGH, St Mary
- *Glass:*   1912–13 east window; 1919–20 east and south windows in Bewicke-Copley chapel
- 1912–15   Chancel & chapel furnishings, chapel screen, pulpit
- 1919–20   War memorial cross in churchyard

TANKERSLEY, St Peter
- 1923–4   High altar & chancel decoration

WARMSWORTH, St Peter
- 1942–5   Proposed altar rails and two clergy stalls

Yorkshire, West

ABERFORD, St Ricarius
- *Glass:*   1920–23 east window
- 1920   Altar design
- 1923   Rood

BIRKENSHAW, St Paul
- 1930–31   New south window with clear glass; limewashing of walls; altar hangings; carved and decorated figure of Risen Christ; pair of altar candlesticks

BRAMHAM PARK, Bramham, Leeds
- 1912   Cherubs

HUDDERSFIELD, St Peter
- *Glass:*   1922 east window
- 1919–25   Ciborium for high altar and refurnishing of sanctuary

KIRKHEATON, St John the Baptist
- *Glass:*   1907

LEEDS, St Hilda
- 1917   Grave cross, banner

LOTHERTON (near Tadcaster), St James
- 1921   Rood beam with figures

MIRFIELD, Community of the Resurrection
- 1928   Four candlesticks & crucifix (from Westbourne Terrace, BAYSWATER, London)
- 1935   Monstrance (from House of Prayer, BURNHAM, Buckinghamshire)

WAKEFIELD, Cathedral of All Saints
- 1950   Loft front, rood and seraphim

WALES

Clwyd

PENTREFOELAS, Parish church (dedication not known)
- *Glass:*   1911; 1932–3 Thomas William Roberts memorial window

Dyfed

LAMPETER, St Peter
> *Glass:* 1939–40 south aisle (Hetty Helen Davies memorial window)

Glamorgan

CARDIFF
★★★ —ALEXANDRA GARDENS (*see page 156*)
> 1923–36 Welsh National War Memorial with additional lettering for WWII

—CANTON
——ST CATHERINE, King's Road
> *Glass:* 1951; 1954 two windows; 1957; (all windows of north aisle with two lights)

——ST LUKE, Cowbridge Road East
> *Glass:* 1957 north aisle, 2 lights & 3 separate lights

—CHURCH STREET, St John
> *Glass:* 1917 east window
> 1909–17 Triptych, Kitchener memorial
> Screen

—ROATH, St Margaret, Albany Road
> 1921–6 Reredos with figures of the Apostles (in wood), Christ (beardless) in centre (alabaster)
> Altar cross & candlesticks
> Proposed war memorial cross

MICHAELSTON-LE-PIT, St Michael & All Angels
> *Glass:* 1955

OYSTERMOUTH, outside Swansea
> *Glass:* 1904 (*whereabouts unknown*)

WENVOE, St Mary
> 1901 Reredos (alabaster, painted & gilt)
> 1901–5 Six candlesticks, crucifix & sanctus bell
> 1920 Lectern & pulpit
> Four candlesticks & crucifix given to Newton Nottage, Porthcawl

Gwent

EBBW VALE, St John
> *Glass:* 1917
> *Church made redundant 1995; all contents, including glass, sold off to a 'church clearer'*

NEWPORT, St John the Baptist
> Glass: 1901; 1942–5 Emma Jane Herbert memorial window
> *c.*1907 Mission House designed by William Bucknall
> 1926 Figure of the Annunciation with canopies, standing in niches near the roof of the chapel
> Proposed decoration of the chapel
> Figure of Virgin & Child
> 1945–8 Reredos and figure of St John the Baptist

WONASTOW (near Monmouth), St Gwynllyw
    Glass: 1903 east window
    1903   Four chandeliers
WYESHAM (near Monmouth), St James
    Glass: 1906 north window

Powys

BERRIEW, St Beuno
    Glass: 1932 proposed
    1932–3   Churchyard cross (memorial to Miss Florence Howard)
GLASBURY, St Peter
    Glass: 1935

SCOTLAND

Aberdeenshire

ABERDEEN
★★★ —CATHEDRAL OF ST ANDREW (*see page 176*)
    Glass: 1938; 1942 east window
    1928–30   Proposed design for Bishop Seabury Memorial Cathedral
    1934–41   Ciborium & altar furnishings, hanging pyx, light fittings, heraldic ceilings
★★★ —CONVENT OF SISTERS OF ST MARGARET (*see page 31*)
    Glass: 1893; 1898; 1907 two side lights in east window; 1908 east window; 1919; 1964 J. M. Neale Memorial (JSB)
    1891–2   Chapel (conventual buildings only partially built)
    Convent closed 2002, though Guest House continued to be occupied by single Sister (this arrangement appears to have ceased in 2006)
—REGENT QUAY, for ST CLEMENT
    1922   Proposed new mission church and hall on a site acquired at Regent Quay, next to Water Lane
—ST JOHN
    1935–7   Reredos, candlesticks, hangings, carpet
★★★ —ST MARGARET OF SCOTLAND (JNC's father's church) (*see page 21*)
    Glass: 1893 chapel of St Nicholas; 1907 'Comper Aisle' east window
    1889   Chapel of St Nicholas with wrought-iron screen (JNC's first building)
    1907–9   Chapel of the Holy Name (the 'Comper Aisle'), a memorial to his parents, with oak screen with 2 figures and heraldic painted ceiling
    1924–5   Pulpit, rood, candlesticks (for high altar), statue of BVM
    1937   Figures of BVM and St Katherine
    JNC made designs for a rebuilding of the church but only the west end was built, of which the Chapel of St Nicholas is part
★★★ BRAEMAR, St Margaret
    Glass: 1901 five windows; 1910 east window of south aisle; 1912 over vestry; 1913 south window; 1914 west window; 1927

1895–1909
    Church; Lightfoot aisle, high altar and sacrament house
    Brass (Salmon memorial)
1919–22 Rood screen
1922 Brass (in memory of Bishop Lightfoot of Durham)
    Closed early 1960s; reopened 1979; in 1986 requiring financial help for urgent
     repairs; in 2006 closed with many windows boarded up, and suffering
     from damp

FORGUE, St Margaret
 Glass: 1901 two windows
    Church closed 1986, windows in situ 1987

INVERURIE
—PLACE OF TILLIEFOURE
    Entrance gates (undated)

—ST MARY
 Glass: 1930–33 south side of church (Mitchell memorial window)

★ OLD DEER, St Drostane
 1895 Reredos
 1896 Chancel extension

STONEHAVEN, St James the Great
 Glass: 1927–30 apse of the baptistery (MacDonald memorial)

WHITEHAUGH, Deaconess Institute
 Glass: 1893

★ WHITERASHES (near Fraserburgh), All Saints
 Glass: 1898 chancel – east window and windows on north and south; 1905
    south window; 1909 south window; 1910 south window; 1919 north
    window
 1898 Reredos

Angus

BRECHIN, Cathedral, dedicated to the Triune God
 1944 Crozier, leather case, linen mitre (SSB)
    Riddels, hangings & frontal (Bishop's chapel)

DUNDEE, Cathedral of St Paul
 1919 War memorial

★★★ KIRRIEMUIR, St Mary
 Glass: 1919–21 south window (Gordon memorial); 1921–5 east window (war
    memorial); 1924 window on south side of chancel; 1926–31 west
    window; 1928 north window; 1936–8 window on north side of
    chancel (Ogilvy memorial); 1942–3 window on south side of chancel
    (MacDonald memorial); 1948 east window of north aisle (memorial
    to JNC's father) and west window
 1903 Church built
 1919–21 Gravestone (Mrs L. A. E. Raymond Philip)
 1921 Kneeling-stone for the Philip family gravestone
 1926 Gravestone (Jane Kydd Duncan)
 1942–3 Stone figure of Virgin & Child in a niche of the south porch
    Fittings

1919–21   In 'The Den', a public park: proposed memorial to 'Sydney' Wilkie (sundial and stone seat on bridge over stream)

Dumfries & Galloway

APPLEGARTH, Parish church (no dedication)

1906   Grave cross

1919, 1925–9

Gravestones (initially to Dorothy Jardine, then to members of Jardine family, who were cousins of JNC)

LOCKERBIE, All Saints

Glass: 1919

1927–32   Reredos and fittings

Fife

(★★)   ROSYTH, Royal Naval Church of St Andrew & St George (*see page 108*)

1921–7   New church designed by JNC and built in collaboration with W. A. Forsyth. It was built of reinforced concrete. Only the east part was completed.

Last service 24 August 1986. Land sold. Church demolished. No furnishings of importance.

Highland

CROMARTY, St Regulus

Glass: 1931 Chadwick memorial window; 1951

1931–2   Memorial stone to Revd A. Chadwick

1947   Gravestone (Madeleine Chadwick, JNC's sister)

INVERNESS, St Michael & All Angels

Glass: 1928 east window

1905   Font cover

1927   High altar & tester

NAIRN, St Columba

Glass: 1913; 1916

★★★   ROTHIEMURCHUS (Aviemore), St John the Baptist

1928–31   New church designed by JNC and JBSC with furnishings including ciborium, altar frontal, altar rails, altar cross, carpet, seats, curtain

Midlothian

EDINBURGH

—CATHEDRAL OF ST MARY

1929–30   Cope (presented for the silver jubilee of Bishop Reid's ordination)

—ST MICHAEL & ALL SAINTS

Glass: 1892 two windows, including west window of south aisle

1894   Banner

—THEOLOGICAL COLLEGE

Glass: east window of chapel (early)

PENICUIK, St James the Less

Glass: 1912; 1918

Perth & Kinross

CRIEFF, St Columba
  1918   Bishop's chair
GLENALMOND (north east of Crieff), Trinity College (now Glenalmond College)
                Chapel
  Glass: 1920 north-east side of chapel (Waddell memorial)
  1918–23   Reredos, war memorial panelling, kneeling stool, electric light fittings
  1924–6   Officers Training Corps – Captain's Shield
  1938–40   Neish memorial – a heraldic panel and two cherubs in oak
(★) PERTH, Cathedral of St Ninian
  1922–5   Fittings, including: stone screen and rood (*removed 1980s*), font cover
                Processional cross for the Bishop
                Vestments
  1930–31   Memorial tablet to Robert Morison Pullar, plate
  1946–7   Banner
PITLOCHRY, Holy Trinity
  Glass: 1920
  1893   Reredos & fittings

Shetland

LERWICK, Home of Aberdeen Sisters
                No longer exists. The glass and possibly the other furnishings now (1973) in
                    St Magnus, Lerwick
  Glass: 1905
  1905   Altar & candlesticks
                Riddels & frontals

Stirling

DUNTREATH CASTLE, Blanefield (near Glasgow)
  Glass: 1903

NORTHERN IRELAND

CLANDEBOYE, Grounds of Clandeboye House
  1946   Memorial stone to the Marquess of Dufferin and Ava

JERSEY

ST HELIER, St Simon
  1920   Altar cross and 6 candlesticks

OUTSIDE THE UNITED KINGDOM

AUSTRALIA, Melbourne, St Mark
   Glass: 1955; 1958
BARBADOS, Codrington College
   1948   Memorial tablet in chapel
BURMA, Rangoon (now Yangon), Cathedral of the Holy Trinity
   1951   Altar cross with gilt figure and candlesticks; painted panel above altar
CANADA
—NEWFOUNDLAND, Cathedral of St John
   1923   Proposed banner for the Girls' Friendly Society
—QUEBEC
   1915   Proposed scheme for General Wolfe memorial chapel
CHINA, Tientsin, All Saints
   Glass: 1937 nine separate lancets around apse
EIRE
—BLACKROCK (Co. Dublin), All Saints
   Glass: 1923–4 Dudgeon memorial window
—CAHIR (Co. Tipperary), St Paul
   Glass: 1928–30 Smith memorial window
—CARNALWAY (Co. Kildare), St Patrick
   Glass: 1898
   1903–7   Reredos
—DERRYLORAN (Co. Tyrone), St Luran
   1964   Banner (JSB) (SSB) (*destroyed by fire, 1996*)
—DUBLIN
——CATHEDRAL OF ST PATRICK
          1899–1900 Frontal high altar
          1900 Alms bags
          (Frontal and alms bags executed by the Royal Irish School of Art
             Needlework)
——VICE-ROYAL LODGE, Private chapel for the Vice-Regal chapel
          1902 Frontal (executed by the Royal Irish School of Art Needlework)
          (*now in St Patrick's Cathedral*)
—KILBRIDE (Co. Wicklow), (Church of Ireland)
   Glass: 1918; 1922–7 Price memorial; 1930
—KILDARE, Cathedral of St Brigid
   1897–8   Frontal (executed by the Royal Irish School of Art Needlework)
—KILKENNY, Cathedral of St Canice
   1929–31   Frontal (SSB)
—KILTERNAN (Co. Dublin), Parish church (Church of Ireland) (no dedication)
   Glass: 1919–21 Trouton memorial
FRANCE
—DOMREMY
          Statue of St Joan of Arc (*no trace in 1985*)
—ESTAIRES (N. France), near church
   1920   Statue of St Barnabas
—PARIS, Cathedral of Notre Dame
   1913   Vestments (SSB) made for Sir Stuart Coats, Papal Chamberlain, later
          given to Notre Dame; mitre added (*now no trace*)

—RHEIMS

    1934   Figure of Dom Perignon (2ft 3ins) of wood holding flask of wine. Figure placed on table for annual Champagne Thanksgiving in Rheims (*no trace 1987*)

INDIA

—CALCUTTA, Cathedral of St Paul

    1904   Choir stalls (SC)

—POONA (now Pune), Church of the Holy Name

    1934–7   Ciborium, crucifix, and figure of risen Christ for high altar

—SANAWAR, Punjab, The Lawrence Military Academy (now the Lawrence School)

    Glass: 1914 heraldic panel in Council Chamber for Lord Harding; window in west gallery of chapel

★★★ —YERENDAWNA, near Poona (Pune), St Crispin

    1903   Church built (for SSJE) by Bucknall and Comper

    1938   English altar, octagonal font, wall paintings

MALTA, Valletta, Pro-Cathedral of St Paul

    1936–7   Gravestone and memorial brass to Elizabeth Anne Coldwell

NEW ZEALAND, Geraldine

            Lectern

PAKISTAN, Lahore, Cathedral of the Resurrection

    Glass: 1935–7 two lights & single light & rose window (Croal memorial)

PORTUGAL, Madeira, Capella da Consolação

    Glass: 1935–6 window for Harry Hinton

    1937   Memorial brass for clock, in consultation with Sir Stephen Gaselee

SOUTH AFRICA

—BLOEMFONTEIN, Cathedral of St Andrew and St Michael

    1892   Crozier (Barkentin & Krall)

    1935   Pectoral cross for Bishop Walter Carey

—CAPETOWN, St Philip (Architects: Herbert Baker & Massey)

    Glass: 1901

SRI LANKA, Colombo

            See EDINGTON, Wiltshire, England

SWITZERLAND, Territet, St John the Evangelist

    1922–3   Reredos panels

USA

★★ —BOSTON, Mass., Emmanuel

    The Lesley Lindsey Memorial Chapel (Architect: Ralph Adams Cram)

    Glass: 1921–4 complete glazing scheme – seven windows

    1921–4   Altar, altar screen and reredos, cross and candlesticks, two chalices, silver-gilt flagon, statue of Virgin & Child

—NEW YORK

——CATHEDRAL OF ST JOHN THE DIVINE

            1929 Reredos & banner pole

——CHURCH OF THE RESURRECTION

            1925 Pall & vestments

——EAST HAMPTON, Long Island, St Luke

            1917 Embroidered funeral pall & vestments

—PHILADELPHIA, St Mark

    1902–5   Altar ornaments including silver crucifix, 3 sets of vestments and frontal (SSB) (restored 1990s)

Bibliography
Anthony Symondson SJ

Sources

J. N. Comper's drawings, professional correspondence and some personal papers, covering the years 1894–1952, were deposited by Sebastian Comper in the British Architectural Library, Royal Institute of British Architects, in 1967. Later John Bucknall, his great-nephew, deposited a number of painted glass drawings and a little correspondence. The papers were catalogued by Angela Mace and details from her work have been included in the gazetteer. They are composed of 396 files, listed in alphabetical order by place-name, with miscellaneous files at the end. They are kept in ninety-eight boxes, CoJ/1–98. The works featured in these files vary from large and small projects, the complete furnishing of new churches, through various restoration and redecoration schemes to the provision of small items of furniture. The contents include copy letters by Comper, J. B. S. Comper, and Arthur Bucknall; letters from correspondents; some estimates, accounts and copy specifications of works; rough sketches; snapshots, guide-books, dedication leaflets and press-cuttings. While this collection contains the bulk of Comper's office papers, it is not a complete record of his work. His early and late works are not fully represented in the collection and there are no ledgers. In 1944 Comper's drawing office was damaged during an air raid and much early correspondence was destroyed. The ledgers and later files were retained by Sebastian Comper and John Bucknall. The RIBA collection forms an extensive body of architectural papers and has been used as a basis for the introduction to Comper's life and work, in company with research in other archives, newspapers and periodicals, parish chests, cathedral muniment rooms, and interviews and correspondence with those who knew Comper.

Writings by Comper

Practical Considerations on the Gothic or English Altar and Certain Dependent Ornaments, Aberdeen, Scotland, Albany Press, 1893

The Reasonableness of the Ornaments Rubric Illustrated by a Comparison of the German and English Altars, London, Harrison & Son, 1897

Further Thoughts on the English Altar, or Practical Considerations on the Planning of a Modern Church, Cambridge, W. Heffer & Sons, 1933

The Bishop Seabury Memorial, Aberdeen, St Andrew's Cathedral, 1941

Of the Atmosphere of a Church, London, Sheldon Press, 1947 (reprinted above, page 231)

Of the Christian Altar and the Buildings Which Contain It, London, Society for Promoting Christian Knowledge, 1950

Select bibliography

Anson, Peter F., 'The work of John Ninian Comper: a pioneer architect of the modern liturgical movement', *Pax*, 27 (1937), 177–84

—*Fashions in Church Furnishings 1840–1940*, Faith Press, 1960

—*The Call of the Cloister*, SPCK, third revised edition, 1964

Betjeman, John, 'A note on J. N. Comper: heir to Butterfield and Bodley', *The Architectural Review*, 85 (1939), 70–82

—*First and Last Loves*, John Murray, 1952

—'Architecture', in *Edwardian England, 1901–1914*, ed. Simon Nowell-Smith, Oxford, 1964

—*Letters: Volume One: 1926 to 1951* and *Letters: Volume Two: 1951 to 1984*, edited and introduced by Candida Lycett Green, Methuen, 1994 and 1995

—*Coming Home: An Anthology of Prose*, selected and introduced by Candida Lycett Green, Methuen, 1997

—*Trains and Buttered Toast: Selected Radio Talks*, edited and introduced by Stephen Games, John Murray, 2006

Callender, Ann, ed., *Godly Mayfair*, The Grosvenor Chapel, 1980

Clarke, Basil F. L., 'Ecclesiastical architecture: some notable architects of the early twentieth century', *Journal of the Royal Society of Arts*, cxxi, March 1973, 222–37

Cornforth, John, 'Last Master of the Gothic', *Country Life*, clxxxii, 14 January 1988, 64–5

Curl, James Stevens, *Piety Proclaimed: An Introduction to Places of Worship in Victorian England*, Historical Publications, 2002

Gray, A. Stuart, *Edwardian Architecture: A Biographical Dictionary*, Duckworth, 1985

Gray, Donald, *Percy Dearmer: A Parson's Pilgrimage*, Canterbury Press, 2000

Hall, Michael, 'The later Gothic Revival in England: a national or international style?', in *Gothic Revival: Religion, Architecture and Style in Western Europe 1815–1914*, eds. Jan de Maeyer and Luc Verpoest, Leuven, 2000

—'What do Victorian churches mean? Symbolism and sacramentalism in Anglican church architecture, 1850–1870', *Journal of the Society of Architectural Historians*, vol. 59, no. 1, March 2000, 78–95

Hillier, Bevis, *Young Betjeman*, John Murray, 1989

—*John Betjeman: New Fame, New Love*, John Murray, 2002

—*Betjeman: The Bonus of Laughter*, John Murray, 2004

Homan, Roger, *The Art of the Sublime: Principles of Christian Art and Architecture*, Ashgate, 2006

Irvine, Gerard, 'Comper, Sir (John) Ninian (1864–1960)', *Dictionary of National Biography*, Oxford, 1971

James, Dom Augustine, *The Story of Downside Abbey Church*, Stratton on the Fosse, 1961

Mayhew, Peter, *All Saints: Birth and Growth of a Community*, Society of All Saints, 1987

Richardson, Margaret, *Architects of the Arts and Crafts Movement*, RIBA Drawings Series, Trefoil Books, 1983

Robinson, John Martin, *Treasures of the English Churches*, Sinclair-Stevenson, 1995

—and David Neave, *Francis Johnson Architect: A Classical Statement*, Oblong, 2001

Service, Alastair, ed., *Edwardian Architecture and its Origins*, Architectural Press, 1975

—*Edwardian Architecture*, London, 1977

Schoeser, Mary, *English Church Embroidery 1833–1953. The Watts Book of Embroidery*, London, 1998

Stamp, Gavin, *An Architect of Promise: George Gilbert Scott Junior (1839–1897) and the Late Gothic Revival*, Shaun Tyas, 2002

—'Sacred architecture in a secular century', *The Twentieth Century Church: Twentieth Century Architecture 3*, Journal of the Twentieth Century Society, 1998, 7–16

—'The last Gothic Revivalist', *The Spectator*, 30 January 1988, 33–4

—and Anthony Symondson, *Clumber Chapel*, The National Trust, 1982

Symondson, Anthony, 'Sir Ninian Comper', *Macmillan Encyclopaedia of Architects*, New York, 1982

—*The Life and Work of Sir Ninian Comper (1864–1960)*, exhibition monograph, RIBA Heinz Gallery, London, 1988

—'John Bucknall', obituary, *The Independent*, 22 August 1989

—'John Betjeman and the cult of J. N. Comper', *The Thirties Society Journal*, 8 (1991), 3–13, 52

—'Art needlework in Ireland: Sir Ninian Comper and the Royal Irish School of Art Needlework', *Irish Arts Review Yearbook*, 10 (1994), 126–35

—'Theology, worship and the late Victorian church', in *The Victorian church: Architecture and Society*, Manchester, eds. Chris Brooks and Andrew Saint, 1995, 192–222

—'Sir (John) Ninian Comper', *The Dictionary of Art*, 7, ed. Jane Turner, Macmillan, 1996

—'Look with your ears: some 20th-century attitudes to the late Gothic Revival', *The Victorian Society Annual 1996*, ed. Sarah Whittingham, London, 1997

—'Unity by inclusion: Sir Ninian Comper and the planning of a modern church', *The Twentieth Century Church: Twentieth Century Architecture 3*, Journal of the Twentieth Century Society, 1998, 17–42

—'Medievalism in the twentieth century: St Cyprian's, Clarence Gate, London', *The Victorian*, the Magazine of the Victorian Society, 14 (2003), 12–15

—'Sir (John) Ninian Comper 1864–1960', *Oxford Dictionary of National Biography*, 12, Oxford, 2004

Tocher, Francis, 'Sir Ninian Comper', *Leopard*, Aberdeen, October/November 1979

Wiseman, J., 'John Comper: a memoir', in John Comper, *Church Principles: or the Scriptural Teaching of the British Churches*, 1904, xiii–xxxviii

Wright, Andrew, 'Ninian Comper: St John the Baptist, Rothiemurchus,' *Architectural Heritage*, the Journal of the Architectural Heritage Society of Scotland, xii (2001), 62–6

Index to places in the Gazetteer

This is an index to the Gazetteer in Part 2 of the book. It shows the county or other heading under which each place in the Gazetteer falls. See the General Index on page 326 for places discussed in Part 1 of the book.

General index

This is a general index to Part 1 of the book (extending to the Foreword to Part 2). This index does not give references to places listed in the Gazetteer, for which see page 321.

References here are to page numbers: those in **bold** type refer to main entries for a subject, and those in *italic* to illlustrations (which are indexed by the place shown in the illustration, not by the nature of the items shown). Sir Ninian Comper is referred to as 'JNC'. His entry in the index is subdivided into sections; so a cross-reference such as '*see* JNC/3b, liturgical planning' refers to the entry 'liturgical planning' within section 3b of the index entry for Sir Ninian Comper. The abbreviation 'OAC' refers to *Of the Atmosphere of a Church*; and 'Context' refers to the essay by Anthony Symondson, '*Of the Atmosphere of a Church* in context ....', starting on page 206.